DEEP MEDIATIZATION

Andreas Hepp takes an integrative look at one of the biggest questions in media and communications research: how digital media is changing society.

Often, such questions are discussed in isolation, losing sight of the overarching context in which they are situated. Hepp has developed a theory of the re-figuration of society by digital media and their infrastructures, and provides an understanding of how profound today's media-related changes are, not only for institutions, organizations and communities, but for the individual as well. Rooted in the latest research, this book does not stop at a description of media-related change; instead, it raises the normative challenge of what deep mediatization should look like so that it might just stimulate a 'good life' for all.

Providing original and critical research, the book introduces deep mediatization to students of media and cultural studies, as well as neighboring disciplines like sociology, political science and other cognate disciplines.

Andreas Hepp is Professor for Media and Communications at the ZeMKI (Centre for Media, Communication and Information Research), University of Bremen, Germany.

KEY IDEAS IN MEDIA AND CULTURAL STUDIES

The *Key Ideas in Media and Cultural Studies* series covers the main concepts, issues, debates and controversies in contemporary media and cultural studies. Titles in the series constitute authoritative, original essays rather than literary surveys, but are also written explicitly to support undergraduate teaching. The series provides students and teachers with lively and original treatments of key topics in the field.

Cultural Policy
David Bell and Kate Oakley

Reality TV
Annette Hill

Culture
Ben Highmore

Representation
Jenny Kidd

Celebrity
Sean Redmond

Global Cultural Economy
Christiaan De Beukelaer and Kim-Marie Spence

Marx
Christian Fuchs

Deep Mediatization
Andreas Hepp

For more information about this series, please visit: www.routledge.com/Key-Ideas-in-Media--Cultural-Studies/book-series/KEYIDEA

DEEP MEDIATIZATION

Andreas Hepp

Routledge
Taylor & Francis Group
LONDON AND NEW YORK

First published 2020
by Routledge
2 Park Square, Milton Park, Abingdon, Oxon OX14 4RN

and by Routledge
52 Vanderbilt Avenue, New York, NY 10017

Routledge is an imprint of the Taylor & Francis Group, an informa business

British Library Cataloguing-in-Publication Data
A catalogue record for this book is available from the British Library

Library of Congress Cataloging-in-Publication Data
A catalog record has been requested for this book

ISBN: 978-1-138-02498-4 (hbk)
ISBN: 978-1-138-02499-1 (pbk)
ISBN: 978-1-351-06490-3 (ebk)

Typeset in Times New Roman
by Deanta Global Publishing Services, Chennai, India

To my son Levi Daniel

CONTENTS

Acknowledgment

I would like to dedicate this book to my son Levi Daniel Hepp. As I make the final revisions to this manuscript, he is preparing for his departure from home, and I hope that at least some of the thoughts I have formulated will be stimulating for him.

I would like to thank above all my wife Beate C. Koehler, not only for the design of the cover picture for this book and the photograph it contains. I would like to express my special thanks for the opportunities I have for writing and research, for the sheer amount of encouragement and support I have received, as well as for her companionship in visiting professorships, stays abroad and various travels abroad. Without Beate's love, acceptance, support and help – especially in turbulent times – this book would not have been possible.

This book is the result of a great deal of research, much of which was carried out in collaboration with colleagues whom I would like to thank. Its figurational approach was developed within four academic contexts: first, while working with Nick Couldry on the *Communicative Construction of Reality*. I would like to thank Nick for more than ten years of collaboration and for the opportunity to think ahead with our joint ideas. The second is the research network *Communicative Figurations*, in which we conduct empirical research on the media-related re-figuration of society. I would like to thank all of those involved, in particular Andreas Breiter, Uwe Hasebrink, Leif Kramp and Wiebke Loosen, for their stimulating work in our joint projects, which has repeatedly opened up new thematic areas for me, especially in the field of pioneer communities and pioneer journalism. Third, the DFG priority program *Mediatized World* was important for the development of this book, in which we spent six years researching the mediatization of various social domains. I would also like to thank all members of this program for our joint work and the many stimulating discussions, especially Ronald Hitzler, Friedrich Krotz and all the 'wild youngsters' who raised early questions on datafication. Fourth, this book is based on more than 15 years of empirical research on mediatization at the Center for Media, Communication and Information Research (ZeMKI) at the University of Bremen. Here I would like to thank all my colleagues for their constructive and stimulating cooperation over so many years, especially the members of the lab *Mediatization and Globalization* with which I also discussed earlier versions of this book: Susan Alpen, Alessandro Belli, Matthias Berg (who in the meantime has left), Julia Gantenberg, Stephan Görland, Andrea Grahl, Katharina Heitmann, Marco Höhn, Florian Hohmann, Sigrid Kannengießer, Heiko Kirschner, Leif Kramp, Hendrik Kühn, Anke Offerhaus, Cindy Roitsch and Anne Schmitz.

In addition, the manuscript also contains various suggestions from conferences and research stays, for which I would like to express my thanks. Chapter 3 of this book was written during a visiting professorship at the *Université Paris 2 Panthéon-Assas*. In this respect I would like to thank my colleagues there, in particular Tristan Mattelart, without whom my stay would not have been possible and for his constructive feedback while I was there. I wrote Chapters 5 and 6 when I was visiting professor at the Department of Media and Communications of the London School of Economics and Political Science. Here, too, I would like to thank my colleagues, especially Bart Cammaerts, Nick Couldry, Sonia Livingstone and Robin Mansell – not only for making my stay possible but also for the suggestions that they gave during many conversations. Furthermore, I was able to present parts of this book's manuscript at many conferences and workshops, partly as keynotes and at times as panel papers. Here I would like to thank everyone who extended their generous invitations, those who participated in the many extensive discussions as a result and those anonymous reviewers for the hints I received. A big thanks also to the Mediatization Section of the European Communication Research and Education Association (ECREA), which for many years now has offered a perfect home to discuss questions of mediatization.

I would like to thank Göran Bolin, Nick Couldry, Knut Lundby, Wiebke Loosen and Kim Schrøder for their very helpful comments on the first draft of this book. Their hints on vagueness of argumentation, missing examples and references and pure errors of thought enabled me to further improve the manuscript.

A considerable help in the completion of the manuscript were various student assistants. I would like to thank Jeanette Asmuss, Linda

Siegel and Kian Reiling for their visits to the library, their visualizations of data and their proofreading. All three supported me considerably in my work. A very special thanks also to Marc Kushin, who supported me with the language revision of my manuscript and turned my broken English into a more polished prose. His comments, hints and suggestions for reformulations have contributed greatly to the quality of the book and to the sharpening of my arguments.

But all these words of thanks must not hide the fact that I am the one responsible for any remaining errors, ambiguities and simply bad writing. It is now up to the reader to decide on the quality of this book. I hope, in any case, that it will be stimulating for many people and that it will generally advance our collective reflection on deep mediatization.

Bremen, August 2018, Andreas Hepp

1

INTRODUCTION

Popular media frequently presents us with fictional characters like Mia, a young woman living in the year 2037: one morning, Mia is woken from a deep sleep with friendly words spoken by Ben, her artificial companion. Ben is an artificial intelligence software application existing primarily in 'the cloud'. Mia can access Ben at all times through her smart watch, her mobile phone and other devices. Mia also lives in a 'smart home': when she enters her bathroom, the lights turn on automatically; at the edge of the mirror is displayed a curated stream of updates and messages from her social media accounts as well as a selection of health information and personal metrics including her heart rate, the quality of her previous night's sleep and how many calories she burned during the previous day. The food in her kitchen is prepared automatically; artificial meat is cultivated in bioreactors and the refrigerator is automatically filled from purchases made online. Mia travels to work on a high-speed train. If she wants to move through the city more privately, she can do so in an autonomous electric car. She works in a support center for autonomous vehicles and it is her job to commandeer a simulator to control a driverless lorry through busy city centers when human support is required. Mia only has to work four hours a day thanks to the productivity benefits afforded by robotics and artificial intelligence technologies. In their free time, Mia and her friends enjoy virtual reality experiences, travelling to faraway places, perhaps to an outpost on Mars for a drive over the Red Planet's undulating dunes.

The scenario above was originally recounted by two journalists writing in the German news weekly, *Der Spiegel*, in collaboration with futurologists from the Ars Electronica Future Lab. The article positions itself as an 'optimistic vision of the future, though, not necessarily the most realistic'.[1] Despite the oft portended risks and harms associated with mass digitalization, the authors here are more concerned with 'the opportunities offered by the future', based not on their 'unrestrained imagination' but, rather, on suggestions inferred by 'current research' to offer a vision of the future that reflects current innovations in media technology.

There are several reasons why I have begun this book with Mia's story. First of all, Mia's everyday life demonstrates what a deeply mediatized life might look like. Some of the features described in the scenario are already part of our lives today: while Ben's functionalities are more extensive than current assistive technologies, we already have similar companions embedded in our smartphones, our smart watches and in other smart devices; they can be seen in Amazon's Alexa, Microsoft's Cortana or Apple's Siri. They are already capable of logging our appointments, we can dictate messages and emails, search for information and make purchases using simple voice commands. These companions already 'live' in 'the cloud' and it seems that we might be well on the way to a scenario akin to the one described above.

But this scenario is also interesting in terms of what is does *not* address – namely, the potentially problematic aspects of a life so richly augmented by always connected media technologies. For example, these artificial companions continuously collect data on us while we use them. In many cases, the automated analysis of these data is the core business model behind their manufacture. Technologies such as those that control vehicles and other equipment via simulation interfaces are already common in more professions than we might think. But again, it is not made clear in *Der Spiegel*'s vision of the future in which areas simulation control are currently most widespread and if we were to investigate its use more thoroughly we would find that their predominant field of use is in the American military and its control of Unmanned Aerial Vehicles (UAVs).[2] On the one hand, therefore, Mia's story is perhaps not so different from contemporary life where digital media and technology already saturate everyday life. In the context of media and communications research, this increasing 'entanglement' (Scott & Orlikowski 2014: 873) of our social world with pervasive media technologies can be referred to as deep mediatization. On the other hand, *Der Spiegel*'s tale of an everyday life simply made better and more efficient thanks to digital technologies remains myopic of the possible negative ramifications of a life molded by deep mediatization.

This utopian description of a technological future is consistent with many mainstream depictions of media-related change that present us with their imaginaries of possible futures. Journalists and futurologists alike promise a 'brave new world' made possible through media technology. Their world is 'white', it is 'clean' and just 'better', because it is created by 'white', 'clean' and 'better' media technologies. We can trace these myths back to the beginning of digitalization. As early as the 1950s, 1960s and 1970s, tales were told of digital media technologies that would bring a plethora of 'positive' transformations to society, we would engage with a 'new economy' (Alexander 1983), for example, and live and interact with each other in 'virtual communities' (Rheingold 1994).

In this sense, deep mediatization is not simply 'produced' by technology companies and 'appropriated' by users. It is also imagined by various actors and driven forward by visions such as those described above which often adopt positive future scenarios. We are dealing here with a highly dynamic and multilayered process.

FROM MEDIATIZATION TO DEEP MEDIATIZATION

Mediatization, a concept often harnessed by the social sciences and cultural studies, refers to an experience everybody is acquainted with in his or her everyday life: technological communication media saturate more and more social domains which are drastically transforming at the same time. More specifically, mediatization refers to the relationship between the transformation of media and communication on the one hand and culture and society on the other (Couldry & Hepp 2013: 197). With reference to everyday experience, it can be said that mediatization has 'quantitative' as well as 'qualitative' characteristics.

Quantitative observations are concerned with media's ever-increasing proliferation through society. They can be measured temporally (media were once only available at certain times of day; they can now be accessed 24 hours a day), spatially (media in the past were often static; they are now accessible in more and more places) and socially (our social practices become entangled with and augmented by a variety of media) (Krotz 2007a: 96). Some media scholars have argued that media have become so pervasive we can refer to the 'mediation of everything' (Livingstone 2009: 1).

A qualitative analysis of mediatization focuses its attention, both empirically and theoretically, on the specific consequences of this saturation of everyday life by media and to what extent this affects social and cultural change.[3] But mediatization research does not deal with the effects of individual media content, rather, it is more concerned with the ways in which society and human practices are transformed more generally by media's ability to mold and shape them. Mediatization can therefore be understood as a 'sensitizing concept'.[4] A sensitizing concept 'gives the user a general sense of reference and guidance in approaching empirical instances' (Blumer 1954: 7) and draws their attention to (present) phenomena in culture and society. On these terms, mediatization 'sensitizes' us to fundamental transformations we experience in the context of today's media environment, and this occurs in three ways in particular: the historical depth of the process of media-related transformations, the diversity of media-related transformations in different domains of society and the connection of media-related transformations to further processes of modernization (Lunt & Livingstone 2016: 465).

A more recent focal point within mediatization research is media's digital character and a need to rethink the whole idea of mediatization because of it. While initial contributions on this matter have been fairly general in tone (Finnemann 2014, Miller 2014), the discussion has intensified and become more specific as digitalization has advanced the processes of mediatization. The reasons for this are multifaceted. Mediatization research has become aware that media is characterized less by the dominant influence of one (digital) medium but more about the differentiation of highly connected digital media and how this affects communication. The focus has shifted, therefore, to life's 'polymedia' (Madianou 2014: 323) character and the 'media-manifold' (Couldry 2012: 16) nature of today's media environment. Against this background, and in order to understand how media shape the entire scope of social domains, it is necessary to consider digital media in terms of their interrelatedness with each other. Furthermore, mediatization research is attentive to the fact that digital media are not merely means of communication. By virtue of being digital, they are at the same time means of generating data while they are used for communication tasks. These data are used as a source for various forms of automated processing which has become a fundamental part of the construction of our social world.

To emphasize, digitalization has seen us emerge into a new stage of mediatization which we can identify as *deep mediatization*. Deep mediatization is an advanced stage of the process in which all elements of our social world are intricately related to digital media and their underlying infrastructures (Couldry & Hepp 2017: 7, 34). As previous research has shown, mediatization is not a linear process, it occurs in various 'waves' of fundamental change to the media environment. If we look at the past few hundred years, we can identify at least three primary waves of mediatization that have affected society in quite startling ways: mechanization, electrification and digitization.

Mechanization refers to the changes in media practice and distribution engendered by mechanical processes typically exemplified by the invention of the printing press in the 1400s as well as more modern mechanical media such as the typewriters and cameras that came along in the 19th and 20th centuries. Electrification is concerned with the development of electronic media over the course of the 20th century; to a large extent, radio and television are the first things that come to mind, but we can also think about technologies such as the phonograph and the telephone. We can plainly see that, through processes of 'remediation' (Bolter & Grusin 2000), older technologies are refashioned into new ones; just as photography remediated painting, the electrical powered off-set printer, and eventually the photocopier, remediated Gutenberg's press; the typewriter was refashioned into the electric typewriter and the computer keyboard, cinema into television and so on. The most current wave of mediatization is digitalization, which stimulated the trend toward increasing datafication.[5] Media are increasingly computerized and objects not previously considered as media, a car, for example, are made media by virtue of their digital connectivity. Since these digital media are now software-based and can be automated by means of algorithms – rules for operation, such as those laid down in computer programs – they are no longer simply communicative tools, they also act as generators of data demonstrating clearly how the advanced stage of deep mediatization is firmly grounded in media's digitization.

The waves of mediatization described above are intrinsically contradictory and have manifested themselves as the consequence of forces beyond themselves at different stages throughout history. However, it is clear that media's pervasiveness in our lives is made possible largely as a consequence of them being refashioned into the digital realm. These software-based media are shaped in a wide variety of digital devices. 'Radio' as a medium, for example, is no longer tied to the radio set. With a variety of software solutions, we can use a whole range of digital devices to listen to the radio. Some still look like radios (the digital radio as a discrete device), some are representations on our screens through specific software (a radio app on a smartphone) and we can apply the same principle to television, telephony and the entire breadth of media services and devices we make use of.

Deep mediatization presents a challenge to mediatization research as it must incorporate the analysis of algorithms, data and digital infrastructures. Investigating algorithms becomes necessary because in a state of deep mediatization facets of the mediated construction of the social world occur through automated data processing. The classification of data, for example, on certain consumer groups when shopping online or personal recommendations based on download histories must be analyzed in a different way compared to political discussions on talk shows, for example.[6] Attention needs to be paid to the digital infrastructures that underpin contemporary media.[7]

As mediatization is a concept that sensitizes us to the more recent changes in digital media we must rethink its current research paths once again because we are forced to further integrate analytical concepts that address questions of algorithms, data and digital infrastructures. In light of this analytical requirement, the term deep mediatization also resonates with various other uses of 'deep' such as 'deep learning' (which is understood as a new level of automated learning processes based on algorithmic processes) or 'deep analytics' (which is applied to data mining). The use of deep mediatization as a term is, therefore, deliberate because it is the stage of mediatization in which the analysis of algorithms, data and artificial intelligence become crucial to our understanding of the social world.

TRADITIONS AND PERSPECTIVES

With my focus on deep mediatization, I position this book within a certain perspective of the discourse on mediatization. In doing so, I will refer to two lines of thought that can be distinguished in previous and current research, these are the institutionalist and the social-constructivist traditions.[8]

The institutionalist tradition on mediatization arose from mass communication and journalism research. Research carried out in this tradition focuses on the role media – understood as a 'semi-independent institution' (Hjarvard 2013: 21) – play in influencing other areas of culture and society that are apparently external to it, a process that often harnesses the metaphor of 'media logic'. Originally developed by David Altheide and Robert Snow in 1979, media logic theory describes the influence discrete mass-media formats have on other areas of society such as politics or religion. More recently, media logic has been utilized more broadly and is often pluralized so that as an analytical tool it may consider the existence of numerous media-related dynamics.[9] Media logics, then, act as 'a metaphor and short-hand for the various modi operandi that characterize the workings of the media' (Hjarvard 2017: 11). Approaches to media logics refer to the operationalization of media forms (genres, framing etc.), the logics of organizational rules (work routines, decision making) and the logics of media's technological affordances (the material characteristics of devices and platforms, etc.). In harnessing the media logics metaphor, media influence is not conceptualized as a more-or-less direct effect but is instead considered as a more complex process of interrelating logics: non-media institutions (in the fields of politics, religion etc.) have their own 'logics' which in turn have the potential to work against media logics which can result in a certain inertia and resistance against a changing media environment.

The social-constructivist tradition finds its origins in media practice research with a focus on media use as well as media production. It emphasizes the role of media in the communicative construction of social and cultural reality and mainly explores mediatization from the perspective of the everyday (Knoblauch 2013, Krotz 2014). Researchers in this tradition investigate how social practices change when they are entangled with media. Here, we can see another way of theorizing the influence media may have which moves beyond the idea of media logics and the direct influences of media's materiality. Media influence is conceptualized as an 'institutionalization' and 'materialization' of social practices (Couldry & Hepp 2017: 32). When it comes to individual media, institutionalization refers to a stabilization of the patterns of communication and of expectations in the process: we know how a certain medium is typically used for communication, we communicate with the help of this medium in that way and we expect others to do the same. This goes hand in hand with materialization, which means that such patterns are themselves inscribed in the media technologies and the (digital) infrastructures that accommodate them. Messenger software, for example, materializes a certain way of 'talking' through its software-based user interface. Institutionalization and materialization are not, however, a one-way street. Each social domain (community, organization etc.) already has its own orientation in everyday practice which is partly supported by media's processes of institutionalization and materialization and partly challenged by them. One can take the family or school as an example. Many of their constitutive practices are now subsumed by digital media. We can look at the practice of creating family albums, which is replicated in the structuring of corresponding photo software, or the digitized school administration system, which replicates the organizational structure of the school. At the same time, the constitutive practices of family and school are challenged by digital media when direct family communication at the dining table is confronted with the parallel communication of children using their smartphones or when the school's organizational communication shifts to messenger services that are beyond the control of the organization. The social-constructivist tradition of mediatization research is concerned with reconstructing the dynamics of these changing conditions of social construction without assuming certain logics from the outset.

Perhaps we are witnessing a convergence of these two traditions and related perspectives. This convergence might have its cause in the latest changes in media technologies which have implications for both traditions: as digital media saturate various domains of society and as they are closely entangled with each domain's practices, it is difficult to assume that media are 'semi-independent institutions' as they are considered in the institutionalist tradition. Digital media are entangled with the practices that produce institutions in such a way that it is hardly possible to juxtapose media logics with institutional logics. At the same time, we must also bear in mind that investigating digital media does not simply mean that we research everyday practices and the communicative construction of society at the level of media use, but we should also bear in mind the role played by large corporations such as Alphabet, Amazon, Apple, Facebook and Microsoft and the infrastructures that they (and others) build. At this point, the original social-constructivist arguments need extending by, among other things, giving greater consideration to the role of institutions in the 'making' of deep mediatization.

In general, it would be misleading to equate the term mediatization in one or both of these traditions with a closed theory of media change. At this point it is helpful to remember again the argument that mediatization is a 'sensitizing concept', that is, it sets out to sensitize us to current social transformations. As such, the term cannot stand on its own as a self-contained theory but another point of view might be more helpful: Mediatization is a sensitizing concept around which various researchers have gathered, researchers who are interested in an empirically based investigation of the significance of the role media plays in the transformation of culture and society. What these researchers have in common is that they are looking for approaches that go beyond simple models of effect and try to see the current change in a more long-term, historical perspective and across various media.[10] From this point of view, the term mediatization refers to an open, ongoing discourse of theorizing social and cultural transformation in relation to media and communications.

Within this discussion, this book takes a position that Nick Couldry and I have described elsewhere; one of 'materialist phenomenology' (Couldry & Hepp 2017: 5–8). Like Raymond Williams (1990) with his idea of 'cultural materialism', we emphasize that it is fundamental for any analysis of media and communication to consider *both* the material and the symbolic. In times of deep mediatization, the consideration of both is likely even more urgent than was already the case with television which Williams referred to in his work: The 'materiality' of today's media concerns not only the various devices, cable networks and satellites. As I already emphasized above, since today's media are largely software-based, it is important to consider that complex tasks can and most likely will be 'moved' to algorithms. It is necessary, therefore, to think much more rigorously about the materiality of media and to also pose questions on which kind of agency is involved and at what times. A *materialist* phenomenology scrutinizes media technologies and infrastructures through and on the basis of contemporary communications.

Despite the important role played by data and algorithms, questions of *human meaning* and *sense-making* are still a central issue for any analysis of social construction. Financial products that make up much of today's globalized stock exchanges, for example, are often completely based on processed data and are wholly intangible without a visual, computer-based representation of the processed data.[11] But the processed data is only given significance as a financial product through the attribution of meaning, meaning given to it by people. For this reason, it is important not to lose sight of the symbolic: the construction of meaning in times of deep mediatization. The material *phenomenology* approach means understanding that, whatever its appearance of complexity and opacity, the social world remains accessible to interpretation and understanding by human actors. Indeed, it is a structure built up, in part, through those interpretations and understandings.

One of material phenomenology's key concerns should be the respective actors involved, whether they be individuals or supra-individual actors such as corporations and collectives.[12] To accommodate this concern this book explores mediatization from an actors' point of view: Mediatization is not a process that just 'happens'. While this process involves a variety of technologies and some of the most complex infrastructures in history, it remains one made by humans who give it meaning: *individual actors* as single humans, *corporative actors* as organizations, companies and state agencies as well as *collective actors* as communities or social movements. Adopting an actors' point of view on deep mediatization means trying to gain an understanding of how mediatization takes place where a variety of actors intersect.

Deep mediatization is characterized by the extent to which the practices of these different actors are *entangled* with digital media and their infrastructures (Scott & Orlikowski 2014). As media saturate the various domains of society, they have also become part of the practices through which these social domains are constructed. Practices perhaps not considered media-related in the past are becoming media practices.[13] In the office and the laboratory, at school and at university, with family or among friends, our current practices are characterized by the fact that we also conduct them with and through media. This foregrounds one particular situation that is revealed by deep mediatization; that practices involving physical activity – handiwork, cleaning, driving, cooking and so on – are closely interwoven with practices of communication (Reichertz 2009: 118–220). When we do things together, we coordinate our actions and orientate our knowledge through communication, and we project our goals through communicative means. With the entanglement of general social practices with media, the separation between communicative action and physical action becomes blurred. The analytically more interesting question is probably more one of how the two refer to each other – and physical practices become media practices as well. A good example for this is the automated tracking of walking, cycling and sleeping by the help of smart watches.

By tracing a material phenomenological route through our analysis, we can understand deep mediatization as a process of *recursive transformation* (Couldry & Hepp 2017: 216–218). Recursivity, a term whose origins lie in logic and computer science, indicates that rules are reapplied to the entity that generated them (Kelty 2008). We sustain it and make necessary adjustments when problems arise, by replaying once again the rules and norms on which it was previously based.[14] Today's recursivity is heightened in an environment characterized by deep mediatization and many forms of practice now involve the use of software and its associated algorithms that do their work through recursive functions.[15] Since software must operate in the wider space of connection even apparently simple acts carried out by social actors depend on many levels of recursion. The transformation of society becomes a *deeply* recursive one: rules for how something should change are inscribed into data processing algorithms which are reapplied to the social phenomena they collect data on and through these recursive loops they are themselves an influential factor in the transformation of social phenomena.

THE CHAPTERS OF THIS BOOK

It is from this point of view that the arguments that follow will flow. If this introductory chapter has provided an initial presentation of the concept of deep mediatization and situated it within further mediatization research, the chapters that follow aim to elaborate in more detail the processes involved in deep mediatization's social and technological formation and attempt to grasp it empirically.

Chapter 2, 'The making of deep mediatization', begins from an actor-centered perspective and sets out to discuss the emergence of deep mediatization. In this chapter, corporate actors (tech corporations and governments) as well as collective actors (the various pioneer communities that have advanced the development of technologies) are harnessed as key points of interest. My main concern is to show that the 'making' of deep mediatization cannot be reduced to the activities of large companies and governments, as is often the case made by a political economy approach to the media. We are already dealing here with a recursive interplay of corporate and collective actors and can only grasp the emergence of deep mediatization if we are acquainted with these dynamics. At its current stage, this interplay has led to five quantitative trends: the differentiation of a variety of end devices as media, their intensifying connectivity through the internet, the rising omnipresence of these media through mobile communication technologies, an accelerated pace of innovation and finally, the emergence of datafication.

Chapter 3, 'Media as a process', argues that it is impossible to grasp deep mediatization without an appropriate concept of media. My main concern in this chapter is to understand media as a process; media are not simply 'there', but they arise in the ongoing process of institutionalization and materialization of communication. Looking at media in this way sheds new light on the discussion on 'media logic'. It becomes clear that media's processual character became most significant at the moment they became digital: based on algorithms and infrastructures, they are generated in narrow recursiveness loops and exist in a state of continuous 'beta'. While media mold the social world through their institutionalization and materialization, we would be indulging in a certain reification if we were to speak of fixed logics as inert properties of media. Rather, one must sharpen one's eye to the processes playing out in their development and use, especially since digital media's capacity to shape the social world never stems from one single medium. We are confronted with a media manifold which is concretized by media ensembles within different social domains and in the media repertories of individuals.

Chapter 4, 'A figurational approach', discusses my principal approach to deep mediatization. Put simply, figurations are exemplary constellations of humans such as can be found in families, communities, organizations or around certain media. My main argument in this chapter is that if we want to understand deep mediatization, our analysis should not start with media themselves but by comparatively analyzing the figurations of different social domains. However, today's figurations are comprehensively interwoven with digital media and their infrastructures. When it comes to society, the main argument of such an approach is that its transformation is best understood as a process of recursive transformation which we can name re-figuration: of a structural change of figurations as well as their interrelatedness to each other in which digital media and infrastructures speed up the loops of recursivity. In sum, a figurational approach has close links to a 'non-media centric perspective' which first analyzes human practices and then the role digital media and infrastructures play within them and the transformations that can occur as a consequence.

Chapter 5, 'Deep mediatization's re-figuration of society', focuses on societal change as a process of transforming figurations and their interrelatedness to each other. The main topics include the changing interrelatedness of figurations through myth, data and infrastructures, the transformation of existing figurations such as organizations (which are discussed through the examples of public debate and news production) and communities (which are discussed through the example of local and transnational families) and the emergence of new figurations (platform collectivities, connective action and global financial markets). Across these examples we are dealing with the 'activation' of the media ensemble for individual figurations and how automation and communicative robots become part of their social construction.

In all, my aim with this chapter is to show that deep mediatization is at the same moment a transformation process that 'works' across figurations but has its particularities in relation to the specificities of figurations.

Chapter 6, 'The individual in times of deep mediatization', flips the perspective of figurations as whole to the embedding of the individual within them. Here I will discuss the consequences of involvement in a multiplicity of figurations and how this shapes individual news repertoires and media practices. One particular change that takes place at the level of the individual is that the digital traces he or she leaves across different figurations are accumulated in the form of 'data doubles'. Such data doubles are highly ambivalent, an individual's data double provides opportunities for surveillance by companies and corporate actors as well as for the 'interveillance' of each other in partnerships, groups or communities. But data doubles also can be a resource for managing and changing one's own life course as the example of self-tracking shows. The particular foci of this chapter are, therefore, the ambivalences of deep mediatization for the individual and the question of how far this relates to a changing social character or habitus.

The conclusion of this book, Chapter 7, is entitled 'Deep mediatization and the good life'. In this chapter, I discuss deep mediatization from a normative point of view. While the 'making' of deep mediatization was closely related to the idea of forming a generation of digital natives which would change the world for the better, the analysis within this book has demonstrated that it is a highly contradictory meta-process of change. But despite these issues, it would be a mistake to assume that the process of deep mediatization could simply be 'switched off'. Therefore, we are confronted with the question of what form deep mediatization *should* take to make a 'good life' possible under the conditions it produces. Here, I refer to the *Gestaltung* of deep mediatization – a German term I use to address the impending formation of mediatization in a normatively better way.

My hope is to be able to give a general insight into the discussion on deep mediatization with this compact volume. My aim is to explain the ambivalence of deep mediatization as a process we are all confronted with, albeit in different ways. It is only possible to form this process of change in a productive way if one deals with it analytically and precisely. This book is sets out to provide an inspiration toward achieving that goal.

I do not see this book as a standard introduction to a scientific field. This would be difficult, even impossible, to achieve as research into deep mediatization is only just beginning to find its feet. My aim with this book is to invite the reader to an emerging discussion. With this in mind it may be helpful to consider this book alongside a number of other publications: those interested in mediatization in general will find access to this discussion through introductory publications such as the monograph by Stig Hjarvard (2013), a handbook edited by Knut Lundby (2014a), an anthology by Frank Esser and Jesper Strömbäck (2014), a book I wrote myself (Hepp 2013) and the publications of the Mediatization Section of the European Communication Research and Education Association (Driessens et al. 2017, Thimm et al. 2018b). These titles do more than enough to provide a clear yet thorough intro-duction to the *general* discussion on mediatization.

As mentioned above, this book aspires to be much more specific in that it is about providing access to the idea of *deep* mediatization. As this discussion is mostly about an advanced stage of mediatiza-tion in which questions of algorithms, data and digital infrastructures are relevant, new interdisciplinary relationships will emerge and this book encourages media and communications research to engage with a range of fields including software studies, sociology of technology and science and technology studies. If anything is brought to light by deep mediatization and digital media's entanglement with so many facets of social and technological life, it is with a certain urgency that the field ought to bridge the gap between itself and an ever-increasing number of academic disciplines.

At its core, my arguments are closely related to a series of other publications I have written with various colleagues. In *The Mediated Construction of Reality* (Couldry & Hepp 2017), Nick Couldry and I developed the concept of deep mediatization and the basis for a *figurational* approach to its analysis. From the research network *Communicative Figurations*, a number of other publications have been published, namely the anthology *Communicative Figurations: Transforming Communications in Times of Deep Mediatization* (Hepp et al. 2017b), a thematic issue on digital traces in context (Hepp et al. 2018b) and another thematic issue on social constructivism in media and communications research (Hepp et al. 2017). Our aim in these publications was to operationalize research on deep mediatization and I will refer to them frequently.

NOTES

1 See, www.spiegel.de/wirtschaft/deutschland-in-der-zukunft-wie-wir-2037-leben-wer den-a-1183331.html (accessed: May 1, 2019, author's translation).

2 Another vivid fictional account of this kind of working environment is portrayed in the film *Eye on Juliet* (2018), in which the main character, Gordon, works as a spider drone operator and supervisor of a Middle Eastern oil pipeline. See, http://eyeonjuliet-themovie.ca (accessed: May 1, 2019).

3 For a general discussion, see, Lundby (2014a).

4 With regard to this argument, see, Jensen (2013: 206).

5 In our book *The Mediated Construction of Reality*, Nick Couldry and I discussed the possibility that a 'new wave of datafication is under way within the wave of digitalization' (Couldry & Hepp 2017: 41). Extending our original reflections, my following argument is that we best understand datafication as one of the trends within deep mediatization, which, in turn, is a consequence of digitalization.

6 See, for example, Beer (2016) and Gillespie et al. (2014).

7 See, Bowker et al. (2010), Parks & Starosielski (2015b), Karasti & Baker (2004) and Mosco (2017).

8 Göran Bolin (2014, 2017: 19–24) and Knut Lundby (2014b) distinguish three tra-ditions of mediatization research: in addition to the institutionalist and social-constructivist approaches mentioned above, a technological one. However, I share with André Jansson (2018: 2–3) the argument that while we can distinguish a technological perspective in principle, it has not emerged as an independent tradition in mediatization research.

9 For an overview, see, Strömbäck and Esser (2014a) and Thimm et al. (2018b).

10 See, among other publications, the discussion on the mediatization approach in the journal *Media, Culture & Society*: Deacon & Stanyer (2014), Hepp et al. (2015), Lunt & Livingstone (2016) and Ekström et al. (2016).

11 This is discussed by Karin Knorr-Cetina, using the concept of 'scopic media' to emphasize the 'flowing representation' of corresponding information; see, Knorr Cetina (2014).

12 For the distinction between 'individual actors' and 'supra-individual actors', see, Schimank (2010: 327–341).

13 For a general approach to media as practice, see, Couldry (2004) and Couldry (2012). For a discussion on the relationship between communicative action and other forms of human action, see, Reichertz (2008) and Reichertz (2011).

14 This has been shown in the field of ethnomethodology (Garfinkel 1967), to which Anthony (Giddens 1984) also refers in his theory of structuration.

15 For an overview, see, for example, Beer (2017), Gillespie (2014), Manovich (2013) and Striphas (2015).

2

THE MAKING OF DEEP MEDIATIZATION

As outlined in the introduction to this book, one of its principal aims is to look at deep mediatization from the actors' point of view to better reflect on how deep mediatization is rooted in human practices that are increasingly entangled with digital media and their related infrastructures. Adopting this perspective means understanding that deep mediatization is not just an independent 'natural' process. Deep mediatization is a socially bound 'meta-process' (Krotz 2007b: 256); much like processes of individualization, commercialization and globalization, it is an overarching process of social transformation that is solidified within numerous other sub-processes. But, as a meta-process – bearing in mind its own dynamics – deep mediatization remains grounded in human practices and should be analyzed as such. A first step in such an analysis is to consider the *making* of deep mediatization. I use the term 'making' in a wider sense, as the 'production' of deep mediatization, as the 'building' of the digital media and infrastructures that constitute the technological pillar of deep mediatization.

In considering the making of deep mediatization from an actors' point of view, different kinds of 'supra-individual actors' (Schimank 2010: 327–341) require our attention. Supra-individual actors are figurations of individuals with their own agency. This includes 'corporate actors' such as companies and state agencies, and 'collective actors' such as social movements and pioneer communities.

With reference to the making of deep mediatization, *corporate actors* such as media and tech companies are perhaps the first supra-individual actors that come to mind. Looking at the Western world, we would struggle to imagine deep mediatization without noticing the activities of companies such as Alphabet (Google), Amazon, Apple, Facebook and others. If we extend our view to take in the rest of the world other large companies such as the Alibaba Group in China and its subsidiaries such as Taobao (an online auction house) or Alipay (an online payment system) play just as important a role in the emergence of deep mediatization as their Western counterparts do. And there are companies that provide certain service platforms like Airbnb for accommodation or Didi Chuxing and Uber for transport. Furthermore, we cannot understand the success of media and tech companies like these without considering other corporate actors: governments and state agencies that support (or hinder) market engagement. All this brings us to a point where we must reflect on the role political economy plays in deep mediatization's making to comprehensively understand its contemporary processes.

Focusing solely on the political economy of deep mediatization would only give us a one-dimensional view of its making. In addition, we have to consider *collective actors*. The main actors in this sense are what I refer to as pioneer communities. These are groups of media and technology related pioneers that seek to foster media related developments across society. A historical view shows that these pioneer communities have played – and continue to play – a significant role in the making of deep mediatization. One historical example is the Whole Earth Network, while in the present-day movements such as the Quantified Self, Maker and Hacks/Hackers movements continue this legacy. Social movements 'act on media' (Kannengießer & Kubitschko 2017: 1), that is, they understand media not only as a 'tool' to communicate their political messages to a broad audience, but they consider media to be so central to our society that as a social movement they stand up for certain forms of media organizations, media infrastructures and media technologies. In so doing they are more focused on campaigning for equitable media and the appropriate regulation of (digital) media and infrastructures and less on pushing the process of deep mediatization itself. Nevertheless, in carrying out these activities they are crucial to the making of deep mediatization.

What really differentiates corporate and collective actors is the character of their supra-individual agency: the agency of corporate actors such as technology companies and state agencies is rooted in binding agreements which are articulated in ongoing practices. The agency of collective actors like pioneer communities or social movements is rooted in shared patterns of perception, evaluation and imagination as expressed by their participants in similarly ongoing practices. Collective actors are much more fluid than corporate actors.

In the first two sections of this chapter, I would like to deal with the supra-individual actors who have promoted the making of deep mediatization the most: on the one hand corporate actors and state agencies and their engagement with an emerging political economy of digital infrastructures; on the other, pioneer communities and their experimental practices and imaginaries of a deeply mediatized world. While companies and state agencies certainly have the greater power at first glance, we will see that the experimental practices and imaginaries of the pioneer communities represent a driving force that should not be underestimated. That said, it would be too simplistic to understand deep mediatization as the direct outcome of the strategies of these supra-individual actors alone. Rather, we should be aware that these actors' engagement cumulates in certain more general, quantitative trends. These trends are symptomatic of the Global North, yet their prevalence is being noticed in other parts of the world as well.

A POLITICAL ECONOMY OF DIGITAL INFRASTRUCTURES

Mediatization research is often criticized for ignoring the political economy of recent media-related changes. This criticism's main argument is that 'mediatization research has not so far developed a comprehensive analysis of the central role played by the resurgence of market fundamentalist models of capitalism in reorganizing the relations between media and social and cultural life it seeks to address'

(Murdock 2017: 119). More specifically, this argument maintains that many of the transformations related to mediatization are mainly driven by the penetration of market models for media and communications leading to a comprehension of media products solely as commodities. Such processes of commercialization are certainly closely interwoven with deep mediatization, just as individualization is, but at the same time, one must bear in mind that deep mediatization cannot be reduced to questions of economics and the market. The dynamics we are dealing with are much more diverse.

Capitalism and the emergence of the internet

The view that media contents are reproducible commodities has been discussed at least since the Frankfurt School and the works of Walter Benjamin (1977, orig. 1936). With the deregulation of the 1980s, however, such arguments have established an enduring importance. The view that media are commodities gained traction in an era of blanket deregulation that began in the 1980s (Hall 1997: 229–230): radio, (satellite) television and telecommunications were privatized and organized along market models instead of public service ones. The emergence of the internet and digital media coincided with the same dominant perspective on media as a commodity. After an early phase as a military and research network, the worldwide establishment of the internet became a commercial undertaking from the outset. The idea of organizing individual platforms or the infrastructure of the internet as a public service, for example, was not even considered beyond small circles of experts.[1]

This is not only the case for the Global North. Across the world media and communications services are organized more or less along the principles of 'market capitalism' and 'digital capitalism' (McChesney 2013, Herman & McChesney 1997), particularly in the case of the aforementioned media and tech companies such as Alibaba, Apple and Facebook. These companies and the services they provide constitute some of the main forces shaping the datafication of society by pushing data-based value models. Following on from this idea, the core challenge for media and communications research from a political economy perspective would not be ideal for tackling the idea of 'deep mediatization' but rather how it deals with the existence of a kind of 'deep capitalism' (Murdock 2017: 130). With digital media and their infrastructures, a much 'deeper' saturation of everyday life with *capitalist* practices and values would be more possible than ever before. Digital platforms such as Foodora, Amazon's Mechanical Turk or Uber, for example, allow for the precise monitoring of those who offer their labor. Any everyday practice can become a resource of value creation if they leave behind digital traces: the processing of online activity enables a range of corporate actors to construct personalized profiles so that our data may become a serious source of revenue for personalized, granular advertising. Nick Couldry and Ulises Mejias (2019b) have described the harnessing of users' digital traces as a kind of 'data colonialism'. In their description, colonialism relates to both the relationships of global exploitation practiced by states and businesses as well as the 'colonization of the lifeworld' (Habermas 1984: 356), that is, the increasing penetration of the lifeworld by the capitalist system.[2]

These developments play an important role in our understanding of the making of deep mediatization. From an actors' point of view, large media and technology companies in tandem with wider political forces and state agencies have been crucial. Particularly fundamental for the idea of deep mediatization is what we might call the commercialization of the internet: it was the provision of large amounts of both private and public capital that made the internet and deep mediatization's principal infrastructures possible. I will discuss this in more detail in Chapter 4 when I approach deep mediatization's re-figuration of society.

At the same time a broader view of *digital infrastructure* is necessary to understand these transformations – a view that reduces them not only to questions of political economy but includes a more detailed perspective on the practices and dynamics of different social and cultural contexts. While historical studies have already demonstrated the need for just such a broader view,[3] it has become a crucial point for investigating more recent developments in digital infrastructures, especially when analyzing the growth of global connectivity.[4] Terminologically, 'infrastructure' is a 'kaleidoscopic' concept with many implications. This has to do with the fact that any definition of infrastructure depends on the perspective of definition. Railroad tracks, for example, which, for the traveler, represent infrastructure, represent for the railroad engineer the focus and the result of their work. We can conclude, then, that analytically, 'infrastructure appears only as a relational property, not as a thing stripped of use' (Star & Ruhleder 1996: 113). We should rather ask, therefore, 'when' does something constitute infrastructure, not 'what' is infrastructure. Taking this into account and extending the definition by Lisa Parks and Nicole Starosielski (2015a: 4), digital infrastructures are situated sociotechnical arrangements that are designed and configured to support the distribution of digital signal traffic.

Looking back at the history of the internet, the extent to which governments and state agencies have played a role in the development of this digital infrastructures is clear. In its pre-market phase, the internet was supported by the US 'military-scientific complex' (Curran 2016: 50). ARPANET, the precursor to the internet was developed by the Pentagon's Advanced Research Projects Agency (ARPA) and later supported through various National Science Foundation (NSF) programs (Greenstein 2015: 27–30); while in Europe, public bodies such as the European Organization for Nuclear Research (CERN), where the World Wide Web was designed,[5] played a fundamental role in building the internet as we know it today. In 1993 the NSF's final plan for the privatization of the internet emerged and this moment can be seen as the starting point in the transformation of the internet into a commercial digital infrastructure. In this process, a shifting oligopoly of companies dominated the internet's development: during the first phase of its commercialization, the scene was led by WorldCom and AOL while more recently the major players have been Alphabet (Google), Amazon, Apple, Facebook and Microsoft in the Global North. In other regions of the world companies such as Alibaba and Baidu in China hold a dominant commercial position in regard to internet services. The ever-shifting dominance of certain supra-individual actors – their ascent and descent – represents the changing character of the internet.

At this point it is crucial to emphasize that the transformation of the internet into a commercial infrastructure did not happen by accident but was largely driven by political strategies and government policies. It was a *political strategy* of the US government to build the Advanced Research Projects Agency (APRA) with the idea to support interdisciplinary research to strengthen the US position during the Cold War. It was also a *political decision* – in the case of the Clinton administration – to privatize the internet's supervisory institutions, namely the Internet Assigned Number Authority (IANA). The IANA became a division of the Internet Corporation for Assigned Names (ICAN), which is still responsible for the global administration of domain names, the allocation of IP addresses and the coordination of the root server system. These are just a few examples of the fact that behind the individual decisions on the internet's path of development — including its privatization and commercialization — were broader political considerations and that it was by no means a 'natural' process. It was, as Mariana Mazzucato (2013) put it, an 'entrepreneurial state' which built up an 'innovation system' at the interface of the military, academic research and business institutions that made the development of the computer industries and the internet possible. The result of these factors in the development of the internet as a commercial concern represents a paradox in that, on the one hand, 'free markets and innovation from the edges' is widely encouraged while at the same time the 'state-supported formation of large media and technology companies' is championed.

It is evident, therefore, that political economy still matters if we want to understand the making of deep mediatization. But because of the profound changes it provokes we have to move from a political economy of media content to a *political economy of digital infrastructures* which as a global phenomenon needs contextualizing locally, regionally and nationally. If we take a closer look at a classical political economy outlook on the media, we can see that it was developed around the argument that mass media were essential organizations in society for economical and ideological reasons. Structured by a society's economy (base), according to a traditional political economy perspective, these media organizations produce content for communicative self-understanding within wider society (superstructure). Questions of ownership mattered because it represented and defined access to and the possibilities of societal communication. Large media companies had unique capabilities of communicating within society which meant that they had a broad influence on public discourse and dominant ideologies. To criticize the shift from public to private ownership – which was related to the global enforcement of private markets and commercialization – was actually a critique of who was able to communicate which ideology in what society.

Digitalization altered this scenario in many ways and the reasons are fourfold (see for the following, Wittel 2012: 317f.): first, the number of media producers increased dramatically. Using digital media – internet platforms, web pages, cameras integrated into mobile phones and so on – ordinary people became, in principal, producers of media content.[6] Second, digital media offer new social forms of distribution that have weakened large media organizations' monopoly on the distribution of media content to some degree. Furthermore, smaller organizations and even individuals are now able to reach a certain audience, to collaborate with each other and become part of a new practice of 'sharing' (John 2017). Third, as digital media pervade everyday life, new forms of production and distribution matter more for the social world. Fourth, and finally, digital technologies are not just media technologies, they are now built into all productive processes. In light of deep mediatization, the digital economy is not a distinct sphere, as the economy of the mass media once was, but, in fact, encompasses the entire economy. More and more business models of producing, distributing and selling 'things' have their basis somehow in digital media and their infrastructures.

Because of these transformations in media's political economy, a political economy of digital infrastructure matters. In essence, this is a political economy that is concerned with how large media and technology companies structure 'global networks and digital information flows and their consumption' (Mansell 2004: 99) and how state agencies are involved in these processes. These corporate actors are informed by both predominant and alternative principles, values and power relations. Ownership, commercialization and market models of distribution are still important but not just with respect to media content (Freedman 2009). They are of even greater importance because digital infrastructures are at *one and the same time* concerned with the production, distribution and communication of media content *as well as* that of other products. This explains the widening perspective in the recent discourse on the political economy of media, including, for example, the question of how digital infrastructures are transforming labor in the 21st century.[7]

Furthermore, ownership, commercialization and market models of distribution matter because new business models have emerged that are grouped around data. Large tech companies have developed an economic stranglehold through access to and the selling of user data. As a consequence, they can develop highly individualized models for addressing users with targeted advertising as a means of developing high revenues.[8] Once again, the implications of this unique access has effects beyond media when these data are perceived as a *general* source for decision making in society.[9] In this scenario, a political economy of digital infrastructures becomes not 'just about ideology and the manipulation of messages any more (base and superstructure), but also about the ownership of infrastructures, of networks and platforms that allow users to socialize, communicate and collaborate' (Wittel 2012: 318).

Digital infrastructures today

We can understand today's digital media only if we consider them as being embedded within digital infrastructures which have a particular materiality. Mobile communications technologies such as mobile phones, tablets, smart watches and many other devices that constitute a so-called 'internet of things' (Bunz & Meikle 2018, Greengard 2015) bring to light the physical basis of their existence. It is not only the cell towers installed in cities and across the countryside that we need to conside, but the (undersea) cable networks which constitute the main 'routes' for digital communication flows.[10]

Data centers form the basis of 'the cloud', the infrastructure of 'storage, processing, and distribution of data, applications and services for individuals and organizations' (Mosco 2014: 17) forming part of the technical protocols that undergird the internet (Galloway 2004, Mueller 2010). While we typically refer to 'the internet' as one unified object, it is based on a variety of different protocols that technically regulate data transfer.[11] We can see here the fundamental influence infrastructures have on the ways in which mediated communication occurs.

What, then, is the overall picture we are confronted with today? To answer this question, it is worth taking a closer look at the technology companies mentioned earlier. What becomes apparent is that these companies are not content providers, as is typically associated with the concept of media companies in a political economy analysis, rather, these companies are actually providers of digital infrastructure *for* media content as well as other services and products (see Table 2.1).[12]

Table 2.1 Western Technology Conglomerates as Providers of Digital Infrastructure

	Headquarters	Market value	Main products and services
Alphabet (Google)	Mountain View, California, USA	$ 863.2B	Web search, online advertising, video portal, communication services, operating systems, cloud services, network infrastructure, genetic engineering, security technology, artificial intelligence applications, financial services and payment systems
Amazon	Seattle, Washington, USA	$ 916.1B	Online trade (new and used goods), web and cloud services, warehouse automation, digital books, digital video rental, digital music, payment systems, organic food
Apple	Cupertino, California, USA	$ 961.3B	Operating systems, software, computers, laptops, tablets, smart phones, smart watches, cloud services, communication services, digital music, digital video
Facebook	Menlo Park, California, USA	$ 512B	Social network platforms, online advertising, online messaging
Microsoft	Redmond, Washington, USA	$ 946.5B	Operating systems, server applications, productivity applications, business solution applications, desktop and server management tools, software development tools, computer games and online advertising

Sources: The companies' websites, Forbes Global 2000 (as of 10.7.2019).

These leading technology companies – typically called the 'big five' – mostly complement each other in the sense that their main businesses differ. While we see overlaps in areas such as operating systems, online advertising and cloud services, other areas of competition are rather limited. This goes someway to explaining why we are dealing with oligopolistic structures rather than competitive ones. Many customers of these services have very few suppliers to choose from, and since the goods on offer are only limited substitutes, we are dealing with a heterogeneous oligopoly. On the whole, therefore, and despite repeated crises of the 'new digital economy' between 2001 and 2004, 'oligopolistic media capitalism' is relatively stable today. In these circumstances, it only seems logical that media companies 'jointly develop profitable markets, sometimes in competition, sometimes working together' (Prokop 2001: 421, author's translation). Competition is, rather, one between the Western oligopoly of the 'big five' and the Asian oligopoly led by the Alibaba group. They have a market value of $499.4 billion and its main products and services are trade and communication platforms for business to business and business to customers, an online auction house, financial services and payment systems, cloud computing and data management, online shopping and film production.

At the heart of their oligopoly is the high status of digital platforms (Gillespie 2010: 352), which bring together users, advertisers and customers in such a way that their own infrastructures of value creation have been built (Plantin & Punathambekar 2019: 2). At this point we are also talking about a *platform ecosystem* (van Dijck et al. 2018: 11). In the Americas and Europe, respectively, this platform ecosystem is dominated by the five technology companies mentioned above: Alphabet (Google), Amazon, Apple, Facebook and Microsoft. They provide 'infrastructural platforms' (van Dijck et al. 2018: 11) such as the Google and Apple app stores or Facebook's login API or Messenger,[13] on the basis of which other digital media can then be developed and distributed. 'Sectoral platforms' (van Dijck et al. 2018: 12) serve a specific area such as news, transport, food, accommodation and so on on the basis of these infrastructural platforms. This is the area in which companies like Airbnb, Foodora or Uber are active.

While this ecosystem in principle offers everyone the opportunity to contribute their own developments, its dynamic lies in the fact that the introduction of additional apps and services strengthens the platform ecosystem further. The more offers available on an infrastructural platform, the more important it becomes. So-called 'disruptive innovators' such as Netflix or Spotify also remain dependent on the infrastructure of the 'big five', with Spotify services accessing Google's cloud servers and Netflix using Amazon Web Services (cf. van Dijck et al. 2018: 12).

However, we must be wary of developing a limited view of the political economy of digital infrastructures. For example, we cannot reconcile what we call digital infrastructure with the products and services these companies provide. Digital infrastructures go much further. They include satellite networks, underwater cables and mobile masts, without which (mobile) internet access would not be possible. Here it is completely different companies that play a role, for example, when it comes to network routers where companies like Cisco are important or when it comes to the ownership of (submarine) communication cables where national telecommunications carriers still play a major part (Davenport 2012: 202f.). So, while companies such as Alphabet, Amazon, Facebook and Microsoft are major investors in *new* cable, the *existing* infrastructure is still based on the work of other companies and institutions. Furthermore, besides the more familiar infrastructural platforms we can also look at software in terms of infrastructure, for example, as in the case of software systems used in the data analytics industry. In this field, the Hadoop software project became the basis for various data analytics solutions and ended up being much more than a simple application, in fact it currently serves as a key infrastructural system for the sharing of data and computational resources (Beer 2019: 57). Today's digital infrastructures are, therefore, a highly complex, multilevel phenomenon.

From a global perspective, it is important to keep in mind that not all infrastructures are maintained by large companies. In particular, when we think about securing the local digital infrastructure in the Global South, supra-individual actors such as small local providers, local start-ups or social movements often play a considerable role.[14] We can see some notable examples on the African continent where small local businesses and start-ups have emerged in urban areas such as Kigali in Rwanda, Kumasi in Ghana and in the Kenyan capital, Nairobi, that are engaged in building up a digital infrastructures in rural Africa and dedicated to providing services for city dwellers.[15] In Kigali, ARED was founded in 2013 and provides charging kiosks for mobile devices and internet access via Wi-Fi. These kiosks are especially developed for Africa's rural areas, which means they have to be highly robust and powered by solar energy. As electricity is one of the main considerations for mobile phone use in rural areas, the kiosks represent important components in the region's overall digital infrastructure. BRCK in Nairobi specializes in providing hardware (desks, computers, Wi-Fi routers, etc.) that is robust enough to withstand the conditions in certain rural areas.

These examples demonstrate that while the 'big five' have established oligopolistic structures in in the western world, and while comparable patterns can be found in Asia with the role played by the oligopoly of Chinese companies around Alibaba, digital infrastructures as a whole are supported by more diverse corporate and collective actors. We must, therefore, be careful that we do not restrict our gaze to the large tech companies in the Global North.

So, it is clear that a multi-perspective view on the corporate actors supporting today's digital infrastructures is not only necessary but essential. On the one hand, it is a question of keeping an eye on the oligopoly of influential technology corporations that offer many of the products and services that make up our digital infrastructure. These companies have considerable global power, as many individuals, organizations and communities are already dependent on the services and facilities they provide if they want to operate productively in a deeply mediatized world. In addition, these corporations have the financial strength to swallow up and integrate smaller technology companies to conduct extensive research and development of their own, and to introduce and possibly enforce their own products and services with existing market power. On the other hand, it is just as vital that we include other actors in our considerations: these are state actors and the ambivalent role they play as regulators and supporters of new technologies, smaller local companies, start-ups, social movements and the work they do to secure digital infrastructures to disenfranchised regions. In sum, any analysis of digital infrastructures should not engage with economic reductionism.

THE ROLE OF PIONEER COMMUNITIES

As I emphasized at the beginning of this chapter, when it comes to the making of deep mediatization beside corporate actors there is another kind of supra-individual actor that matters, particularly in respect to the introduction of new technologies[16]: collective actors that make up so-called pioneer communities. In the following, I want to shed some light on their role in the making of deep mediatization. My intention is not to neglect the importance of traditional social movements in the field of technology which will receive plenty of attention later in the book. But when it comes to the *making* of deep mediatization, pioneer communities are of particular relevance and of special importance because of their orientation toward future, technology-related developments.

From early pioneers to pioneer communities

To what extent thought leaders and pioneers play a special role in the making of deep mediatization is demonstrated by historical studies. As Fred Turner has shown, we cannot understand the development of the internet and the 'new economy' it gave birth to without considering the Whole Earth Network as an 'extraordinary influential group of San Francisco Bay area journalists and entrepreneurs' (Turner 2006a: 3). This network imagined a world shaped by computers and computer networks far before it became normality to everybody else. The naming of this network references the Whole Earth Catalog, a book-size brochure published by Stewart Brand between 1968 and 1972. The original aim of the catalog was to introduce the New Communalists[17] of US counterculture in the 1960s and the 1970s to the 'tools' that were considered helpful for living in a rural community. Over the years it became a publication that brought the attitude of the countercultural life to a wider audience. The catalog converged scientific research, hippie homesteading, military survival equipment, ecology and mainstream consumer culture to create something akin to a 'network forum' (Turner 2006a: 5) of exchange and encounter.

With the relative collapse of the counter-cultural communes of the early 1970s, the network then turned to computer technology as another way of realizing their ideas of a new community. There are links, for example, to the Homebrew Computer Club, where visions of the personal computer were developed in the mid-1970s,[18] to the hacker movement[19] and later on to the MIT Media Lab as an idealized institution[20] where societal change through digital technology was imagined and fantasized about. After the discontinuation of the Whole Earth Catalog, important media that contributed the influence of this network in the 1980s and 1990s were WELL (Whole Earth 'Lectronic Link), an online network based in the San Francisco Bay Area[21] and one of the oldest online communities and eventually, *Wired* magazine, which launched in 1993, introduced new visions of the digital 'new economy' in its discussion of the deregulated, self-organizing internet with unbridled enthusiasm.[22] In addition, conferences were continuously held on various issues related to emergent technology. Part of this febrile technological atmosphere also meant that a lot of political consulting took place.

At this point, we must be careful not to solely attribute the development of technology in Silicon Valley to the success of the 'Californian ideology' (Barbrook & Cameron 1996) driven by the visions of the countercultural movement. As I have already argued above, it is important to be cognizant of other actors, including the state and its (military) investments in advanced technology. At the same time, the Whole Earth Network's rapidly spreading ideas can be considered as a vital part of the history of digital media and their infrastructures. The uniqueness of this network is, on the one hand, the belief of its pioneers in the changeability of society through technology and, on the other, their position as intermediaries between different worlds of technology development, politics, business, counterculture and everyday media use. As Manuel Castells (2001) has emphasized, science, communitarianism, hacking and entrepreneurship came together historically in the culture of those who produced the internet.

One particular historical fact is that the new communities 'reported' by the Whole Earth Network were not simply 'there' and, therefore, could not be the subject of 'investigative' journalistic coverage. They were first *created* as a product of 'reporting' on them and the conferences that collected their imagined members. In this respect, the engagement of the Whole Earth Network is not simply a matter of technology journalism. Rather, we are dealing with processes of the *curating* of technology-oriented communities: to 'define' these communities' frames of relevance, to 'select' potential members as part of these actor constellations, to 'arrange' individual statements and to 'present' them to different audiences (as well as the emerging pioneer community itself).

The influence these pioneer communities have had in the making of deep mediatization becomes evident in the explicit references to representatives from leading technology companies, for example, to the Whole Earth Catalog or the Homebrew Computer Club meetings as important focal points in their early years.[23] But pioneer communities can still be seen today. These include, for example, the Maker Movement (a community that is oriented toward producing new devices and tinkering with existing ones), the Quantified Self movement (a community oriented toward technology-based self-measurement and self-improvement) or the Hacks/Hackers movement (a community oriented toward practices of publicity and innovative journalism). The lineage of these movements and others can be traced back to the Whole Earth Network.[24]

'Pioneers' in this respect are less the 'extraordinary inventors' of certain technologies heralded as 'disruptive' by innovation researchers, rather, they can be seen as operating at the more quotidian heights of technological change.[25] We should also approach them reflexively and critically and avoid simply adopting and accepting their innovation discourses and ideologies. Such pioneers can be professionals (journalists working in a professional domain, for example), or amateurs (people who tinker, for example, as makers in their spare time).[26] The distinction of 'professional' and 'amateur' is a relative one insofar as amateur pioneers can refine their pioneering domain in such a way that it becomes an area of professional engagement. An example for this would be a maker who 'professionalizes' him- or herself in a way that he or she can earn a living through their pioneering ideas. Furthermore, 'amateur pioneers' are not necessarily amateurs with reference to their education: they are often trained as engineers, programmers or professionally educated in other related fields. But when they act as part of the pioneer community, they are not are not necessarily focused on professional value creation. With this in mind, pioneers can be characterized by the following:

1. Pioneers construct their identity around the idea that they adopt a *forerunner role* within a certain domain and are accepted as such by other members of that domain (but not necessarily all).

2. Within their domain they act as *intermediaries* (Bourdieu 2010: 151),[27] who in their practices connect different spheres of activity (development, everyday media use, politics etc.) – often explicitly advocating the necessity of moving beyond their own field.

3. By virtue of their *experimental practices*, pioneers play a special role in the development of their domain (e.g., in the sense that they also act as trainers or consultants).

4. Pioneers consider *visions of possible future scenarios* that are perceived as the 'sociotechnical imaginaries' (Jasanoff & Kim 2015) of media-related developments. As a consequence, these pioneers often become a topic in the media's broader discourse around related change.

Such pioneers are typically engaged in pioneer communities as 'communities of practice' (Wenger 1999). These communities are oriented towards the future and change and typically constitute themselves around certain experimental practices. As communities, their members share a sense of unity and have established 'structures' beyond situational gatherings (Knoblauch 2008: 75–77). Within pioneer communities, professional pioneers often adopt the role of an 'organizational elite' (Hitzler & Niederbacher 2010: 22) which means that they have a deep involvement in these communities, are experts with detailed knowledge concerning the dominating topic of these communities, and are typically responsible for organizing their activities.

Today's pioneer communities

As noted above, today we can identify three significant pioneer communities that relate to the notion of deep mediatization: the Quantified Self Movement, the Maker Movement and the Hacks/Hackers movement (see Table 2.2). While they relate to one another to some extent, they differ through the orientation of their practices (the self, manufacturing, publicity), their visions of media-related collectivity and societal transformation, their events and the reach of their published works (e.g., websites, journals, reports).

The *Quantified Self (QS) movement* has gained a lot of attention from academic researchers,[28] especially in terms of individual practices of self-measurement.[29] What is now commonly known as

Table 2.2 Examples of Today's Pioneer Communities

	Social domain of community	Visions of collectivity and societal transformation	Important events and locations	Examples of prominent websites and identity-creating publications
Quantified self movement	Predominantly oriented toward practices of the self	• Collectivity and societal transformation based on technologies of self-measurement • Interest in datafication and media omnipresence	• Quantified Self Conferences • Meetups	• Wolf (2009): Know Thyself. In: *Wired*, June 22/2009. • Quantified Self website (http://quantifiedself.com), since 2007
Maker movement	Predominantly oriented toward practices of manufacturing	• Collectivity and societal transformation based on technologies of making and sharing • Interest in pace of innovation and connectivity	• Maker Faires • Maker spaces, hack spaces, fab labs	• Anderson (2012): *Makers: The New Industrial Revolution*. New York, London: Random House • *Make: Magazine*/website (http://makezine.com), since 2005
Hacks/Hackers movement	Predominantly oriented toward practices of publicity	• Collectivity and societal transformation based on new forms of reporting • Interest in differentiation and datafication of media	• Hacks/Hackers conferences • Meetups	• Gray/Chambers/Bounegru (2012): *The Data Journalism Handbook*. Beijing, Cambridge: O'Reilly Media • Hacks/Hacker website (http://hackshackers.com), since 2009

'self-tracking' was once called 'life-logging',[30] a practice that began as an artistic and self-experimental comment on human-technology interaction. However, the term 'quantified self' refers to a more specific and well-defined community. Following a face-to-face meeting of around fifty people with a shared interest in the field in 2007, Gary Wolf and Kevin Kelly – the aforementioned two *Wired* journalists close to the Whole Earth Network – launched quantifiedself.com. Their website brings together producers as well as users of the relevant technologies and hosts conferences based around the possibilities of self-tracking and practitioners' experiences of the various technologies associated with it. Local groups are mainly organized as meetups (meetup.com), linked by QS (online) publications which curate the discourse on the identity of this pioneer community. Since 2011, the QS movement has spread to Europe and has become involved with the health industry.[31] Running parallel to these activities, various industries have designed, produced and marketed devices specifically related to health-related self-tracking.

The QS movement is a pioneer community whose members share an interest in (media) technologies for practices of the self. When it comes to their visions of societal transformation, data-focused productions of the self are thrown into the foreground, selves that are dedicated to a 'new individualism' that 'involves concentrating on the self' (Lupton 2015: 183). We are confronted here with a kind of paradox, on the one hand, the QS movement is focused on the individual. This is most enigmatically expressed by its notion of 'n of 1' (Greenfield 2016: 123), the gathering of vast amounts of quantified data with reference to one person with the aim of improving his or her life. On the other hand, we have to bear in mind that at the core of this movement there remains a community that emphasizes the importance of changing collectivity and society through the adoption of individual self-measurement. As such, this pioneer community was 'successful' in that it contributed to the fact that the idea of continuously measuring oneself, collecting data about oneself to improve one's own practice, has become a generally accepted discourse and widespread pattern in many countries in the Global North.

It is no simple task tracing the origins of the *Makers pioneer community*. When we consider hack spaces and fab labs[32] – and not only maker spaces – as important locations where members meet for the exchange of ideas and technological production, the hacker cultures and their hacker spaces are important precursors to the Makers.[33] A link between the hacker and open-source movements remains to this day.[34] In addition, the Do-It-Yourself (DIY) movement is an important contextual factor in the history of the Maker movement, with its long tradition as a community of practice in Europe and the US.[35] The difference between the two is that the Maker movement has a particular focus, one that is dedicated to change through technological developments. In a narrower sense, the Makers as a pioneer community emerged around 2005 when Neil Gershenfeld's (2005) book on fab labs and 3D printing was published, *Make: Magazine* was launched by O'Reilly, and the first Maker Faires were held in Silicon Valley. Critical to the ongoing spread of this community was the introduction of the Arduino board in 2005, the RepRap Open Source 3D printer in 2007, the first MakerBot 3D printer in 2009, the availability of the Raspberry Pi microcomputer in 2012, and – as a framing discourse – the publication of the book *Makers: The New Industrial Revolution* authored by the former *Wired* editor Chris Anderson (2012).

Anderson's book offered a condensed ideology for the Makers' pioneer community and its visions of collectivity and change. In short, they were represented as a 'community of equally obsessed people from around the world' (Anderson 2012: 15, 73–77, 92–95, see also Hatch 2014), a community that shared the vision that the internet of things and related technologies of production would bring about a 'new industrial revolution' coalescing DIY, handicraft and self-made technological innovations. A considerable factor in the spread of the Maker movement was the San Francisco based company *Maker Media* founded by Dale Dougherty (Dougherty & Conrad 2016), which in 2012 became independent from O'Reilly Media and now owns the *Make: Magazine* and *Maker Faire* brands. Core to the spread of the Maker movement is a kind of 'franchise model' for curating the discourse around this pioneer community, whereby *Make: Magazine* and especially the *Maker Faire* brand were distributed globally by *Make Media*, together with a (semi-) professional engagement with hacker and maker spaces undertaken by a wider group of people (Davies 2017). In June 2019, however, Maker Media ceased operations because of financial problems and Dale Dougherty founded the *Make: Community* for the curation of the pioneer community.

As journalism goes through a period of radical change, the *Hacks/ Hackers movement* is stepping in with a network of journalists and tech enthusiasts to intervene and engage with a new kind of practice. This community finds its roots in a variety of movements that bring new, technology-oriented visions of the future of journalistic work (Usher 2016: 71–100). One of its origins lies in the open data movement that has close links to the more computer-oriented open source movement.[36] The open data movement is in turn related to visions of a new form of open data journalism, towards which the Hacks/ Hackers movement is oriented. It was originally founded in 2009 in the San Francisco Bay area as a network of journalists ('hacks') and technologists ('hackers') whose aim was to rethink the future of news and journalism.[37] It quickly grew in the US and spread internationally with local groups surfacing first in Latin America, then across Europe and in Australia. By May 2019, 116 local groups had been established around the world that found a common home on the movement's website as well as gaining presence through a mailing list and social media platforms and has subsequently 'grown to become the largest organization of its kind' (Lewis & Usher 2014: 384). The movement exhibits an affinity with the digital media industry evident at the launch in May 2015, in partnership with Google, of a series of events they dubbed 'Connect'.

In a wider sense, we can understand Hacks/Hackers as a central community in the more far-reaching field of 'pioneer journalism' (Hepp & Loosen 2019: 1). In one respect, current media change invites the possibility of new forms of journalism that this network is oriented towards to flourish.[38] In another, pioneer journalism has stimulated change through its visions of possible new futures for the craft. Some examples include data journalism (which uses digital traces as a news source), data value chain journalism (which is oriented towards new forms of value generation through data), nonprofit impact journalism (which is based on donations for investigative reporting), chatbot journalism (in which a chatbot provides journalistic content) and sensor journalism (an automated form of journalism based on sensor data).[39]

Irrespective of whether or not ideas like these will result in sustainable models for new forms of journalism, the Hacks/Hackers movement pushes current changes forward as new technologies offer opportunities for richer public discourse. For example, the establishment of new publics through open access data represents the kind of imaginaries discussed at local Hacks/Hackers groups as 'informal trading zones' between journalists and hackers (Lewis & Usher 2014: 388). This is perhaps best expressed by the term 'hacker journalist': from their own subjective point of view, the 'hacker journalists' help people learn about their world and are engaged in actions to see how civic media might contribute to some sort of democratic or social good and making the world a better place.[40] The main idea being that an experimental use of data will support a new kind of public engagement and as a result new ways of building and sustaining collectivities can emerge.

By considering pioneer communities such as those described above, the extent to which, as collective actors, they can contribute to the making of deep mediatization is rendered visible. In their self-perception as forerunners in their respective fields, the members of these pioneer communities advance recent media-related developments in their constant search for the latest, technological innovations. Typically, their visions of future possibilities are ahead of their time which often results in their ideas failing to come to fruition, but they can just as often lead to radical solutions. More important than the question of whether a single idea will prevail, is the fact that such pioneer communities can open up spaces of possibility for imagining technology-based changes. It is through these visions of spaces of possibility and the retrospective reporting of them that pioneer communities develop influence in their respective domains. The QS movement, for example, experimented with practices of self-measurement and related technologies way before they entered the mainstream. The 'translation' of these experimental practices into general media coverage of self-tracking and self-measurement was often framed critically and dismissively as a dystopian 'tracked society', especially in left-wing and middle-class media. At a deeper level, however, the pioneer community's assumption of the simple changeability of society through technology was adopted in this public discourse.[41] In a similar way, many practitioners in the Maker movement develop novel products which may never find a market but they still continue to play and experiment with new ideas. Again, it is through media coverage of these new forms of making, engagement in local maker spaces and their integration into educational networks that the visions of the Maker movement are able to spread. Likewise, pioneer journalists have been pushing the boundaries. For example, a type of automated journalism called sensor journalism, that to adequately function requires ready-made sensor interfaces that don't yet exist, is still able to open up spaces for reflection on the future of journalism. With these examples in mind, we can consider pioneer communities as *laboratories for the making of deep mediatization*: often their exploits fail and yet on occasion they develop successful products. What they do best is experiment with possibilities and developing imaginations of a deeply mediatized future.

In so doing, pioneer communities act as intermediaries. A hybrid of social movement and think tank, they typically connect producers and developers with users, research, politics, journalism and industry. They provide a 'layer' that sits across distinct corporate actors such as established media and technology companies or state agencies. This can be seen in the case of the QS movement (in which the founders of start-ups are as active and as passionate as regular users, organizing events in both the academic and the political fields), the Maker movement (whose open concept of maker spaces has become an approach widely adopted by private companies, libraries and schools) and the Hacks/Hackers movement (that connects pioneers from established media and tech companies, start-ups and individual journalists). As *intermediaries*, pioneer communities are crucial to the ongoing curation of ideas for state-of-the-art digital media technologies, often long before they result in established products or services.

That said, we should be wary of failing to apply critical oversight on collective actors in the vein of those mentioned above. Firstly, skepticism of possible technological futures is glaringly absent among pioneer communities. The typical solution to a media-related problem such as data loss or misuse is to find a superior technical solution. Pioneer communities' unshakeable faith in technology tends to be myopic of its potential side-effects. Here we see echoes of the 'Californian ideology' (Barbrook & Cameron 1996: 44) combining the free-wheeling spirit of the counterculture and the entrepreneurial zeal of the tech industries into a vision of technological feasibility. As collective actors pioneer communities are highly fluid in their compositions and, to a large extent, they lack democratic structures. Typically, the consulting they carry out for state agencies goes unnoticed by the wider public and more often than not a high level of insider knowledge is necessary to grasp their influence. In a certain sense, pioneer communities are collective actors who, in their efforts to advance the notion of deep mediatization, only manage to do so in a very introverted way.

DEEP MEDIATIZATION'S QUANTITATIVE TRENDS

In the previous two sections, we have seen the role corporate and collective actors play in the making of deep mediatization. However, understanding this process of making is something much more complex than simply analyzing the political economy of powerful companies and state agencies or the influence of pioneer communities. To really grasp deep mediatization's diverse trajectories, it is important to understand how the different strategies and practices of corporate and collective actors cumulated in the meta-process of deep mediatization. As a first approximation, we can identify at least five quantitative trends to which the strategies and practices of the various corporate and collective actors cumulate:[42] first, the *differentiation* in the vast amount of digital media; second, an increasing *connectivity* of and through these media, offering the possibility to individually and collectively 'connect' across space and time; third, an escalating *omnipresence* of media stimulating the possibility of being permanently connected and in multiple places; fourth, a *rapid pace of innovation*, that is, the emergence of 'new' media and services over ever-shorter periods of time; and fifth, *datafication*, the representation of social life through computerized data across media devices and their underlying software and infrastructures.

These trends can neither be reduced to the engagement of one corporate or collective actor nor can they solely be thought of as discrete, media phenomena. Rather, they are all inextricably linked, *altogether* they are characteristic of deep mediatization's quantitative shifts. We must also be aware that these trends do not occur in a linear fashion and it is by no means certain whether or not these trends will continue and what other trends will emerge. Despite these complexities, overall, the distinction of these trends provides us with an initial understanding of the media-related changes we are confronted with in different social domains.

Some data

The *differentiation* of media has seen both their variety and their assorted functionalities steadily increase over the past few decades. During digitalization's infancy one of the major discussions centered around 'convergence' to argue for the 'coming together' of different media into the 'union' of one device: the 'multimedia computer'. The discourse around convergence soon widened. Henry Jenkins, for example, used the term 'convergence culture' to describe the media-related changes he was researching. In his definition, convergence does not refer to its original Latin meaning in the sense of 'moving toward union or uniformity' – as the merging of distinct technologies, industries, or devices into a unified whole of the personal computer as a kind of 'hybrid medium' (Höflich 2003: 65) implies. Rather, Jenkins understands convergence to mean 'the flow of content across multiple media platforms, the cooperation between multiple media industries, and the migratory behavior of media audiences who will go almost anywhere in the search of the kinds of entertainment and experiences they want' (Jenkins 2006: 2). The meaning of 'convergence', therefore, is less a merger of all media devices into one kind of super-device, it is considered more as convergence at the level of content which, being digital, becomes communicable across multiple devices, some newer, some older.[43]

Digitalization brought with it a variety of very different media, media that are invariably based on software and are fundamentally digital in the ways they make the communication of various kinds of content possible across them all (see Manovich 2013). We can connect this idea back to the early visions of pioneer communities who imagined life as something entirely digital.[44] 'Being digital', as far as the co-founder of the MIT Media Lab, Nicholas Negroponte's vision of the future was concerned back in 1995, included the idea of making all things 'digitally active' (Negroponte 1995: 209). He talked about teacups, clothes, toys and cars all becoming absorbed into the digital realm many years before the idea of the internet of things became a talking point, let alone feasible. This resonates today with the strategies of the large tech corporations that try to widen the fields they do business in. They either expand their product range to include additional digital devices as 'smart' devices, or they offer the infrastructure and software required to connect the various devices of the emerging internet of things.

The internet of things vividly illustrates the ongoing differentiation of digital media. At its core, it is an umbrella term for technologies that make up today's digital infrastructures networking physical and virtual objects allowing them to work together through information and communication technologies.[45] We are dealing here with a variety of networked 'things', ranging from communication media in the narrow sense of the term to devices that we have not previously understood as communication media, but which are thus integrated into internet-based communication processes. The latter can be, for example, sensors that automatically transmit weather data or the sensors in our network-connected cars. As 'smart cars', they can be controlled differently than before and data records of their movement – like other data – can be integrated into many other processes of datafied communication.[46] On the other side of the coin, industrial production plants can be controlled and monitored via internet of things technologies as discussed with reference to 'industry 4.0'. In this sense, the internet of things exemplifies the fact that the boundaries of what we call digital media have become blurred as a consequence of their differentiation.

The scope of this development is difficult to measure because there are no reliable figures related to the internet of things. While IBM predicted one trillion connected devices by 2015, more conservative industrial sources assume significantly lower figures. These range in 2016 between Gartner's estimate of 6.4 billion (a number that does not include smartphones, tablets and computers), the International Data Corporation's estimate of 9 billion (which also excludes these devices) and the technology market analyst IHS Markit's estimate of 17.6 billion (which includes common computational devices).[47] These figures, however, are not so decisive if we are to understand a differentiation trend. What is of more significance is that the internet of things demonstrates how digitization was not associated with the convergence of all digital media into one ultimate device. The decisive change is that more and more devices are *also* becoming digital media – that is: means of communication and data production – when they are integrated into the digital infrastructure of the internet.

Statistically, we can link the quantitative trend of differentiation to the allocation of internet protocol addresses (IP). Unique IPv4 addresses continuously increased from 329.1 million addresses world-wide in 2017 to 814.4 million in 2008 which is a growth of around 247 percent (see Figure 2.1). As these addresses are typically allocated dynamically we can expect that growth at the level of digital media devices will be even greater. But a much bigger shift is the upgrade in internet protocol from IPv4 which allocated 4.3 billion unique addresses to IPv6 which statically could provide for 3.4x1038 addresses, that is 340,282,366,920,938,463,463,374,607,431,768,2 11,456 unique IPs (see Greenfield 2010: thesis 27).[48] If we look at the actual and predicted growth of IPv6-capable devices which are connected (see Figure 2.1) the numbers are remarkable: in 2014 2.01 billion devices were globally connected; in 2017 this more than doubled to 4.32 billion; and for 2021 the predicted number is 8.4 billion devices. All in all, this demonstrates well what is meant by the trend of differentiation of digital media.

A second quantitative trend is an intensifying *connectivity*. By connectivity, I refer to the interconnectedness of various digital media as a consequence of their digitalization and the infrastructure of the internet. This can apply to 'old' media such as television and the press which subsequently went down the digital route but is doubly relevant for a 'new' generation of personal communication technologies, digital platforms and mobile apps. Again, today's comprehensive connectivity refers to the pioneering vision of networking all human knowledge through technical systems. Well known examples include the Memex

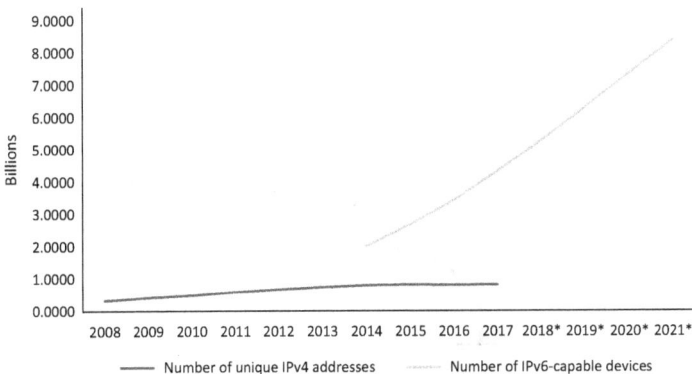

Figure 2.1 Number of unique IPv4 addresses and IPv6-capable devices

(Memory Extender), an easy-to-use knowledge discovery and exploitation system introduced hypothetically by Vannevar Bush (1945), or Ted Nelson's hypertext project *Xanadu*, founded in 1960, which aimed to create a universal library with countless interconnected documents. As we have seen, today's internet connectivity is no longer just about the World Wide Web (WWW), that is, hyperlink structures between individual documents. Connectivity takes place across many levels, not least in regard to the ongoing processing of data.

Considering that the internet represents the principal infrastructure of this multi-level connectivity, we can understand its underwater cable connections as a sign of how connectivity has developed in recent decades. The map below visualizes which regions of the world are connected to internet infrastructure by submarine cables (see Figure 2.2). In the meantime, these underwater cables are no longer only the primary connections between North America and Europe but extend across the entire world. Africa and South America are now much better developed in terms of connectivity than they were just a few years ago. However, these material cable networks are still not distributed equally across the world but privilege one portion of the globe with faster overseas online communication over others (Starosielski 2015: 65–66). While people living in the Global North are afforded immediate connectivity through their access to a broad infrastructure, for

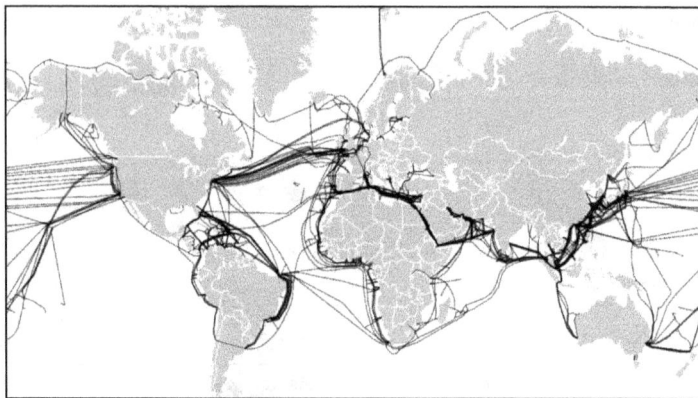

Figure 2.2 Internet underwater cable connections. Source: Open Street Map figure, based on https://www.submarinecablemap.com (accessed: May 1, 2019)

others in Africa or Asia the same infrastructure shapes or molds a decelerated pace of communication across continents.

This underwater cable infrastructure also corresponds to the increase in the number of internet users worldwide from 2010 to 2016: if we follow the statistics published by the International Telecommunications Union (ITU), the worldwide number of internet users increased from 1.991 million in 2010 to 3.896 million in 2018.[49] In 2005, the percentage of the global population accessing the internet totaled 15.8 percent, yet we can see a clear demarcation between usage in the Global North at 51.3 percent and in the Global South at 7.7 percent. By 2018, these numbers had increased to 51.2 percent of the world population, with the Global North amounting to 80.9 percent and the Global South 48.3 percent. There is clearly an issue with these figures in that they are very general and to all intents and purposes remain abstract. Differences and inequalities in connectivity exist particularly at the local level, not only when comparing global regions, but especially when looking at the difference between urban and rural areas. Nevertheless, these numbers provide a broad understanding of how media connectivity has increased globally.[50]

Besides their differentiation and connectivity, the upward trend in media's *omnipresence* is a clear expression of the quantitative changes in the media. Face-to-face meetings, talks and lectures, walking and other social situations, which for a long time were not particularly related to media, have become so in one way or another. These dynamics have gained particular momentum thanks to the spread of mobile communication technologies.[51] In regions of the world with the respective infrastructure it is now possible to be 'always on' (Chen 2011: 63) and 'constantly in touch' (Agar 2003: 22); that is, being reachable at any moment in time.

Therefore, just as the internet stands for increasing global connectivity, mobile communication represents the increasing omnipresence of media. Ultimately, this corresponds to the possibility of being able to access media in a wide variety of situations and locations, at least in principle. The establishment of mobile communications is again not only a phenomenon exclusive to the Global North. Rather, it is a general fact in the so-called Global South as well. This is made clear on the current world map of mobile-cellular subscriptions per 100 inhabitants (see Figure 2.3).

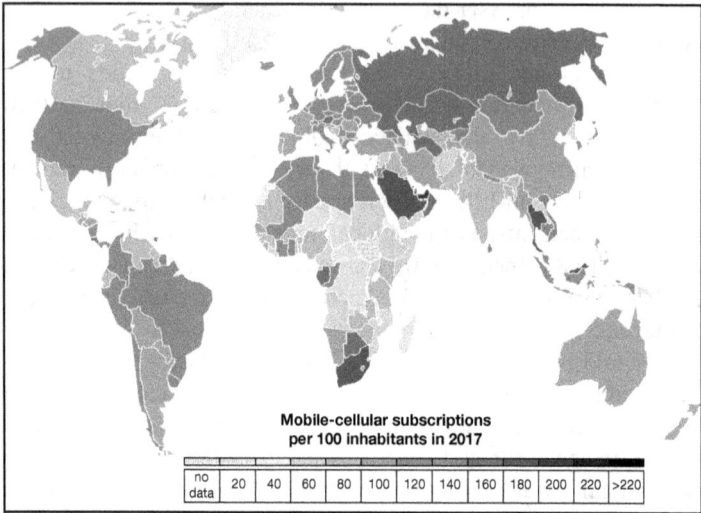

Figure 2.3 Mobile-cellular subscriptions per 100 inhabitants in 2017. Source: International Telecommunication Union (ITU) (2017): Measuring the Information Society Report (2017). Volume 2. ICT country profiles. Geneva: International Telecommunication Union[52]

The map is based on current figures from the International Telecommunication Union (ITU). Again, two things stand out. Firstly, the spread of mobile phones is not just a phenomenon in the Global North. In virtually no country were mobile-cellular subscriptions below 40 percent in 2017. Nevertheless, and secondly, there are still inequalities here too: while coverage exceeds 100 percent in the Global North – i.e. there are more than 100 contracts per 100 owners, meaning people have more than one subscription – African countries in particular reach about 40 percent. These lower figures must not obscure the fact that mobile communications in particular has contributed to a change in the media environment in most African societies. This concerns the possibilities of keeping in touch with family as well as payment services based on mobile phones or content offerings (Nwankwo & Ogbu 2018: 6–8). Especially in African societies, the omnipresence of media through mobile communication is increasing.

Another quantitative trend is a rapid *pace of innovation*. This means that the time sequence of fundamental media innovations has – at least in the *perception* of many media users – shortened considerably over the past few decades (Rosa 2013: 71–74). These cycles of innovation are driven both by ideas that develop within pioneer communities that can lead to innovative start-ups, and by the broad investments made by large technology companies and state institutions in the development of certain technologies.

Again, we can use statistical data to substantiate this trend. Figure 2.4 visualizes the share of smartphone operating systems worldwide (for each year in its first quarter) and of fundamental system updates. When it comes to the pace of innovation, this figure is of interest in at least three respects. Firstly, it demonstrates the important role played by the development of the touchscreen-based

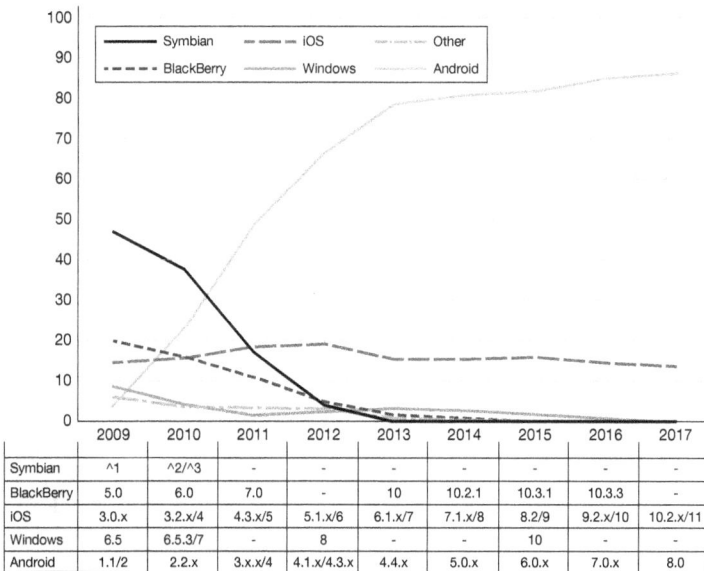

	2009	2010	2011	2012	2013	2014	2015	2016	2017
Symbian	^1	^2/^3	-	-	-	-	-	-	-
BlackBerry	5.0	6.0	7.0	-	10	10.2.1	10.3.1	10.3.3	-
iOS	3.0.x	3.2.x/4	4.3.x/5	5.1.x/6	6.1.x/7	7.1.x/8	8.2/9	9.2.x/10	10.2.x/11
Windows	6.5	6.5.3/7	-	8	-	-	10	-	-
Android	1.1/2	2.2.x	3.x.x/4	4.1.x/4.3.x	4.4.x	5.0.x	6.0.x	7.0.x	8.0

Figure 2.4 Shares and updates of smartphone operation systems worldwide. Notes: shares of smartphone operation system worldwide until 2017 (in percentage of retail sales). The source does not provide data on sales for every year. The data for 2011 has been calculated based on reports by Gartner (Q1 for the respective year)

smartphone. In the period between 2009 and 2012, the touchscreen pushed aside the leading devices and their operating systems at the time – BlackBerry and Symbian – resulting in iOS and Android's market domination. Secondly, the chart visualizes the fact that neither Android nor iOS remained static in their composition. These operating systems are updated regularly with the result that older devices can become obsolete every two to four years. Users are either left having to deal with less powerful and less secure phones or are forced to 'upgrade' to the next generation of device and the version of the operating system that accompanies it. Thirdly, smartphone operating systems are extraordinary examples of products that are in 'constant flux' (Cheney-Lippold 2017: 90): data that users transmit through their use of smartphones are used continuously to further develop the various apps, even as information to enhance the functionality of applications (such as map apps or platform-based apps) and to further develop the devices themselves. It is precisely this last point that indicates how data analytics has generally contributed to accelerating technological development. This is associated with an 'envisioning of speedier practice' (Beer 2019: 46) through automated data processing, which ultimately results in a continuous pressure to adapt software-based media.

The fifth and final significant trend that must be considered is *datafication*. Datafication insinuates itself as more and more of our media become software-based leaving behind exponentially larger quantities of 'digital traces' (Karanasios et al. 2013), data that, when processed algorithmically, can be aggregated. This is the case across the whole gamut of digital media platforms.[53] In dominant public discourse, this is mainly discussed with reference to the concept of 'big data', that is, the possibilities of automated processing of large amounts of data culled from digital traces.[54] This means that the representation of social phenomena by quantified data plays an increasingly prominent role in societal self-understanding and self-conception.

From the perspective of digital infrastructure, datafication refers first and foremost to the existence of appropriate data centers that enable the centralized collection and processing of data 'in the cloud'. Examples include the data centers of the internet's major players: Alphabet (Google), Amazon, Apple and Facebook. Looking at their localization practices at a global level (see Figure 2.5), two things stand out: on the one hand, a broad digital infrastructure has been established for 'cloud storage'. On the other, Western companies are mainly oriented towards the Global North. Even if one considers that other companies such as Alibaba are decisive in Asia, it becomes clear that the extent of datafication, as we perceive it in the Global North, may be less dominant in other regions such as South America or Africa. However, investments in this area suggest that this trend will continue to spread globally.

Another way of describing the trend of datafication is by looking at 'cloud traffic' (Mosco 2014: 15–76). This term refers to the exabytes of data being transferred to and from cloud servers. According to existing statistical data, there was a massive increase in cloud traffic in North America and Europe between 2014 and 2015, a period when cloud-based online systems were beginning to take off in a significant way. Cisco Systems, a company that produces routers and switches and one that clearly benefits from the widespread use of

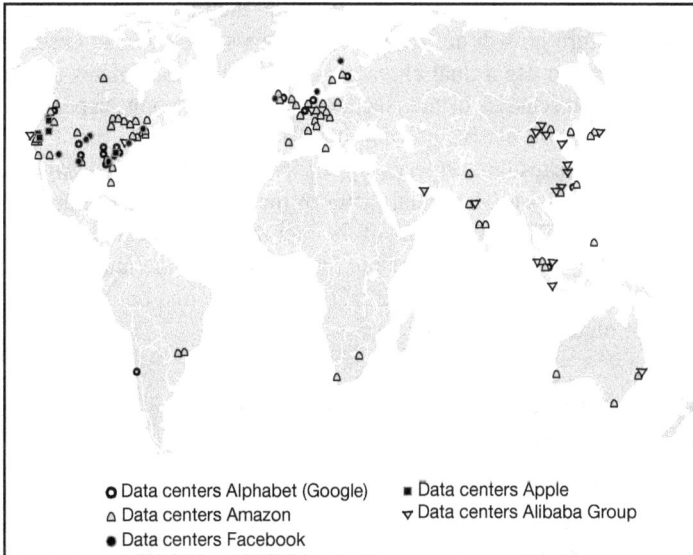

o Data centers Alphabet (Google)   ■ Data centers Apple
△ Data centers Amazon   ▽ Data centers Alibaba Group
● Data centers Facebook

Figure 2.5 Data center locations of the major tech companies (2018). Source: company web pages (accessed August 2018)[55]

cloud computing, has published interesting statistics on this growth:[56] North American cloud traffic in 2015 measured 1.891 exabytes per year, in the Asia Pacific 908 exabytes per year, in Western Europe 718 exabytes per year, in Central and Eastern Europe 124 exabytes per year, in Latin America 140 exabytes per year, and in the Middle East and Africa 69 exabytes per year. The estimated growth in their forecasts for 2020 is enormous: North American cloud traffic in 2020 is expected to reach 6.844 exabytes per year, in the Asia Pacific 3.469 exabytes per year, in Western Europe 2.528 exabytes per year, in Central and Eastern Europe 485 exabytes per year, in Latin America 448 exabytes per year, and in the Middle East and Africa 304 exabytes per year.

We should be wary of forecasts like these as they form part of a process that communicatively constructs the need for investment in this area. Despite the vested interests contained in such figures, it adequately exemplifies data storage in the cloud as a core moment of datafication in both its present expression and projections of its future: on the one hand there is a remarkable, but relatively lower degree of actual increase in traffic; while on the other, high expectations for future growth are expressed. In this sense, we can observe that datafication has a dual character — a duality that relates to the other trends discussed in this section: the term not only captures a trend in the sense of changes that have already occurred but it also manages to encapsulate expectations of its own stability and growth. Such expectations are a crucial factor in the public discourse around all five trends. This reminds us of the fact that deep mediatization is also driven by visions of a possible future – born in the imaginations of not only pioneer communities and corporate actors but also in the minds of regular citizens.

The contradicting nature of deep mediatization's quantitative trends

As I have already mentioned, care must be taken when examining and speculating on dominant trends: these are preliminary interpretations based on current directions in media and communications research. We must also be cautious when making statements about the global nature of these trends. The figures above regarding the five trends already show that there are differences between the Global North and the Global South at the aggregation level of countries alone. But there are other differences that make up a 'digital divide'. In some countries, for example, we can identify considerable differences between urban and rural regions. While in urban regions – also in the Global South – the expansion of the digital infrastructure is well advanced, in rural regions – also in the Global North – this looks, in part, clearly different.[57] Residents in these areas may not even have access to broadband internet or to high-speed mobile networks. We must, therefore, be cautious that we do not lose sight of these further-reaching spatial differences between urban and rural zones.

Furthermore, there are also differences between groups of the population in terms of ethnicity, gender and class – these criteria of inequality will often overlap in an intersectional way. Not all individuals and groups have equal access to the media and communication technologies described here and are, therefore, involved in these quantitative trends in different ways. This has to do partly with economic conditions, for example, with the resources that people can invest in the use of such technologies. But some empirical facts are counterintuitive. For example, media devices owned by migrants are often of a higher quantity and quality than those belonging to other population groups even though migrants often have comparatively scarce financial resources.[58] This may be because migrants attach greater importance to communicative networking with their families and associated diasporas and are, therefore, prepared to invest considerable parts of their financial budget in such technologies. But even if this contradicts the more intuitive assumptions, it is still an indication that there are differences between groups that are not reflected in the summary of figures discussed so far.

Therefore, all five trends are certainly not globally homogeneous and differ in terms of their intensity and their characteristics region to region and domain to domain. This can be seen as a further indication that the process of deep mediatization must always be examined in a context-specific manner. But the absence of such homogeneity cannot, conversely, be equated with the fact that these trends are a highly particular phenomenon. They are global in the sense that they pass through the various regions and social contexts of the world as trends, albeit with different characteristics.

In sum, the five quantitative trends demonstrate that comprehending the making of deep mediatization means more than merely understanding a political economy of digital infrastructures or describing the strategies and practices of corporate and collective actors. They reveal, moreover, how different forms of agency cumulate in the emergence of something much more all-encompassing and transformative. When it comes to a detailed analysis, the differentiation of media, their increasing connectivity and omnipresence, the rapid pace of innovation and the swift progress of datafication, these are all trends that can best guide us in understanding the making of deep mediatization. Yet, the empirical challenge remains that we must investigate the specific contextual solidification of these trends.

NOTES

1   In particular, compare the following publications on the history of the internet: Abbate (1999), Bunz (2009) & Naughton (1999). If one reflects on the 1960s and 1970s – the period before 'deregulation' – and assumed that a platform like Facebook was established during this period, in most European countries such a service would probably only have been possible as a public service. The reason for this is that it would have been considered far too powerful to be placed in the hands of a private company.

2   These are aspects of the digital economy that I will discuss in more detail in Chapter 5.

3   See, for example, Hughes (1983), but we can trace this line of argument back as far as Harold Innis (1951).

4   See, for example, Parks & Starosielski (2015b) and Larkin (2008).

5   The first site on the world wide web (WWW) can be found at info.cern.ch. It went online on August 6, 1991. It is an unadorned website with black writing on a white background, without pictures and animations. The site provides information on the history of the WWW.

6   These changes were reflected in media and communications research particularly with the concept of the 'produser', see, for example, Bird (2011), and Bruns & Schmidt (2011).

7   See, for example, Burston et al. (2010), Fuchs (2014) and Scholz (2013).

8   Joseph Turow examined this in detail (cf. Couldry & Turow 2014, Turow 2011, 2017).

9   See, for this discussion especially, Amoore & Piotukuh (2016), Elmer et al. (2015a) and Schäfer & van Es (2017).

10 First and foremost, undersea cables enabled the internet to become a global phenomenon as 'almost 100 percent of transoceanic Internet traffic is carried via fiber-optic undersea cables' (Starosielski 2015: 54).

11 This is not only the TCP/IP protocol, the Wi-Fi Protocol, the Routing Information Protocol (RIP) and the Exterior Gateway Protocol (EGP) are just but a few examples. In a careful analysis of the functioning of the EGP, Paul Dourish (2015) demonstrated how, despite the internet being commonly perceived as an open decentralized structure, different protocols shape communication practices by building more centralized and institutional network spaces.

12 For a more detailed discussion of the merger between the content providing parts of the media industries and technology companies see, Bolin (2011: 45–66).

13 See, Grenz & Kirschner (2016) and Nieborg & Helmond (2018).

14 See, for a general discussion on datafication and the Global South, Milan & ten Oever (2017) and Taylor (2017). Detailed examples are discussed by Payal Arora, for example, in the case of LAN houses in Brazil (Arora 2019: 30–37). She also argues for the necessity of completely different innovations and start-ups in the Global South than those imagined in Silicon Valley (Arora 2019: 127–151).

15 The significance of such local social movements, providers and start-ups is vividly illustrated in the film 'Digital Africa – Ein Kontinent erfindet sich neu' (English: A Continent Reinvents Itself, ZDF/ARTE 2018). See also, Nwankwo & Ogbu (2018).

16 Robin Mansell (2004: 99) has argued that political economy research would benefit by intersecting with innovation studies.

17 The New Communalists stand out from the New Left in that they do not rely on political institutions to change society and participate in political confrontations, but by changing communities of coexistence and thereby individuals (Turner 2006a: 33–39).

18 The Homebrew Computer Club was founded by Gordon French and Frederick Moore, the latter being affiliated to the Whole Earth Network, from which funds from the sale of the Whole Earth Catalog may have flowed into the HCC (Turner 2006a: 102).

19 The first book written about hackers was by Steven Levy (1984) who also wrote reviews for the Whole Earth Catalog. Inspired by this book, the first hacker conference was then held by members of the Whole Earth Network, including Stewart Brand and thus the hacker movement began to be curated (Turner 2006a: 132–140).

20 In addition to the publications of Nicholas Negroponte (1995), the founding director of the MIT Media Lab, Stewart Brands' book about the creation of the Media Lab (Brand 1987) contributed to the perception of the MIT Media Lab as a model for societal change.

21 Howard Rheingold, himself involved in WELL, developed his idea of the 'virtual community' with reference to this online network, see, Rheingold (1994).

22 For an analysis of the discourse in Wired, see, Frau-Meigs (2000).

23 A prominent example of this is Steve Jobs who, in a speech at Stanford University on June 12 2005, called the Whole Earth Catalog 'one of the bibles of my generation' and a 'Google in paperback form, 35 years before Google came along' (see, https://youtu.be/UF8uR6Z6KLc [accessed: May 1, 2019]).

24 Dale Dougherty, who is a central figure in the Maker movement, for example, is a former co-founder of O'Reilly Media, or Kevin Kelly, who founded with Gary Wolf

the Quantified Self movement, is one of the co-founders of *Wired*. For the Maker movement, Fred Turner (2018) demonstrates this history in a detailed analysis of key texts.

25 See also, Sven Kesselring and Gerlinde Vogl's (2004: 47) research on 'mobility pioneers': individuals who use the internet and digital media in pursuit of a highly mobile life-style, commuting between widely dispersed localities. Another example of note are electronic artists who are pioneers in appropriating experimental technologies: 'explorers, investigating the cutting edge of new technologies' (Gaved & Mulholland 2008: 19; see also, Kangas 2011).

26 However, we must be careful at this point not to 'celebrate' the role of the amateur (see, for such a critique Keen 2007). The point I want to make here is that these pioneers do not necessarily act in professional contexts when it comes to the domain they are pioneering.

27 For more examples of intermediaries in the media field, see, Negus (2002), Nixon & du Gay (2002) and O'Connor (2013).

28 For an overview, see, Lupton (2016) and Neff & Nafus (2016).

29 See, the relevant chapters in Abend & Fuchs (2016), Ajana (2017) and Strübing et al. (2016).

30 See, Crawford et al. (2015) and O'Hara et al. (2008).

31 See, Nafus (2016) and Selke (2016).

32 The term 'fab lab' was coined by Neil Gershenfeld (2005) as an abbreviation for 'fabrication laboratory': a small-scale workshop offering (personal) digital fabrication.

33 See, for a discussion of hacker cultures the original book by Levy (1984) as well as Hunsinger & Schrock (2016) and Lange (2015). For an analysis of 'hacker spaces' see, Kostakis et al. (2015) and Maxigas (2012).

34 See, for this, Krebs (2014): 20 and Coleman (2013).

35 See, Atkinson (2006), Hemphill & Leskowitz (2012) and Ratto & Boler (2014).

36 See, Baack (2015) and Lewis & Usher (2013).

37 For more detailed information on this network see, http://hackshackers.com (accessed: May 1st, 2019).

38 Most research is focused on the questions how journalists take advantage of these technologies and the organizational pressures brought about by them; cf. especially: Anderson (2013), Broussard (2015), Creech & Mendelson (2015), Knight (2015), De Maeyer et al. (2015) and Flew et al. (2012).

39 See, for a detailed analysis, Hepp & Loosen (2019).

40 See, Stray (2011) and Lewis & Usher (2013: 603).

41 We have shown this in detail in a discourse analysis of practitioners from Germany and the UK, see, Hepp et al. (2018a).

42 See, for the differentiation of these trends, Hepp & Hasebrink (2017).

43 For a detailed discussion of 'convergence' see, Jensen (2010) and the chapters in Storsul & Stuedahl (2007).

44 The idea of 'ubiquitous computing' was coined at the end of the 1980s by Mark Weiser, who worked at Xerox PARC in Palo Alto. At the core of his idea is a vision

of integrating computation and networking into the array of everyday objects; this is most commonly associated today with the internet of things.

45 For a detailed analysis of the internet of things as a core moment in digital infrastructure cf. Grisot et al. (2018).

46 See, Miller (2017) and Sumantran et al. (2017). For a general overview, Miller (2019) emphasizes the need for mediatization research to focus more on the internet of things.

47 See, https://spectrum.ieee.org/tech-talk/telecom/internet/popular-internet-of-things-forecast-of-50-billion-devices-by-2020-is-outdated (accessed: 30th August 2018).

48 Many thanks to Marc Kushin who hinted me to this fact and to Jeanette Asmuss who checked the data.

49 See, for these statistics https://www.itu.int/en/ITU-D/Statistics/Pages/stat/defa ult.aspx (accessed: May 1st, 2019).

50 These dynamics are made particularly clear in Payal Arora's (2019) analysis of 'digital life beyond the west'.

51 For further background on this trend see, Goggin (2011) and Ling & Donner (2009).

52 The figures for some countries are based on estimates, not on measurements by the ITU. This includes the following countries: Antigua and Barbuda, Republic of the Congo, Nauru, Philippines, Sierra Leone, Somalia, South Sudan, Swaziland, Tajikistan, Tonga, Turkmenistan, Tuvalu.

53 See, van Dijck & Poell (2013), Gillespie (2018) and my argument in Chapters 3 and 4.

54 For a more utopian approach to big data, see, Mayer-Schönberger & Cukier (2013), for a critical academic reflection of this discourse see, boyd and Crawford (2012) and Lohmeier (2014).

55 To provide more detail, this figure is based on the following web pages (accessed: May 1st, 2019): Alibaba Group, Alibaba Cloud (2018): Document Center. Regions and zones. URL: https://www.alibabacloud.com/help/doc-detail/40654.htm; Alphabet Inc. (Google): (n.d.): Google Rechenzentren. Standorte von Rechenzentren. URL: https://www.google.com/about/datacenters/inside/locations/?hl=de; Amazon Web Services (AWS) (2018): Globale AWS-Infrastruktur. URL: https://aws.ama zon.com/de/about-aws/global-infrastructure/; Datacenters.comSM (2018): Data Centers, Apple Inc. Complete List of Colocation, Cloud Services & Disaster Recovery Locations. URL: https://www.datacenters.com/locations?selected_pro vider=200203&selected_specialty=cloud+node; Facebook, Inc. (2018): Company Info. Stats. URL: https://newsroom.fb.com/company-info/.

56 See, https://www.cisco.com/c/en/us/solutions/collateral/service-provider/global-cloud-index-gci/white-paper-c11-738085.pdf (accessed: May 1st, 2019).

57 See, for example, the EU report 'Broadband coverage in Europe 2017', https://publications.europa.eu/en/publication-detail/-/publication/0f079a7b-6ac8-11e8 -9483-01aa75ed71a1/language-en (accessed: May 1st, 2019).

58 See, Hepp et al. (2011).

3

MEDIA AS A PROCESS

While Chapter 2 was dedicated to the making of deep mediatization – that is, to understand how the current quantitative trends of deep mediatization come together from the strategies and practices of corporate and collective actors – this chapter focuses on media themselves. Looking at deep mediatization from an everyday perspective, it is evident that 'doing something with media' makes a difference compared to practices that are not entangled with digital media. But what exactly is this difference? How can the media's capacity to mold the social world be adequately captured?

Posing these questions, it is important to be aware that mediatization as a concept predominantly directs to media's role in the transformation of culture and society — but without theorizing this role as the result of 'media effects'. Research on media effects investigates the impact of certain 'media content' (news, fiction and so on), more on the level of the individual and less so on the level of wider society.[1] By contrast, mediatization research has a broader perspective that runs parallel to medium theory. As in medium theory, researchers on mediatization understand their approach as 'an alternative to the dominant paradigm of media effects' (Meyrowitz 2009: 517). Connected to names like Harold Innis, Marshall McLuhan and Joshua Meyrowitz, medium theory shifted the focus 'from the content of media as the prime source of influence [...] to the nature and capacities of each medium itself' (Meyrowitz 2009: 517). As a consequence, the main question is *not* to ask 'What are the effects of certain media content?' but 'How do the characteristics of a medium shape communication and perception?'. This is also the case with mediatization research. But mediatization research opens up an even wider perspective by focusing much more on the context, diversity and dynamics of different media. And in so doing it does not so much neglect the question of 'content' but tries to avoid narrowing down on them as is traditional in media effect research.

Mediatization research asks more generally how important media are as means of communication and as an influence on the social construction of reality. This social construction is understood as an ongoing, multilevel process. Consequently, mediatization research's perspective is one that places emphasis on dynamics and interrelations, it moves 'beyond a simple causal logic dividing the world into dependent and independent variables' (Schulz 2004: 90). With mediatization research, it is essential to have an adequate understanding of media's propensity for shaping reality – their molding forces – as a multi-level phenomenon.

To take this step, it is first necessary to develop an idea of media. As I want to argue in this chapter, it is particularly helpful to understand *media as a process* if one wants to grasp current processes of mediatization. This idea has a certain proximity to the one of 'liquid media' as developed by Mark Deuze (2007: 30–33). Deuze's starting point is a reference to Zygmunt Bauman's (2000) analysis of 'liquid modernity'. Bauman argued that postmodernity is characterized by the 'liquification' of the institutions previously associated with what he terms the era of 'solid' modernity. The traditional institutions still exist but they have become more flexible, less hierarchical and more consumer-oriented – all the while re-articulating social inequalities. This liquidity is driven by economic deregulation or more concrete re-regulation by prioritizing private markets. From the perspective of the individual 'liquid modernity' is rendered into a 'liquid life': a precarious life as a consumer, characterized by ongoing, disorientating velocity under conditions of constant uncertainty (Bauman 2005: 1–10). Media not only became an omnipresent factor in this 'liquid life'; they became as 'liquid' as modernity's other institutions. And being liquid, digital media have saturated all areas of everyday life; as Deuze puts it, media became 'pervasive and ubiquitous, forming the building blocks for our constant remix of the categories of everyday life (the public and the private, the local and the global, the individual and the collective)' (Deuze 2011: 137). There is a paradox at the center of this pervasiveness and ubiquity, he argues, as media – because of how they have spread and the role the central roles they play in our lives – are invisible as far as their social functions are concerned. Therefore, we lose sight of the objects that shape our lives the most.

The idea of deep mediatization is associated with a similar perspective on the pervasiveness of digital media. This ubiquity contributes to media's significance, their importance in today's social world. In using the expression 'media as a process', I am concerned with something that relates to this ubiquity and invisibility but attempts to explain it. Digital media and their underlying infrastructures can be so ubiquitous and invisible because they are simply not 'static' (and never have been), media are an ongoing process. As my remarks in Chapter 2 on digital infrastructures made clear, this perspective does not mean losing sight of media's materiality. On the contrary: we can only adequately grasp digital media – as with media in general – if we have their materiality in mind. However, even this materiality is not simply a given but is produced in a continuous process.

Seeing media as a process is an appropriate starting point from which to grasp their molding capacities on an ever-changing construction of the social world. Media have never been static, but with deep mediatization their processual character is made even more plain, which has something to do with the fact that the 'processual nature' of media has become amplified in light of digitalization. This is partly linked to the aforementioned character of digital media considered as existing in a 'permanently beta' state. As already emphasized when I discussed the trend of the accelerating pace of innovation, because digital media such as online platforms or smartphone apps are based on software and algorithms, they are much easier to adapt to varying situations while they are still in use. Algorithms contribute to an additional processual dynamic when they are able to 'self-learn', for example, on the basis of user data. The automated processing of data has become part of what media are.

Taking this as a point of departure, I develop in this chapter the following argument: first, I will consider 'media logics' as an important and established metaphor in mediatization research to grasp the molding capabilities of media. My argument in this section is that the metaphor of 'media logics' was important for mediatization research because it demonstrated the complexity of media's molding forces. For an analysis of the current phase of deep mediatization, however, this metaphor becomes problematic because it remains ambiguous and obscures media's processual character. This raises the question of how we can adequately conceptualize media and their molding forces from a processual point of view. To address this question, I theorize media on the basis of two ongoing processes: institutionalization and materialization. While these processes are quite flexible when a medium 'emerges', they increasingly consolidate with its establishment. This is also apparent with today's digital media, especially if we include algorithms, automation and communicative robots in our considerations. This leads directly to the third section of this chapter, namely the processual dynamics *between* different media. In times of deep mediatization, media do not appear as individual media, we are constantly confronted with media manifold. For empirical research and critical analysis, it is necessary to place this media manifold into some sort of scale: firstly, there is the level of the media environment, that is the totality of media that are available at a certain point in time. Secondly, there is the level of the media ensemble. These are the media that are 'used' within a certain social domain. Thirdly, there is the level of the media repertoire. These are the media that an individual appropriates and uses in his or her everyday practices. The molding forces of media – their institutionalization and materialization – must be seen in concrete terms in relation to these different levels.

QUESTIONING MEDIA LOGICS

There has always been a certain ambivalence around the idea of media logics in mediatization research. On the one hand, the concept had large appeal because it inspired a certain way of thinking about how media change might have long-term influences.[2] On the other hand – and maybe exactly because of this inspiration – it has remained vague. This is the reason why 'media logic' in mediatization research is often described as a 'catch-all term' (Asp 1990: 48) or as a 'metaphor' (Hjarvard 2017: 1221).

We can understand much of the writing on media logics as an attempt to bring some clarity to this vagueness. It has been important to move from 'media logic' in the singular (which always had the problem of assuming one logic for all media) to 'media logics' in the plural (which opens us up to a reflection on the various dynamics that are at work). This shift relates to the changing character of media: while most attention was initially paid to mass media and mainly television, mediatization research's interest has widened to include all kinds of media, especially digital media.

One reason why the metaphor of media logics has such a wide appeal is that it resonates very well with a more general discussion in social sciences and humanities about the 'logics of practice', 'logics of action', 'institutional logics' or 'cultural logics'.[3] Often, 'logic' is used in order to indicate that there is somehow an underlying 'structure' or 'pattern' which should become a matter of analysis. But the idea of logic can be taken even further. Bourdieu, for example, argued that there is a *general* 'practical logic'. In relation to each practice this logic 'is able to organize all thoughts, perceptions and actions by means of a few generative principles, which are closely interrelated and constitute a practically integrated whole' (Bourdieu 1992: 86). Arguing on a very general level, 'logic' for Bourdieu works as a category to name a fundamental organizing principle of the social world.

Systematizing the present discussion, we can notice at least three approaches to media logics in mediatization research (see Table 3.1):[4]

Table 3.1 Three Approaches to Media Logics

Approach	Concept of logics	Concept of influence
Interaction	Forms of interaction	Adaptation to media forms
Organization	Organizational rules	Adaptation to the rules of media organizations
Technology	Material affordances	Adaptation to media's material affordances

first, there is the approach to media logics that relates to *interaction*. The idea at this point is that each medium – in contrast to the multi-plicity of its contents – offers particular forms of interaction: its ways of presenting, its genres and its aesthetics, which altogether are under-stood as the logics of the medium. The influence of a medium is then conceptualized as the way in which interaction in general adapts to such media forms. Second, there is the *organization* approach. Here, the emphasis is on considering media as organizations with specific organizational rules and media's rules of organizing are understood as their logics. The related concept of influence is that of an adapta-tion of non-media organizations to media's rules. Third, there is the *technology* approach. Here, media logics are understood as material affordances. The related concept of influence practices adapts to these affordances in various social domains.

Distinguishing between these three approaches to media logics, it is important to be aware that they cannot be put against each other. While 'forms of interaction' were originally the principal focus when analyzing media logic(s), all three approaches overlap with one another because media are at the same time means of communication (which relates to the interaction approach), institutions (which relates to the organization approach) and materialities (which relates to the technology approach).

Forms of interaction

It makes sense to start our reflection on different approaches to media logics with interaction because this is where the metaphor of media logics has its origins. Interaction on these terms finds its roots in sym-bolic interactionism theory, a sociological approach which focuses on the analysis of actions between persons and the production of mean-ing. Symbolic interactionism is grounded in the basic idea that the meaning of social objects, situations and relationships is constructed in the symbolically mediated process of communication. The underly-ing concept of interaction is correspondingly broad. Interaction refers to the meaningful process of 'acting together' by people, both in direct communication as well as communication mediated through media.

Referring back to the more general sociology of Georg Simmel (1972), the idea is to differentiate the 'content' of an interaction and its 'form'. In media and communications research there are various concepts to describe these forms of interaction: genres, aesthetic patterns or formats are the most common ones. The fundamental idea linked to the term of form is that the way we as humans communicate – with or without media – is based on patterns that are independent from the content of a single interaction. David Altheide and Robert Snow originally introduced the idea of '*media logic* [...] [as] a form of communication' (Altheide & Snow 1979: 10, emphasis in original).[5] In their definition, a media form is how 'material is organized, the style in which it is presented, the focus or emphasis on particular characteristics of behavior, and the grammar of media communication' (Altheide & Snow 1979: 10). Media logic becomes, therefore, a codification of how media work as a form: what their 'underlying interactive order' is (Lundby 2009: 108).

This approach to media logics as forms of interaction provides us with an opportunity to link the general sensitizing concept of mediatization to already established, analytically more specific definitive concepts in media and communications research – to refer at this point back to the aforementioned distinction made by Herbert Blumer (1954). For example, we can understand news values as being based on specific media forms such as the format of a news show (Hjarvard 2018: 64). Mediatization research, then, analyzes how these formats and related news values have changed over time, thereby shifting media's influence. The same can be said, for example, for research on the changing forms of presenting celebrities in the media (Driessens 2014), or research on the changing forms of visual self-presentation on social media (Neumann-Braun & Autenrieth 2011). From the perspective of mediatization research, media's forms of interaction are not simply interesting in themselves. It is about analyzing them in terms of how other domains of society are molded by them and how this refers to the transformation of culture and society as a whole.

Organizational rules

A second approach to media logics is to look at them through the lens of organization. Beyond media and communications research the idea of organizational logic is very much related to the discussion on neoinstitutional theory.[6] In this line of argument, an 'institutional logics perspective' means to investigate the 'socially constructed, historical patterns of cultural symbols and material practices' (Thornton et al. 2012: 2). This includes the assumptions, values and beliefs through which individuals and organizations provide meaning to their daily activity.[7]

While the institutional logics perspective offers certain models for analyzing organizational influence,[8] in mediatization research different ways of theorizing organizational demands and orders are more common. For example, media organizations such as broadcasting companies, editorial departments, or social media firms are – in the tradition of Niklas Luhmann (2012) – theorized as 'systems', which are based on their own, autopoietic organizational rules.[9] Such organizational rules also refer to certain forms of interaction ('programs of presentation' in this tradition), how, for example, journalistic genres (news, commentaries) should be produced. However, the idea of organizational rules goes much further in that they also include decisions as to what, for example, appears as news at all, the principles according to which work is divided up or the timing of news production. Media logics are then understood as the 'modus operandi' (Hjarvard 2013: 17) of media as organizational systems. From this point of view, media logics never determine the operations of other social systems such as politics or economics but trigger reactions against them. These reactions are conceptualized as being self-regulated because these systems also have their own autopoietic organizational rules on the basis of which these organizations operate. As a consequence, irritation of other systems by the system of media does not lead to an effect but to 'self-preservation and self-transformation' (Eskjær 2018: 94).

Following W. Richard Scott (2001), it is possible to distinguish four different types of organizational rules: normative rules regarding expectations of the ways actors should behave in specific organizations; representational rules that help to construct shared understandings of organizations; constitutive rules that help to create organizations as social phenomena; and regulatory rules for enforcement reasons. In organizational terms, media logics, then, are the totality of these rules being at work at specific media organizations; the influence of media logics is the reaction to these organizational rules (Donges & Jarren 2014: 188).

As part of these rules, organizational media logics can also imply other meta-processes of change such as commercialization as it occurs in news production, for example, 'according to economically motivated rationales' (Strömbäck & Esser 2014b: 19).[10] Following on from this, commercialization is not necessarily working *against* media logics but can be part of them because most media organizations are commercial organizations, which has significant implications for all the processes of production.

Material affordances

A third approach to media logics is look at them through a technological lens. With increasing digitalization this material dimension of media has come into focus in general media and communications research (Katzenbach 2012: 125–126) and in mediatization research in particular (Thimm 2018: 113). The most common way to conceptualize media logics with this approach is to theorize technology as media's material affordances.[11]

Again, we see a theorizing of media logics that links this general sensitizing concept with a definitive concept of media and communications research. Originally, the idea of affordances has its origins in psychology where it is used to capture animals' and humans' perception of the specific 'offerings' of a natural or cultural environment: a cave that can be used as a shelter, for example (Gibson 1967). This idea was picked up in sociology to describe the shaping character of technological artifacts, where affordances are understood as 'functional and relational aspects which frame, while not determining, the possibilities for agentic action in relation to an object' (Hutchby 2001: 444).

In media and communications research,[12] the concept of affordance was further developed to describe the materiality of media technologies, how they shape the practices of media users and at the same time are shaped by them. Materiality at this point refers to 'the physical properties or features of objects and settings that 'invite' actors to use them in particular ways' (Lievrouw 2014: 23). Because the idea of affordance offered on the one hand an approach to analyze what users gain from a technology and on the other hand how their practices are molded by it, its spread in media and communications research has been rapid.[13]

The main idea of affordance is to investigate how (digital) media as technologies 'have the potential to alter the form and function of communication' (Schrock 2015: 1230). A core anchor point at this stage is to understand this not as a one-way street, that media 'do' something to human communication practices as a direct outcome of their materiality; rather, they shape *possibilities* in an interaction between designers and users of technology (Bucher & Helmond 2018: 236). A good example to explain this is Facebook. Facebook affords users the ability to make some choices to influence their news feed, which then molds their experience of using this platform (Nagy & Neff 2015: 4). On the one hand this experience remains embedded in their everyday practices, for example the practices of making friends, informing oneself or contacting others (Bucher 2012). On the other hand, it is the decision of Facebook designers which possibilities of interaction they build into their platform; decisions that are constantly evaluated against what are observed as user practices. Potential affordances even become more complicated as the users' knowledge of a digital platform's invisible algorithms is more often than not based only on everyday experience[14] and the individual outcomes of algorithms remain unpredictable to them. Accordingly, an analysis of affordances is always concerned with the question of expectations, or lack thereof, of technology.

The problem of media logics

Up to this point I have reconstructed the use of the term 'media logics' in its multiplicity. The line that connects the approaches of forms of interaction, organizational rules and material affordances is the assumption that each medium has particular characteristics through which it is molding individual practices as well as social domains. This molding process is not understood as a simple effect but takes place in a multifaceted interaction. The key point remains, however, that the idea of media logics is mostly about a property of a medium that is ascribed to it.

My argument here is that static attribution is an issue. This becomes evident when we take a closer look at the question of perception, as it is referred to in the discussion on material affordances. The term affordance refers to the mutuality of an actor's perceptions of a technology and its capabilities that provide the potential for a particular practice.[15] Affordances are constituted in the interrelation between an individual's perception of a medium and its qualities as a technology.[16] Researching affordances also means addressing 'imagined affordances' (Nagy & Neff 2015: 5, 7): the users' imaginations of what the specificities of media technologies are and what they might offer to them.

Generally speaking, and also in the case of forms of interaction and organizational rules, we can say that media logics come into play partly by perception, that is, not just by the definitive characteristics of media but by their attributed – and therefore, imagined – functionalities. From this perspective, the idea of media logics across all three approaches *also* refers to the perceived expectations of certain media. Typically, this is referred to as 'perceived media logic' (Nölleke & Scheu 2018: 197) or 'media logic as an orientation frame' (Schrott 2009: 49) which results in instances of 'self-mediatization' (Strömbäck & Esser 2014b: 21).[17] With this in mind, media logics can be explained as a response to what actors perceive as media's molding force and not necessarily to how media function.[18] As a consequence, research on mediatization has tended to focus on individual or supra-individual actors' perception of media's influence instead of only centering actual media characteristics.

Coming from this direction, we are already foregrounding process because perception is a highly dynamic phenomenon. The need for an even more far-reaching process perspective on media is clearer if we focus on platforms like Facebook and Twitter in more detail. They are typically characterized as possessing a 'social media logic' (van Dijck & Poell 2013: 2) or a 'network media logic' (Klinger & Svensson 2015: 1241, Klinger & Svensson 2018: 1). This shift in terminology expresses the differing characteristics of these platforms compared to earlier media forms as a new 'programmability' (van Dijck & Poell 2013: 5). Their *material affordances* are mainly based on software. Social media platforms' underlying algorithms define 'popularity' (van Dijck & Poell 2013: 6) in a new way: the popularity of certain users and their content is constructed through algorithmic filters. These platforms are linked to new *forms* of presenting oneself, starting from the way photos are taken for Facebook and ending in how 'successful' posts are written.[19] This relates to particular *organizational rules*: the business models of platform media companies are based on the monetarization of user data as they gain their revenue by 'selling' detailed knowledge about users for online advertising (van Dijck & Poell 2013: 9). Furthermore, it is not possible to see social media platforms isolated from other kind of media. In part, we can only analyze the dynamics of platforms if we also consider that their content spreads with the help of 'traditional' media such as television or radio which hint to 'important events' taking place on social media platforms:[20] Social interaction here is mediated by a dynamic of mass media, social media platforms and offline institutional processes.

Therefore, neither what constitutes a platform like Facebook nor its perception, use and interrelationships with other media are a static phenomenon. We are dealing with the ongoing processes of articulation and rearticulation of that what we call media. It is only through processes that the ability of media to mold the social world emerges and unfolds. Here, one arrives at a general problem for the metaphor of media logics, namely that it tends to reify the dynamic of these ongoing processes. The metaphor of media logics implies that media in and of themselves would stand out by structuring human practice in a certain way – precisely according to logics of form, organization or affordance. The human actors involved – those who continually produce the media as well as those who appropriate them – are lost sight of as well as media's processual character. Media become a 'static object' that is powerful in itself.

THINKING ABOUT MEDIA AS A PROCESS

Emphasizing the processual character of media is something that is crucial for understanding digital media: based on software, their changeability and speed of adaptation have increased considerably. The rapid change of what we call digital media makes us aware of their processual character every day. While this is also the focus of my following argument it is worth contextualizing this historically. A look into the past sharpens our view on the present. Or to put it another way: media have *always* had a processual character. In this respect, 'media as a process' is a general term used to bring this processual perspective front and center. However, as digitalization has intensified this processual nature has become even *more dominant*. It is in this respect that the expression 'media as a process' emphasizes a contemporary phenomenon.

There are many standard writings on media history, typically addressing early media 'networks' such as postal or broadcast services including mail or radio and television.[21] In contrast to these general narratives I want so take a more specific, relatively obscure historical example because of its historical duration exemplifies media's processual character very well. Grimeton, a Swedish radio station formed in the 1920s and active until 1995 was part of a network of longwave transmitting stations that 'could be called the wireless 'internet' of the twenties' (Johansson 2013: 3152).[22] This network for telegram transmission consisted of nine stations in the USA, Hawaii, Wales, Poland and Sweden. It was owned by the Radio Corporation of America (RCA).

Grimeton radio station went into operation on December 1st, 1924. The station is the only surviving, fully functional machine station in the world and was added to the UNESCO World Heritage List in 2004. In the early days of radio technology, oscillations had to be generated with the aid of a motor, that is, electromechanically by a 'machine'. This required high-speed generators called alternators which made up the core of the machine transmitter. The alternator used in the RCA network was developed by Ernst Fredrik Werner Alexanderson, a Swedish-American engineer and part of a group of pioneers in broadcasting technology. The Grimeton radio station consists of the transmission house, houses for workers as well as the transmission antenna which is suspended from six towers that look like huge high-voltage masts (see Figure 3.1). The location of Grimeton in Sweden was chosen because from there a radio connection without any barriers was possible across the sea to Long Island, USA.

In practice, a message was communicated as follows: a private telegram was posted at the Swedish Post Office. From there, the text was sent by cable as a Morse code signal via the central office in Gothenburg to Grimeton. From Grimeton the message was transmitted wirelessly to the Radio Central of America station in Long Island. The telegrams were then forwarded via wire connection or brought to their addressees with the help of delivery boys. The total information transmitted from Grimeton in 1936 was 1.8 million words, the equivalent of around 10 megabytes of digital data (Johansson 2013: 3152).

Figure 3.1 Grimeton transmission masts and network. Photograph: Beate C. Köhler

After the Second World War, when intercontinental radio links were established via shortwave, the Swedish military used Grimeton to communicate with its submarines as the frequency range of the electromagnetic waves generated by the station were able to penetrate several meters deep into salt water. The character of the medium thus changed: a station in a telegraph network for the aerial transmission of messages to individuals became a transmitting station for sending longwave signals through the sea to submarines.

Grimeton radio station is a perfect example of media's processual character. First of all, we are confronted with the process of 'creating' this medium. It starts with a pioneer community that develops the concept of radio wave transmission and the technicians to practically implement these ideas. While the development phase is very fluid, stability occurs the moment the medium's infrastructure is built up. This includes material components (the alternator, the transmitter building, the transmission masts, the houses for the workers, the cable connection to Gothenburg), but also institutional components (the construction of the team of workers at Grimeton, the establishment of a telegram department at the Swedish post office, the use of the already institutionalized Morse code for transmitting telegrams, the organization of the network of cooperating radio stations).

The 'emerging stability' of the medium arises through an intermeshing of the processes of *materialization* (the construction of the related media technology and infrastructure) and *institutionalization* (the construction of the related institutions and work practices). However, this stability is always temporary: the medium of transcontinental long-wave telegraphy does not remain the same over time but continues to develop. This can also be seen as an almost disruptive development, as in the case of Grimeton, where the medium of wireless telegram communication became the medium of subaquatic military communication. The stabilization of the medium through its materiality and institutions must, therefore, not be equated with unchangeability. A medium always develops dynamically.

Grimeton radio station embodies what I mean by media as a process: a medium such as that in the case of transcontinental telegram transmission molds the communication that takes place via the medium. But the reason is not that the medium contains certain 'logics' as a static phenomenon (what would Grimeton's 'logics' be?). The reason is that complex processes of institutionalization and materialization intermesh, constituting a constantly changing specificity of the medium.

Institutionalization and materialization

But what exactly do we mean when we refer to institutionalization and materialization? And how can we grasp their interdependency? In order to clarify these questions, it makes sense to define both concepts in general terms and then to make them more tangible in regard to digital media.[23]

When it comes to the process of *institutionalization* I am not equating the idea to comprehensive organizations such as media companies, broadcasters and platform providers, for example. These organizations are, as institutions, part of what constitutes media. But the process of institutionalization already begins prior to this kind of formalization. Generally speaking, institutionalization is a much wider process that involves not only habit at the level of individual actors, but, more subtly, the way actors mutually adjust their expectations of each other:

what Berger and Luckmann, following Schütz, call the reciprocal typ-ification of habitualized actions (Berger & Luckmann 1966: 72). Even the family is an institution that typifies particular forms and expected patterns of practice in terms of the types or roles of the actors involved ('father', 'mother', 'current partner', 'child', 'aunt' and so forth).

Therefore, using the idea of 'institutionalization' when consider-ing media does not only mean that we are thinking just about media organizations. At stake are processes of institutionalization that are more far-reaching in everyday life, such as in mobile telephony, which institutionalizes a communicative triadic relationship: 'caller', 'called' and 'bystanders'.[24] This does not mean that there is no space to focus on media organizations as powerful corporate actors when analyzing deep mediatization. In concrete terms, we can hardly grasp the molding forces of mobile telephony without also involving mobile phone providers in our considerations. They define certain standards, create and maintain the infrastructures needed (which in turn influ-ence the quality of reception in both urban regions and rural ones). However, we must go one step further and keep in mind other media-related processes of institutionalization such as the afore mentioned triad relationship of caller, called and bystander. This relationship is clear in the practices of mobile telephony, for example, when at the beginning of a telephone call on confidential topics callers and receiv-ers communicatively ensure that no one listens to the telephone call, or when a bystander turns away or signals on their own not to listen if he or she realizes that the telephone call is confidential. Media institu-tionalize our communicative practices on a variety of levels: how we arrange ourselves in a media use situation, our forms of communica-tion, that is, of interaction through media, and the organization of the technology and infrastructure, to name just a few.

Closely related to these processes of institutionalization is the *mate-rialization* of media. I use the term 'materialization' in a comprehen-sive sense, referring here both to the material presence of each medium and at the same time the norms and beliefs surrounding 'how things are' in relation to it. Each medium has a characteristic materiality which is built up in an ongoing process. This is not only the material-ity of the device as such (the TV set, the mobile phone, the computer, etc.), but also the materiality of the underlying (digital) infrastruc-tures: the cable networks, the satellites, the broadcasting stations and so on. This materiality is a process as it must be 'kept working'. This means that not only do digital infrastructures and technologies have to be preserved as an ongoing materialization process, but also that the institutions that ensure them need to be considered.

At this point, materialization as a process intermeshes with institutionalization while both remain independent processes: at the moment when the institutions that sustain the infrastructures disappear – the teams of workers and telegram offices in the case of Grimeton – only 'monuments' remain. As a materiality these remind us of a bygone functionality but are no longer media that are able to mold culture and society as in the case of Grimeton.

As soon as a medium is formed it appears to us as a 'natural' phenomenon. 'Natural' here means that certain institutional and material aspects of media, over time, have come to be so essential to everyday practice that they seem 'self-evident'.[25] For example, it feels 'natural' to use radio as a broadcasting medium directed toward a particular communicative 'center' because its existing infrastructure and institutionalized forms of communication suggests so. In the same sense it appears 'natural' to use internet platforms for curated exchange because they are coded as such and the technology companies behind the platforms promote them through the institutionalization of moderation.[26] Naturalization can intensify to reification. At this point, a medium is considered 'as a thing on its own', as something that 'lacks all human properties and capacities' (Honneth 2008: 148) and no longer as something that is articulated through ongoing human practice. In part, this is what happens when static media logics are assumed: a reification takes place when logics are ascribed to a medium as fixed characteristics. That these characteristics are produced in ongoing processes of institutionalization and materialization of human practice is, thus, overlooked. Ascribing emphasis on these processes means to understand media as 'points of passage in social practice' (Göttlich 1996: 254), a phrase that goes back to the writings of Raymond Williams.[27]

In order to grasp the intermeshing of institutionalization and materialization in the constitution of media, it is helpful to revisit the three approaches to media logics — forms of interaction, organizational rules and material affordances. In so doing it becomes apparent that institutionalization and materialization are interdependent when considered in the context of all three approaches.

When it comes to forms of interaction, I have already given some examples of how institutionalization can be understood, namely as the institutionalization of certain practices of communication: patterns according to which we write letters or e-mails, telephone, or online chat threads. Furthermore, the communicative roles we take are institutionalized, both in terms of roles of interaction (speakers, listeners, discussants, etc.) and in terms of organizational roles (editors, producers, reporters, etc.).

Adopting a processual perspective means being aware of how particular forms become specific to a certain medium that have to be rearticulated continuously. This is especially apparent when we look more closely at the emergence of specific media. For example, soap operas existed long before television came onto the scene as a narrative genre for radio. These were taken up by television and developed as visual genres when these forms of popular storytelling were considered as characteristic for the medium of television. The WELL network, as one of the first online platforms, institutionalized forms of interaction – a division of labor in the creation of content by many 'amateur' contributors – that goes back to how the content production of the Whole Earth Catalogue was organized: its principles of participation, its inclusion of various authors and the role of its operators in curating a range of voices. The institutionalization of individual media does not develop from 'nothing', but from already institutionalized forms of interaction which, in a sense, 'migrate' from one medium to the next, a process through which their institutionalized form is transformed.

These institutionalization processes go hand in hand with materialization: media, as technologies and infrastructures, are built according to an institutionalization of practice. Television was made viable by its vast array of masts and broadcasting stations in such a way that shapes it as a perfectly *centralized* medium for storytelling and drama. This is the reason why it was possible that 'drama as an experience [became] […] an intrinsic part of everyday life, at a quantitative level which is so very much greater than any precedent as to seem a fundamental qualitative change' (Williams 1990: 59). The same can be said of digital platforms: the way users are curated, how information about them is structured, how timelines are organized, how 'liking' and 'commenting' are possible – all these are materializations of already institutionalized practices.

Institutionalization and materialization also concern the media as an organization. Thus, one dimension of any medium is that there are media organizations – broadcasters, platform operators, etc. – that 'carry' the medium. These media organizations are complex formalized institutionalizations, not only of forms of individual practice, but also of cooperation, work organization, decision making and implementation. From a processual perspective, organizations are multi-layered figurations of 'organizing' (Weick et al. 2005: 409). And organizations rely on their materializations: the aforementioned buildings and other 'things' that 'belong' to them, whose continuity they secure, but which at the same time also secures their agency.

Often the material affordances of digital media are reduced to their technological characteristics, because the 'newness' that first catches the eye first is technological.[28] When discussing a medium's technology, its materiality as object or artifact is generally what is focused on. However, it is crucial that we do not consider these materializations independently of related institutionalization processes.[29] This is about the institutionalization of human practices that are necessary to constitute and maintain media artifacts and infrastructures, for example, the institutionalized practice of software programming, the (constant) development of end devices, the refinement of broadcasting standards and so on. Here, figurations of people are involved in different degrees of organization: development teams, innovation groups, workshops and mobile task forces. We cannot understand the materialities of a medium beyond the institutionalized figurations of people, neither in its creation nor in its existence.

Algorithms as process amplifiers

The examples discussed so far should make clear what it means to speak of media as a process: It is a helpful starting point to understand media as articulated in the intermeshing of institutionalization and materialization. While this also appears to be an appropriate approach historically, it is becoming even more important today when digital media are based on algorithms.

If we understand algorithms as a set of steps to accomplish a task, or more precisely as a recipe that specifies the exact sequence of steps required to solve a problem, the term is more comprehensive than that of merely 'software'.[30] That said, software is based on algorithms and understanding this is fundamental for a thorough understanding digital media. This is the reason why the overall discussion on algorithms has recently intensified in media and communications research. An increasing amount of research is dedicated to 'algorithmic culture' (Striphas 2015) and 'algorithmic life' (Amoore & Piotukuh 2016). With reference to digital media, the term 'algorithm' indicates that media are based on 'encoded procedures for transforming input data' (Gillespie 2014: 167). However, there is a certain shift in the character of algorithms: while originally this definition continued to discuss 'a desired output, based on specific calculations' (Gillespie 2014: 167), with self-learning algorithms and artificial intelligence, the latter became more complex in the sense that the output is defined much more dynamically than it was before (cf. Loosen 2018b).

We also should consider algorithms as articulated by an intermeshing of institutionalization and materialization: an algorithm is not an 'object that exists outside of [...] social processes' (Beer 2017: 4). By contrast, they are rooted in institutionalized social practices: practices of defining and coding them as well as practices of their use. Therefore, in specifying the possible molding power of algorithms it is important to keep in mind that the organizations – companies, state agencies, administrations – that commission the coding of software have certain purposes and interests as well as explicit and implicit models of the social which become inscribed in the algorithms they produce.[31] In conceptualizing algorithms in such a way, it becomes evident that they have further amplified the processual character of media. This concerns the development of digital media on the one hand, and their further maintenance on the other.

In the 1950s and 1960s, electronic media were mainly developed industrially 'behind closed doors' before they were made available to a wider audience. Initially, such an approach to media development was widespread in the development of digital media as well: until the late 1980s, software development was carried out by documenting specifications in 'requirement documents' (Turner 2016: 257). These defined the demands on the software over several pages, which were then processed step-by-step before the 'finished' product came to market.

Since the 1990s the focus on software development has somewhat altered, especially when it comes to digital media. Important keywords here are 'participatory design' and 'co-creation', that is, the gradual development of software together with prospective users.[32] In this process, 'prototypes' play an important role as does (co-operative) 'prototyping'. The latter is the practice of a step-by-step software design that is based on the continuous development of its concept through successive prototypes. Prototypes of software are a complex construct:[33] they are not just working models of new software and new devices on which to run them. As 'socio-material configurations' (Suchman et al. 2002: 163) they represent social practice in a certain way. They model idealized forms of social practice and new institutionalized forms of social organization. Prototypes are 'in need of development' and 'solicit the collaboration of users and others in the building of a particular future' (Turner 2016: 266).

With the development of digital media through participative approaches and prototyping, the dynamics of 'making media' have intensified since the times of legacy media;[34] this means that it makes even more sense to emphasize the processual character of the creation of a medium.

When they are developed, digital media are much more process-like than their legacy counterparts mainly because of their adaptability: it is much easier to edit software than hardware. It is often highlighted that algorithms are 'black boxed' (Pinch & Bijker 1984: 404), which means that their operations are opaque to the end user (and partly to the designers).[35] This 'blackboxing' is part of technology's process of materialization: a technology as black box is rarely questioned but taken for granted as something 'quasi-natural' which is 'just there' and 'just works'. With algorithms, however, the durability of this black boxed technology became a much more relative one in the sense that changes can be implemented much faster than they can with non-digital media.

Compared to pure hardware algorithms provide a simple way of modifying the functionality of a digital medium such as a social media platform, and this is an ongoing process as Facebook or Twitter clearly demonstrate. Software-based media can be 'tweaked and re-coded where the outcomes are seen to be in need of adjustment' (Beer 2017: 4). Digital media are therefore 'forever in beta stage' (Manovich 2013: 1) and in a 'constant flux' (Cheney-Lippold 2017: 90).[36] Coded algorithms can be changed 'easily, instantly, radically, and invisibly' (Gillespie 2014: 178) while still being operational. So-called self-learning algorithms even modify their data processing principles based on the data they process.

In sum, algorithms are *process amplifiers* for a variety of reasons: as today's digital media are primarily defined by software, their creation has become an iterative process in which users are much more involved than was the case with electronic media. But even after digital media have been developed, they are much easier to modify as software can be adapted and further refined while they are in use. The intermeshing of institutionalization and materialization has become much more dynamic than it was in the age of legacy media and this processual character even becomes more dynamic with the rise of automation.

Automation and communicative robots

At several points in the previous section, we talked in passing about automation. Automation is a key aspect of digital media as algorithms are designed to be 'functionally automatic, to act when triggered without any regular human intervention or oversight' (Gillespie 2014: 170).[37] Because of this, some use the term 'automated media' (Napoli 2014: 340) instead of digital media. Automation is a fairly broad phenomenon, referring to media use as well as media production.[38] When it comes to media use, algorithms serve to enable users to navigate complex, highly connected media by means of 'automated orientation aids' such as recommendation and aggregation systems. When it comes to media production, automatically generated user data constitute an important basis for decision-making. But even certain forms of media content, such as weather forecasts, are produced automatically on the basis of information from databases.

Considering the latest developments in media technology and artificial intelligence, the possibilities of automation come together in the emergence of what we might call *communicative robots*. From a user's point of view, communicative robots are not an isolated phenomenon but have to be seen in the broader context of the spread of robots in the domestic and private spheres. Fortunati argues that we are witness to an incipient 'robotization' (Fortunati 2018: 3) of private and domestic life. Service robots such as automated vacuum cleaners, lawn mowers and window cleaners are beginning to seep into the popular imagination and into our homes. This is the context in which we should see 'social robots', that is autonomous systems that are *designed* to interact with humans (Böhle & Pfadenhauer 2014: 3).[39] A domain in which these social robots are growing in popularity were nursing homes, in which robots with the appearance of small seals were used to care for dementia patients (Pfadenhauer & Dukat 2015).

Research on social robots has over time faced a fair amount of criticism due to the tendency of focusing on artifacts and underestimating the relevance of communication.[40] For this reason I prefer to apply the term 'communicative robot'. Broadly, communicative robots are (partially) automated communication media which operate — often but not always on the basis of artificial intelligence — autonomously with the purpose of quasi-communication with human beings in order to enable further algorithmic based functionalities. I use the term 'quasi-communication' quite deliberately: it emphasizes the fact that the main function of communicative robots in their relation to human beings is not 'that the machine is able to think but that it is able to communicate' (Esposito 2017: 250). Furthermore, this phrasing makes explicit that the form of communication which takes place is an attribution of communication by humans to a machine and not communication in the sense of a human symbolic exchange as it is theorized in symbolic interactionism. And finally, this phrase emphasizes that we are dealing with a recursive loop here as well. Thus, human communication served as a model for the development of human-machine interfaces the analysis of which now reveals that machines are perceived and treated by humans in a similar way to interaction partners. As Andrea Guzman aptly puts it: 'The technologies that are now inspiring communication scholars to pay attention to human-machine communication are the result of decades of research guided by the idea of communication outside the discipline' (Guzman 2018: 7, see also Guzman & Lewis 2019: 5). In all, most communicative robots are not physical artifacts but are in fact purely software-based.[41]

In today's everyday life, we can currently identify three types of communicative robots: artificial companions, social bots and work-bots. *Artificial companions*[42] include Amazon's Alexa, Apple's Siri, Google's Assistant and Microsoft's Cortana. Much rarer artificial companions take the form of a physical artifact. One is Anki's Vector, a robot in the form of a small moving caterpillar that can be queried and take photos. What really makes it stand out from other virtual assistants, though, is that it also expresses its 'emotional status'.[43] This is also a feature of the Sony Aibo robot dog which was produced between 1999 and 2006 and subsequently updated and reissued in 2017.[44] Such companions present themselves as 'conversational visà-vis, artificial playmates and interdependent actors' (Böhle & Bopp 2014: 164).

The typical structure of artificial companions follows a general theme: they have a software-based interface between itself and the user via which he or she can communicate with the system through the means of (spoken) language. This is done either through a smart-phone app, an application on the computer or through voice commands directed at an 'intelligent' speaker. The spoken commands or questions are not then processed 'in' the device but transferred via the internet to data servers – in a sense they are sent 'to the cloud'. Once a command reaches a server speech recognition configured by artificial intelligence processes takes place, the questions and commands are processed and the result is transferred back to the device. The output then takes shape either in the form of a specific activity (execution of a software command) or a spoken response (output of relevant information).

These artificial companions are not simply media in the sense that they serve as interaction nodes between people. Because their functionality is based on datafication, that is, the collection and processing of large amounts of data, they are part of an automated, data-based construction of reality. The Shazam application, which was adopted by Apple in 2017/18, and is a kind of specialised artificial companion for music use, is a clear example of this taking place: the app identifies songs via the smartphone's microphone; a snippet of the song is recorded, the resulting audio file is transmitted to 'the cloud', compared to an existing database of already digitized songs and, if recognized, the result is communicated back to the user through the app (otherwise a message appears that the song could not be recognized). Shazam saves these search results in a user database and on this basis creates personal playlists, recommends new music titles, highlights new releases and suggests new songs. What is happening here is what Barile and Sugiyama refer to as the 'automation of taste' (Barile & Sugiyama 2015: 413) through an artificial companion. On the one hand, Shazam provides users with extended control of their music consumption. Searching and selecting music becomes an individual act augmented by technical support. On the other hand, the accompanying automated processing and taste classification directs individual variation and gives the communicative robot a considerable position in the composition of the respective music repertoire.

Besides artificial companions, *social bots* are a widespread form of communicative robots. In essence, most social bots are automated social media accounts that operate as if 'real' people were doing the communicating. More precisely, social bots are 'software processes that are programmed to appear to be human-generated within the context of social networking sites such as Facebook and Twitter' (Gehl & Bakardjieva 2016: 2). The history of social bots goes back to at least 2008, when the first experiments with scripts imitating Twitter users began to be developed. These scripts tweeted text elements that were synthesized from other tweets by human users. In 2017, it is discussed that between 9 percent and 15 percent of active Twitter accounts might actually be bots.[45] Instagram is assumed to have similar numbers.[46] According to Facebook, in the same year around 10 percent of its users were 'fake' accounts, which does not mean that each of them is also a social bot (some are human-operated accounts running under a 'false' identity).[47] Such numbers, however, are highly speculative, as there is no real possibility of identifying bots accurately (Lazer et al. 2018). Nevertheless, this phenomenon is becoming more relevant and can be linked with what Sherry Turkle called the 'robotic moment'. Turkle describes how that 'even before we make the robots, we remake ourselves as people ready to be their companions' (Turkle 2015: 338). In the case of bots, this means that with platforms such as Facebook, Twitter or Instagram, users are represented in a highly structured manner as are their interactions, hashtags and other elements of their communicative practices on the platforms, the representation and communication of humans is pre-structured to such an extent that their replication by machines is comparatively simple. Therefore, these platforms represent a 'leveled middle ground' where humans and robots appear on a 'significantly equalized footing' and where social bots 'have good chances to be successful in presenting themselves as humans' (Bakardjieva 2015: 248).

Furthermore, there are *work bots*: bots which are used for automated labor. There are several examples of this, even in journalism: the LA Times' Quakebot is an automatic article-generating program that uses algorithms to turn e-mail alerts from the US Geological Survey (USGS) into news stories.[48] The San Francisco based Hoodline generates hyperlocal news articles from scraped public databases using work bots.[49] Quill is an application developed by Narrative Science which transforms data into contextually-rich information.[50] Quill can be used to produce journalistic content as well as other forms of content such as product information for online catalogs. In the field of media and communications these work bots are typically discussed in terms of 'robot journalism' (Thurman et al. 2017: 1251; Clerwall 2014: 519) or 'automated journalism' (Loosen 2018b: 11). This kind of automated reporting is principally about 'algorithmic processes that convert data into narrative news texts with limited to no human intervention beyond the initial programming' (Carlson 2015: 417). Or put another way, algorithms arrange data and information from different sources in a way so that the outcome is a text, video or any other kind of media product (Dörr 2016).

The example of work bots demonstrates that we are probably less confronted with a simple replacement of humans by communicative robots. Rather, these work bots become something akin to colleagues: companions in content production that reveal transformations to the journalistic work process. This concerns the role of the journalist, who, when using, for example, Narrative Science technologies, is thought of more as a 'meta-writer' or 'meta-journalist' (Carlson 2015: 423) to facilitate automated stories. In their application of these technologies, journalists have to preprogram their stories' scripts (the line-up of players, the match result and so on) into an appropriate descriptive language. These scripts push the 'meta-journalists' into the use of a certain compositional form as offered up by the software. If the data processed by these scripts rely on existing databases, the underlying data models also have a comprehensive influence over which 'stories' can be told and how.[51]

Taking the phenomenon of communicative robots, we can see that advanced automation has once again increased the media's processual dynamics. First of all, this concerns data processing. In the examples discussed so far, the core aspect of automation is the automated processing of data (language, images, etc.) through the utilization of databases.[52] What we are dealing here with are new forms of institutionalization and materialization based on processes of categorization. Relational in their structure, the databases used are often highly flexible and only loosely connected objects can be ordered in a potentially unlimited number of ways.[53] Because of this flexibility, categorization is important as even metadata is not strictly 'raw' in nature but already somehow organized and, therefore, structured (cf. Gitelman & Jackson 2013). This categorization constitutes a powerful semantic and political intervention because 'what the categories are, what belongs to a category, and who decided how to implement these categories in practice, are all powerful assertions about how things are and supposed to be' (Gillespie 2014: 171). Overall, categorization is an ongoing process with its own dynamics as new data are added based on the assignments made. We are thus confronted here with processes of an automated, data-based construction of the social world: a type of 'data structuring' (Flyverbom & Murray 2018: 1) which is based on the qualities of databases.

Secondly, it becomes apparent that this automated processing relies on procedures of continuous feedback. In a certain sense, a special quality of communicative robots is that they are designed to communicate data to humans in a targeted manner and along predefined scripts. Targeted communication can take on a variety of forms: it could be the precise answer to a question addressed to an artificial companion, but it is also possible that a bot communicates information on an event – an earthquake, a goal scored during a football match, an exceeded limit value of air pollution – almost instantaneously. Furthermore, it can mean that information about one's self (tastes, habits and so on) is collected on an ongoing basis and that suggestions for visiting events, buying new books or reading additional information are made based on the automated processing of such data. With communicative robots we as humans are confronted with a process of dynamic feedback through machines.

What characterizes media as a process?

How can we sum up the considerations we have made so far? What characterizes media as a process? The Grimeton radio station example demonstrates that a processual approach to media is not only appropriate for today's digital media. The establishment of this radio station as part of a wireless telegram network was connected with the construction of various institutions and material conditions. They then had to be maintained in an ongoing process, a process that also included a disruptive change in the medium from one of terrestrial radio communication towards one of subaquatic communication. Looking back, we can see that an approach to media as a process seems much more appropriate than implying more or less fixed logics. The reason is that it becomes possible to examine in more detail the intermeshing of institutionalization and materialization, how different individual and supra-individual actors are involved and the consequences media's resulting molding capabilities have for different domains of society. The expression 'media as a process' is, therefore, intended to point out that the media should generally be viewed less as a static phenomenon and more as something that is continuously articulated.

But as media became digital — that is, based on software — the dynamics of institutionalization and materialization increased fundamentally. This is the reason why an understanding of media as a process is even more necessary for investigating deep mediatization. Ultimately, algorithms can be understood as a 'process amplifier'. This already occurs in media's creation, which has become more fluid with prototyping and cooperative forms of programming. Today's digital media emerge much more visibly as part of a process. But because they are based on software, process dynamics remain once they are established. Compared to hardware-only electronic media, algorithms can be easily modified without restricting their functionality and continuously collected user data are an important source of information for the purposes of this modification. Platforms such as Facebook, Twitter or Instagram, for example, are constantly changing their characteristics, new possibilities for communication come into being and existing ones are refined or restricted. With digital media it becomes much more evident as to what extent institutionalization and materialization are ongoingly intermeshing processes. This also applies to automation and communicative robots and their ability to continuously generate and process data. This is coupled to a targeted process of automated feedback of data analyses to users and it is here where we are dealing with a further dynamic of media's inherent processuality.

The expression 'media as a process' draws attention to these dynamics. Especially in times of deep mediatization, it is important to take the processuality of media seriously if one wants to grasp their molding capabilities.

SCALING THE MEDIA MANIFOLD

If one considers media in terms of their processuality, it is vital that we reflect one other dynamic, namely, that of media's interrelation with each other: in times of deep mediatization, media do not stand alone, discrete and inert, but are comprehensively connected with one another. It is in this way that their specificity articulated. When it comes to terminology, there are different candidates that are able to capture media's interrelatedness in research. 'Cross-media' (Bjur et al. 2014), for example, is used in journalism and audience research to describe how practices in media production and media use typically unfold 'across' different media. 'Transmedia' (Evans 2011) is used either to describe storytelling across multiple media or audiences' appropriation of media content that is available on various platforms (Berg & Hepp 2018). The term 'polymedia' (Madianou & Miller 2013) captures the ways in which the primary concern of media users shifts from the constraints imposed by an individual medium to an emphasis upon the social, emotional and moral consequences of *choosing* between those different media.

There is a common line between these variations in terminology: all the terms place an emphasis on the dynamic interrelations between media. With deep mediatization these dynamics increase in their mutual dependency which is the reason why we should understand this as the complexity of a *media manifold*.[54] Like the terms above, media manifold emphasizes the diversity of the different media with which we are confronted in times of deep mediatization. But this idea goes one step further. By media manifold we understand the 'large 'universe' of variously *connected* digital media through which (in various figurations) we actualize social relations' (Couldry & Hepp 2017: 34–35; emphasis added). As we have seen, digitalization involves a further deepening of this connectedness, both through digital media's infrastructures and the layering of connected media practices in which individuals, collectivities and organizations are now routinely engaged.

The dynamics of the media manifold are rendered tangible as soon as we consider them from the point of view of individual experience. If we follow Mirca Madianou and Daniel Miller's argument (2013: 175f.), there are three preconditions that clarify a polymedia experience: access, affordability, literacy. There must be general access to the variety of different media, that is, their availability cannot be restricted to certain groups of people. At the same time, access to these media must be affordable; the economic resources available to people must be sufficient to finance the purchase of the corresponding technologies and their use. Finally, an adequate level of media literacy should be commonplace, that is, adequate skills to make an appropriate use of digital media. From an individual's point of view this all results in an 'integrated structure' (Madianou & Miller 2013: 174) which establishes the media manifold from a subjective perspective. It is not simply a matter of making selections from a variety of available media; in addition, the single medium takes on a specific meaning due to its position in this manifold of variety. When the written letter was the only medium for reaching distant relatives, its choice as a medium had no further meaning than the desire to reach loved ones and colleagues. But right now, when there is so much choice and a person decides to write a letter instead of using a messenger app, e-mail, internet video telephony or mobile phone, writing a letter takes on a particular meaning. The same can be said for every other medium: in today's media manifold, these media must be understood in terms of their relationality to each other, a relationality that moves and changes dynamically.

The media manifold also refers to questions of media content. With digital media, content can 'travel' across different devices or technologies and we are confronted with an *ongoing* process of what Bolter and Grusin refer to in a historical perspective as 'remediation' (Bolter & Grusin 2000). This applies not only to professionally produced content, to which this concept originally referred, but also to everyday interpersonal communication: each individual can distribute his or her photos, texts, document scans, audio and video files across different media. This often happens in the everyday life of media appropriation: images and news are communicated via various social media platforms and messenger applications in order to reach as many family members, friends and acquaintances as possible. This digital content and the various online platforms designed for their distribution, are the subject of an additional passing on of media artifacts. This stimulates dynamics in the co-construction of media representations.

Such examples demonstrate very clearly what is meant by the processual interrelationality of the media manifold: it becomes necessary to consider different media in relation to their dynamics with one another, as well as to reflect on the dynamics of co-constructing media representations across media. In order to capture this idea, it is helpful to remain aware of the various scales of the media manifold: first, at the scale of the totality of accessible media in a society, the 'media environment'. Second, at the scale of social domains of collectivities and organizations, where the media manifold solidifies within certain 'media ensembles'. And third, at the scale of the individual for whom the media manifold refers to their personal 'media repertoire'.

Media environment

We can understand the media environment as the entire body of media available at any given time.[55] This operates at the scale of the five quantitative trends of deep mediatization discussed earlier in this book: the differentiation of a vast amount of digital media; the increasing connectivity of these media; the rising omnipresence of media that creates the possibility to be connected permanently and wherever you may be; their rapid pace of innovation, that is the emergence of 'new' media and services in ever-shorter periods of time; and datafication, which is the representation of social life by computerized data through media devices, their underlying algorithms and digital infrastructures. These trends are not to be considered as separate phenomena but as closely linked with each other coming together in the media manifold of the media environment.

Two types of 'formative structures' (Bolin 2017: 45) can be distinguished in the media environment, namely those of media's interrelations as technologies and those of representations. Interrelations of media technologies are about the entire material fabric of digital media and their infrastructures as well as the selected processes of institutionalization. The point here is that the moment we see this media technologies as part of a media environment, their dynamic come to the fore. So, it is not just an individual medium that is of interest, but its dynamics of interrelation to others. If we consider a media environment in its totality, it is a matter of impossibility to capture these dynamics altogether. But for any analysis it is a first step to acknowledge them to avoid any hasty conclusions in relation to one medium.

In addition, each media environment is characterized by a totality of representations that goes beyond the media content of an individual media artifact. These representations are institutionalized to the extent that they are not simply individual expressions, for example, as part of media coverage on a specific event, it is more about the dynamics between these representations which unfold along certain discourses. These discussions are institutionalized patterns of communicating about 'something': what are the forms and ways of representing nuclear power, of sexual practices, cultural differences and so on. We can consider this as a 'semiotic web' that characterizes each media environment, that is, 'a map in which we act as individuals, but which also set up limits, privileges certain kinds of action before others, and guides us in our everyday lives' (Bolin 2017: 46). It is important, therefore, to bear in mind that in a particular media environment patterns of media representation firmly establish themselves. With current levels of connectivity, the underlying discourses develop dynamically across different media.

Each individual is born into a specific media environment. This points to the distinct significance of using the term *environment* in our discussion: just as social phenomenology argues that 'the world of contemporaries' (Schütz 1967b: 30) is what we experience as a social environment into which we are born, the media environment is the mediated world into which we are born, with each one contributing to the shape of life going forward. In this respect, from the point of view of the individual, the human-made media environment sometimes appears as 'natural' and accordingly 'reified': it exists first of all as *it was found*. However, once again one should not make the mistake of concluding that the media environment is a 'naturally' occurring given. It is based on a variety of practices of individual and supra-individual actors and is – no matter how long-lasting it may appear – also prone to change by human actors.

Ultimately, it is also the media environment that political actors address through their regulations and these regulations concern both its media technological aspects (for example, the regulation of the digital infrastructure) as well as its representational aspects (the banning of certain content, for example). On the variety of media and their high degree of interconnectivity, Andrew Chadwick (2017) describes the media environment as a 'hybrid media system'. His argument is that the hybrid media system is based on conflict and competition between 'old' and 'new' media, which at the same time are interdependent on each other. In this hybrid media system, power and influence are shifting. On the one hand, 'grassroots' communication has become more achievable thanks to the infrastructure of the internet. On the other hand, there is a considerable concentration of power among prominent corporate actors which also poses a stark challenge to state regulatory structures. This shift in power dynamics illuminates the extent to which deep mediatization's progress is accompanied by the dynamic character of the media environment and why it is necessary to address questions of media regulation in new ways.

An engagement with the media environment from a comprehensive point of view should also reflect the materiality of the media in another respect, namely in relation to ecology and sustainability. If one focuses on the media technolgical aspects of the media environment, it is clear that one can barely analyze them without also considering questions of natural resources. The production of digital media technologies – smart phones, computers etc. – is dependent on the extensive exploitation of minerals, it requires a considerable amount of energy and it also exploits human labor.[56] For broadband internet access, fiber optic cables need to be laid. The way distribution systems materialize, and their environmental consequences, differs radically from region to region, whether they course through concentrated urban regions, the suburban sprawl, mountainous farmland, or the ocean's depths.[57] It is worth noting the extent to which existing infrastructures such as pipelines can support or run alongside the installation of these cables – and the extent to which new communication infrastructures supports alternative economies. Every time data is accessed in the cloud energy is consumed, as is so with the automated data exchange of connected digital media. The rise of the internet of things will only increase the amount of energy consumed as deep mediatization's tendrils work their way into the objects of everyday life.[58]

When looking at the media environment we need to deal with a range of different process dynamics. First, we have the dynamics media generate among themselves, through which only the totality of a media environment is created. As we have seen, these dynamics have both media technological aspects (media manifest as devices and the infrastructures they depend on) and representational ones (the discourses that unfold across various media). But we are also dealing with dynamics of power, in which the media environment is not only the subject of political debate, but also the subject of regulation. Other dynamics concern the ecology and sustainability of the media environment, that is, its relationship to the wider human environment.

In keeping these different process dynamics in mind, it immediately becomes clear that a fully holistic analysis of the media environment is an undertaking that can hardly be realized. Rather, it is a matter of selecting single dynamics and examining them each in detail. In turn, concrete analyses then allow more general statements about the media environment and the ways it might change because of each dynamic's integration. But the more specific question is how these dynamics manifest within certain social domains. This points to another level of scale for the media manifold, that is, the media ensemble.

Media ensemble

The media ensemble is the subset of a media environment, the array of media that are used within a particular social domain of a collectivity or organization.[59] From a media-sociological point of view, the overall totality of the media environment is not present everywhere in the same way but does tend to be preselected by the social domains in which humans interact. A domain's media ensemble is different than an individual's personal media selection. On the one hand, the media ensemble of a particular social domain can be much more limited than the media being used by an individual. For example, while an individual might use – besides a mobile phone – various kinds of online media for personal communication, the media he or she uses in a certain group of friends might be restricted to SMS and mobile phone calls because these are also the media which are used by the others in the group. On the other hand, as each social domain involves various individuals using different media, its media ensemble might include media that particular individuals within the group do not use. Consequently, the characteristic media ensemble of a social domain can be more extensive than the media being used by the individuals who constitute it. This is the case if we consider organizations where certain media are only used by some of the individuals involved (for example, those working at the reception desk or those in a more administrative position) and where differences exist from one department to another.

If we deepen our approach to organizations, we once again arrive at the technological and representational aspects of media's interrelations. Journalism is but one example where we can see this taking place. Various studies have shown how the newsroom has transformed alongside the technological development of media ensembles. Work practices are altered when computers, digital cameras and e-mail make their way into an organization. Some scholars argue, for example, that with a changing media ensemble the organizational form of the newsroom can become a cross-media one by being able to simultaneously produce content for radio, television and online.[60] With a changing media ensemble new positions have arisen, the 'data journalist', for example, who generates news or visually presents it on the basis of online data and digital traces.[61] It has been argued that the new ensemble of different media technologies breaks down boundaries in the newsroom by involving freelancers in the production process in new ways.[62] Other arguments concern the changing relationship between journalists and their audiences.[63] This relationship is transforming due to the ongoing communication of journalists with the people who consume their content on various platforms (Facebook, Twitter, Instagram, etc.). These studies focus on how media's interrelations are part of the complex process of organizational transformation.

But we cannot understand this organizational transformation without also considering questions of representation, especially the representations of ideas that are related to an organizational appropriation of media ensembles. One important argument suggests that we reflect on the dynamics of 'translating ideas' in reference to organizational transformation. At this point translation is understood as an 'ongoing process through which institutional ideas and practices are created, legitimized, selected and given meaning as they travel across organizations and organizational fields' (Fredriksson & Pallas 2017: 128). In other words, adjusting an organization's media ensemble is always associated with appropriating the representations of ideas on how a changing media ensemble is expected to mold an organization. For example, a social media strategy *should* enable newspapers to reach their audiences more efficiently, or cross-media production *should* make it possible to serve more channels, or a new newsroom editorial system *should* ensure a flatter organizational structure. The translation of ideas is never a one-to-one transfer, rather, these are complex processes of co-construction in which 'locally translated ideas get decontextualized and serve as a source of inspiration' (Fredriksson & Pallas 2017: 131).

Similar things can be said for communities and their media ensembles.[64] Again, the technological interrelations between media are striking: a certain media ensemble is characteristic of each community and the desire of the individual to become a member of this community also means that he or she must 'get involved' with its media. These do not have to be media exclusive to the community. For communities such as circles of friends, cliques or peer groups, the media ensemble typically consists of more widely available platforms or messenger services such as Facebook and WhatsApp. What is crucial, however, is that participation in many communities today goes hand in hand with the pressure on the individual to engage with their community's media and any associated rules of media use: the frequency with which one reads certain news, the way one comments on YouTube content, the ways in which one interacts with another and so on. The rules for media use are often those that refer to the media's interrelations with the ensemble as a whole: for example, what you can 'say' in a phone call but 'avoid' in an e-mail, what is 'expected' in an Instagram comment but is considered 'unseemly' on Facebook. The innate human need for communitization is often a considerable driving force for engaging in 'new' media, namely those that are part of the media ensemble of a collectivity. We can see this as a moment of individualized pressure provoked by deep mediatization: there may be no other way to become part of and interact with a community unless you use certain media in certain ways.

The interrelation of representations can also be identified in communities. In a certain sense, communities are always 'interpretive communities' (Lindlof 1988; Schröder 1994). Even if they do not constitute themselves around individual genres or formats — such as fan communities (Radway 1984) – communities are partly characterized by their practices of appropriating media representations. The reason is that these representations are important points of reference for the construction of a collective identity. For example, certain YouTube channels or Instagram accounts, which young people follow and through which important fashion styles are negotiated in their peer groups, are used in the negotiation of their shared identity. With the increasing differentiation and simultaneous connectivity of digital media, these representations unfold across different media and travel from one medium to another.

Media repertoire

Finally, we can scale media's relatedness to the level of the media repertoire, an individuals' selection from the media manifold as they use and appropriate media as part of their everyday practices.[65] This concept refers to the entirety of media that a person regularly uses. Rather than taking the media-centric point of view that asks which audiences a particular medium reaches this concept emphasizes the question concerning which media a particular person uses. In so doing, it is focused on the idea of entirety. The idea of media repertoires stresses the need to consider the whole variety of media regularly assembled by a person. This helps to avoid misinterpretations of empirical data that result from approaches that emphasize a single medium.

Media repertoires refer to 'relatively stable transmedia patterns of media use' (Hasebrink & Domeyer 2012: 759). In times of deep mediatization, practices become media practices that unfold across media. This can be illustrated by the practice of cooking. Cooking includes a variety of individual acts such as selecting recipes, shopping, cutting ingredients and so on; these acts are typically realized with reference to digital media: one gathers recipes from cooking apps or internet forums, shopping lists are created in a notetaking app or exported directly from the cooking app and the preparation and the resulting dish can be documented in photographs. These images are distributed on platforms as part of the documentation of a family celebration or as 'food porn' to share with friends and, perhaps, a wider audience.

This broad relation of individual practices to digital media results in a certain ambiguity with which the term *repertoire* is used. For example, 'communication repertoire' (Hasebrink 2015) is used alongside 'media repertoire'. This is done in order to make clear that in the analysis of the phenomenon of interest, direct communication is just as significant as mediated communication. Elsewhere, the term 'public connection repertoire' (Hasebrink 2019: 1) is used[66] to refer to the entirety of media with which people realize their communicative connection to the 'public', how they establish their 'public connection' (Couldry et al. 2007). 'Information repertoires' (Hasebrink & Domeyer 2010) refer to the complexity of cross-media practices for informing oneself. When it comes to political information the term 'news repertoires' (Kobbernagel & Schrøder 2016) is also widespread.

This terminology is hierarchical, if we understand media repertoire and communication repertoire as two general concepts which are each accentuated differently: on the one hand, with reference to media practices (all practices related to media), and on the other, with reference to communication practices (all communication practices, mediated or otherwise). On this basis, a range of partial repertoires can be distinguished. These then reinforce an individual's overall media or communication repertoire with reference to a particular social domain.

In all these cases we have to consider the interrelatedness of each repertoire both in regard to media technologies and in regard to representations, while at the same time reflecting the internal structure of repertoires. This can be illustrated by information repertoires.

An information repertoire is internally differentiated (Hasebrink & Domeyer 2010: 54–55). It is, first of all, about *undirected information needs*, that is, a general and continuous observation of the individual's environment in regard to possible opportunities and risks. *Thematic interests* are active orientations towards certain topical areas in which people specialize in order to acquire special expertise (for example, in the professional domain or in regard to certain popular cultures and certain hobbies). Furthermore, there are *group needs* that refer to information from and about the reference groups relevant to an individual, whether they be as part of a couple, peers, family, or other colleagues and friends. Finally, there are the concrete *problem-solving needs* that are at the center of the information-seeking approach. These result from the requirements of concrete situations the solution of which requires certain information at an individual level.

If we emphasize the interrelations of media technologies in these information repertoires, various points are striking (as would be the case in other kinds of media and communication repertoires).[67] From an individual's point of view there is the question of 'proportion of use', that is, how much time is allocated to certain media and for which purposes. A further aspect is that of the 'relevance of components': if we consider the variety of (digital) media which constitute a person's information repertoire, some media are more relevant for them than others. Here the different components of an information repertoire matter in the sense that 'relevance' can differ from one medium to another: the media that are of importance for addressing the general information needs of an individual are different to the ones they might use for thematic interests, group needs or information-seeking. Then there is the question of 'diversity': how diverse are the media that constitute an individual's information repertoire? Is it just the WWW or does it include a wide variety of different media, from books and newspapers to artificial intelligence-based apps? Finally, we can refer to 'functional complementarity', that is, the extent to which (digital) media complement each other from the point of view of the individual. Empirical research indicates that individuals attribute 'highly specific functions' to certain media, 'thus emphasizing a high degree of functional complementarity within their repertoire' (Hasebrink & Domeyer 2012: 770).

It is quite clear that information repertoires in particular, and media and communication repertoires in general, should be considered in terms of the interrelations between the representations that are produced within them: these representations can be categorized into 'genres, topics, concrete products, brands' (Hasebrink & Domeyer 2012: 760). For information repertoires, it can be said that the topics that interest a person present themselves as different media representations. This concerns undirected information needs as well as thematic interests, group needs and information-seeking: the information that is important for an individual to establish orientation might come from reading online newspapers as well as from conversations and movies. The information on the topic of one's own hobby might be garnered from forums, books and WWW pages. Pictures of shared experiences can be just as important for group communication as well as the exchange of memes (whether that be in the form of cartoons or cat pictures). The search for specific information can also result in the appropriation of different content. What we call 'information' expands across various representations. It then becomes clear that we can only adequately grasp the internal dynamics of information repertoires if we also pay attention to the interrelationality of their representations. This also applies to all other media and communication repertoires: their dynamics of representation are cross-media.

The distinction between the three scales – media environment, media ensembles and media repertoires – provides us with a basis from which to analyze today's media manifold in real terms. Media's institutionalization and materialization unfold as ongoing, intermeshing processes. It is analytically impossible to describe these processes of institutionalization and materialization in their cross-media dynamics in relation to the entire media environment. The reason is that these processes are far too contradictory and complex for the media environment of a society as a whole. But solid analyses of selected dynamics of the media environment, of certain social domains or particular groups of individuals and their media ensembles or media repertoires are, indeed, possible, which in turn allows conclusions to be drawn on the change in the media environment as a whole. The idea of the conceptual distinction proposed here is to make these analyses possible.

NOTES

1   See, for this research tradition Neuman & Guggenheim (2011).

2   The inspiration this concept offers to very different scholars is maybe best represented by the fact that it was a reference point in early publications on mediatization (Asp 1990), and it inspired whole books (Altheide & Snow 1979) and encyclopedia articles (Mazzoleni 2008). Most recently an edited volume of scholars of mediatization research focused on the idea of media logics (Thimm et al. 2018b).

3   In such ways, the term 'logics' is used, for example, by Bennett & Segerberg (2013), Jameson (1991) or Thornton et al. (2012).

4   This distinction is developed in parallel with other differentiations in media logic in mediatization research. For example, Stig Hjarvard (2018: 71) differentiates

three dimensions of media logic: 'technology', 'aesthetics' and 'institutional'. Or Jesper Strömbäck and Frank Esser see, three constituents of 'news media logic': 'professionalism', 'commercialism' and 'media technology' (Strömbäck & Esser 2014b: 19). Others differ on the 'cultural', 'institutional' and 'technological' dimensions of media logic (Eskjær 2018: 88; Livingstone & Lunt 2014; Lundby 2014b). The distinction of the dimensions of interaction introduced here attempts to take these arguments further in the overall frame of media sociology where the term 'institution' or institutionalization' is used in a broader sense that cuts across technology and interaction: technologies imply certain forms of institutionalization while interaction refers to certain institutionalized forms of practice and communication.

5 See also, Altheide (2018: 12). For a detailed discussion on how Altheide and Snow developed their original idea over time, see, Lundby (2009: 101–108), Krotz (2018: 41–44) and Thimm et al. (2018a: 1–2). Lundby's main argument is that 'form' is a key to media logic but we should apply rather more specific conceptual tools (Lundby 2009: 105).

6 Cf. for this approach Powell and DiMaggio (1991), and within that volume especially Friedland & Alford (1991).

7 Examples of some of the main research areas of this institutional logics perspective include investigations into educational organizations (Townley 1997), health care (Scott et al. 2000) and gastronomy (Rao et al. 2003).

8 See, for example, the approach being outlined by Thornton et al. (2012) who structure their analysis around three levels of social systems: organizations, institutional fields and societies.

9 See, Rühl (1969) and Blöbaum (1994); for a broader perspective on media as organizations and for my reflections that follow, see, Donges & Jarren (2014: 187–191).

10 See, for this a point of view – however, taking a more critical position against the idea of 'media logics' – Landerer (2013), who differentiates between 'normative logic' and 'market logic'.

11 See, for example, Hjarvard (2013: 27–33) and Thimm (2018: 119).

12 One major factor for the uptake of affordances in media and communications research was the wide-spread use of the concept in studies on human-computer interaction; see, for the discussion there McGrenere & Ho (2000) and Turner (2005).

13 See, for example, Bucher & Helmond (2018), Crawford & Robinson (2013), Graves (2007), Postigo (2016), Wellman et al. (2003) and Zillien (2008).

14 See, Eslami et al. (2015: 1) and Nagy & Neff (2015: 1, 4).

15 See, Boase (2008: 4), boyd (2010: 39) and Majchrzak et al. (2013: 39).

16 For this reason, it is important to reflect on the wider context of the technologies being used (Oudshoorn & Pinch 2003) as well as the perceptions of the designers and users of these technologies about possible actions they might afford (Gaver 1996). See also, Schrock (2015: 1230).

17 Altheide and Snow partly understood media logic as 'a way of "seeing" and of interpreting social affairs' (Altheide & Snow 1979: 9).

18 See, for this position, Esser & Matthes (2013: 199), Marcinkowski (2014) and Nölleke & Scheu (2018: 199).

19 See, Astheimer et al. (2011), Frosh (2015) and Tifentale & Manovich (2016).

20 For international news operations, Bloom et al. (2016) show that social media are currently being used more for promotional and audience tracking purposes than for newsgathering. And for cases where tweets are a source for coverage in 'traditional' electronic media, it is their stories which become the main focus of interest and not so much the original tweets or the individual user responsible for breaking the story (Murthy 2011: 787).

21 See, for example, Briggs & Burke (2009) or Chapman (2005).

22 Thanks to Göran Bolin, who told me about this station while I was in Sweden. For further information on Grimeton radio station, see, Johansson (2013) and Walde (2006) as well as the official web site http://grimeton.org (accessed: May 1, 2019).

23 In contrast to my earlier writing where I used the term 'reification' (Hepp 2013: 57) I have adopted the term 'materialization' instead to emphasize the fact that it is about the process of becoming 'material artifacts'. This can involve reification in the original sociological sense of the word (Honneth 2008) but does not necessarily do so. Such a focus on materiality is also the reason why the idea of 'objectivation' as it is used in social constructivism falls short because of its ambiguity (Berger & Luckmann 1966: 25–59; Knoblauch 2013: 302–307): It is used for what I call materialization as well as for processes of symbolic objectivation such as, for example, in language. Opening up at this point a further difference between 'objectivation' and 'objectification' (Knoblauch 2017: 165–166) seem to be confusing but hints to the same problem.

24 See, for a discussion of this, Höflich (2016: 167).

25 See, Couldry & Hepp (2017: 33) on this.

26 As Tarleton Gillespie (2018: 111–140) demonstrates in his careful analysis, 'moderation' as a form of institutionalized curation on platforms remains very much 'human labor'. We cannot, therefore, consider moderation as a purely algorithmic process and therefore a materialization; we must reflect the different forms of institutionalization and materialization altogether.

27 Göttlich (1996) formulated this statement based on Raymond Williams' (1983) reflections on 'mobile privatization'.

28 See, for example, the chapters in Jones (1998).

29 In this sense, Christian Katzenbach (2012) argued for the necessity to think of technologies as institutions.

30 See, for example, Cormen (2013: 1) and MacCormick (2012: 2), who both argue from the perspective of computer engineering and informatics.

31 It is important to reflect on the 'governing institutions' (Breiter & Hepp 2017: 391) as being involved in the construction of algorithms.

32 For 'participatory' software design approaches in general, see, Greenbaum and Kyng (1991); for the approach of 'co-creation' in particular, see, Kohler et al. (2011), Nambisan & Nambisan (2013), Piller et al. (2010) and Sanders & Stappers (2008).

33 See, for this, Suchman et al. (2002) and Turner (2016).

34 Bentley & O'Brien (2017), for example, argue similarly.

35 One aspect of this 'black boxing' is that algorithms become in their genesis increasingly difficult for any one person to understand in its entirety (Napoli 2014: 344), and to some extent take on a life of their own (Ullman 1997: 117).

36 As Lev Manovich put it in clear terms: 'Thanks to the practices pioneered by Google, the world is now used to running on web applications and services that have never been officially completed but remain forever in Beta stage'. (Manovich 2013: 1). For a further discussion of this from an organizational point of view, see, Neff & Stark (2003).

37 This 'automatization' of algorithms can be understood as one of the main reasons why Actor-Network-Theory's assumption of non-human, 'material agency' (Leonardi 2012: 35) became so important for media and communications research (cf. Hopkins 2015).

38 See, Loosen & Scholl (2017) and Napoli (2014).

39 For a general discussion on how the 'simulation of being social' takes place, see, Böhlen & Karppi (2017), Böhle & Pfadenhauer (2014), Fink & Weyer (2014), Gentili et al. (2015) and Kaerlein (2015), Meister (2014), Pfadenhauer (2014).

40 See, Bakardjieva (2015: 247) and Fortunati (2018: 7).

41 In this regard, there is a wide discussion that aims to extend the concept of social robots, see, for example, Barile & Sugiyama (2015: 407), Böhle & Bopp (2014) and Esposito et al. (2014: 626).

42 For the term 'artificial companion', see, Turkle (2002) and Böhle & Bopp (2014).

43 See, www.anki.com/en-us/vector (accessed: May 1, 2019).

44 For the history of this robot, see, the following fan page: http://www.sony-aibo.com (accessed: May 1, 2019).

45 See, Varol et al. (2017), who come to these numbers using a bot detection tool they developed. See, also Ferrara et al. (2016).

46 See, www.theinformation.com/articles/instagrams-growing-bot-problem (accessed: May 1st, 2019).

47 See, the company's stock exchange report: http://d18rnop25nwr6d.cloudfront.net/CIK-0001326801/06205619-7ced-42ed-b8c8-4621b5a121c9.pdf (accessed: May 1, 2019).

48 See, Oremus (2014), in 2017 there was a discussion on Quakebot as a software glitch triggered bot that published information on an earthquake that occurred in 1925; see, www.theregister.co.uk/2017/06/22/la_times_bot_spreads_fake_news/ (accessed: May 1, 2019).

49 See, Wang (2018) on this example.

50 For the slogan Narrative Science uses to advertise its product, see, https://narrativescience.com/DesktopModules/EasyDNNNews/DocumentDownload.ashx?portalid=0&moduleid=2058&articleid=1853&documentid=235 (accessed: May 1, 2019).

51 See, Carlson (2015: 423) and Caswell & Dörr (2018: 492).

52 The prominent role of databases is also the reason why they have become an important subject in the debate on deep mediatization. See, in particular, Andersen (2018).

53 See, Rieder (2012) and Burkhardt (2015: 121–148).

54 The following refers to our arguments in chapter 3.3 of our book *The Mediated Construction of Reality*, in which Nick Couldry and I outlined the idea of the media manifold (Couldry & Hepp 2017: 53–56), with reference to an original work by Nick Couldry (Couldry 2012: 43–46).

55 For a more detailed discussion of the term, see, (Hasebrink & Hölig 2014: 16), (Jensen & Helles 2015: 292) and (Livingstone 2001: 307). The understanding of media environment outlined above does not correspond to the idea of media ecology, where medium and environment are equated (see, Strate 2017: 112, 194). Another widespread concept is the idea of a 'media landscape', which uses a more 'spatial metaphor' (Bolin & Hepp 2017: 321).

56 See, Cubitt (2017: 164), Maxwell & Miller (2012: 86–108) and Qiu (2016: 53–118).

57 See, Starosielski (2017: 41).

58 See, Mosco (2017: 148–156).

59 See, Hasebrink & Hepp (2017: 371–374). This understanding of media ensemble was already argued by Hermann Bausinger (1984: 349), considering media use in a family setting. In the following I refer to his understanding but extend his original arguments. See also, Morley (2007: 200).

60 See, Loosen (2005).

61 See, for research on data journalism, for example, Anderson (2013), Appelgren & Nygren (2014), Borges-Rey (2016) and Lewis & Westlund (2014).

62 See, for example, Deuze (2008) and Deuze & Witschge (2018).

63 See, Loosen & Schmidt (2012) and Loosen & Schmidt (2017).

64 For the following arguments, see, our own research on the mediatization of communitization, especially, Hepp et al. (2014a, b) and (2017).

65 For a detailed discussion of the idea of media repertoires, see, Hasebrink & Hepp (2017), Hasebrink & Domeyer (2012) and Hasebrink & Popp (2006).

66 This term has recently been suggested by Uwe Hasebrink to research individual's public connection. Jan Fredrik Hovden & Hallvard Moe (2017) have developed the same line of argument while not using the term explicitly.

67 See, for this Hasebrink & Domeyer (2012) and Hasebrink et al. (2015).

4

A FIGURATIONAL APPROACH

Chapter 3 ended with the argument that a processual perspective on media is required if we want to understand deep mediatization with any real rigor. The need for a processual perspective is even more essential when instead of isolating individual media we are, in fact, examining the dynamics between different media. We live in a media environment that is characterized by a media manifold in which we can understand the influences of media only if we consider them in terms of their interrelation. If we take these dynamics seriously, it is less appropriate to begin research on deep mediatization by investigating a (single) medium. We must consider our approach inversely: a helpful starting point for researching deep mediatization is, paradoxically, *not* media themselves, but the social domains and, *in a second step*, the role of media in a domains' construction.

An understanding of society as separated into different domains has a long tradition in the social sciences. The argument generally goes that our present societies are characterized by ongoing social and cultural differentiation.[1] Classical theorists in the social sciences have stumbled upon various terms to categorize society's wide assortment of separate domains. Max Weber, for example, used the term *Wertsphären* (Weber 1988 [1919]: 611) to reflect this differentiation. Pierre Bourdieu (1993) described processes of differentiation by analyzing differences within and across 'social fields'. In system theory, we have the concept of '(sub-)system' as described by Niklas Luhmann (2012 Vol. 2: 4–27), a term that was also used by Jürgen Habermas (1992) to describe social differentiation. Phenomenology places emphasis on different (small) 'life-worlds' (Luckmann 1970: 587; Schütz 1967a: 207–259), with a certain relationship to the 'social worlds' of symbolic interactionism (Shibutani 1955: 566; Strauss 1978). More recently, Luc Boltanski and Laurent Thévenot (2006) argued for different 'orders of justification'. Irrespective of which theoretical approach one takes, the lines between them emphasize the differences and tensions between 'sub-spheres' in (late) modern societies. This point of view is shared by mediatization research when emphasizing the domain specificity of mediatization.

Mediatization research investigates domain-specificity with varying theoretical conceptualizations and different approaches to scale. For example, the discourse on the mediatization of different social fields that follows Bourdieu's understanding of societal differentiation (Couldry 2012: 144–153), or the discussion on the idea of different (sub-)systems in the spirit of Luhmann (Kunelius & Reunanen 2016: 8–12), or the tendency to explore social worlds by adopting phenomenological and symbolic interactionism (Hepp & Krotz 2014: 6–9). The use of the term 'social domain' does not mean to suggest that these different theoretical conceptualizations are the same. Rather, in using the less theoretically loaded term 'domain' it places emphasis on the overarching argument that mediatization differs from one social sphere to another.

At this point we move to a what is called *non-media-centric media studies*.[2] The idea of this perspective is 'to "decenter" the media, in our analytical framework, so as to better understand the ways in which media processes and everyday life are interwoven with each other' (Morley 2007: 200). While this approach has already been developed with regard to electronic media such as television and radio, it has additional relevance for digital media and their infrastructures: in a moment in which digital media are 'everywhere', a focus on *one* of them prevents us from understanding how they influence different social domains as well as individual human beings. Only by taking particular social domains and the individuals' involvement in them as a starting point can we grasp what media 'do'. In this way we can reflect on the processual dynamics of media as embedded in meaningful units of everyday practice.

From this perspective, I want to develop in what follows into a figurational approach on deep mediatization. Taking up the original arguments of Nick Couldry and myself (see Couldry & Hepp 2017), I would like to initially make clear why the concept of figuration is helpful for a preoccupation with media and communication. From there, I will broaden the perspective on society as a whole and explain what a figurative perspective actually is. Then I arrive at the point of describing the media-related transformation of societies as a process of re-figuration.

FIGURATIONS, COMMUNICATIONS AND MEDIA

For a long time in the social sciences there has been a tendency to conceptualize each social domain as a 'stationary object' that would surround the individual human being (Elias 1978: 13). Society is thought of as consisting of entities such as the family, school, the workplace and the state which each arrange themselves 'around' the individual imposing varying degrees of regulation and governmentality on members of society. In opposition to these categorizations, Norbert Elias argued for what we can call a figurational approach. A figurational approach understands the individual and society not as separate entities but as fundamentally entangled with each other (Elias 1978: 129). The various institutions that make up society only exist in and through the social practices of individuals, and the individual only exists in light of the social relations in which he or she engages. Society does not consist of entities external to and independent from the individual. All social institutions are made up of individuals who are oriented to and linked with each other in diverse ways. This is what we can understand as 'webs of interdependencies' or, as Elias puts it, 'figurations' (Elias 1978: 15). If we follow Elias' train of thought the traditional institutions of family, school and workplace are no longer positioned 'around' individuals but are constituted an figurations *of* individuals. Each individual lives at the intersection of the different figurations in which he or she is involved and develops an identity through the subjective narration of the self on the basis of his or her involvements.

Figurations are kept together by a shared orientation of practice by those who comprise them. An individual can be a family member, a school member or a member of various organizations; how he or she acts is mediated through the overall 'doing' within the figuration. The relations in these figurations operate also as power relations that, typically, have a certain stability in the sense that the roles of those in power have corresponding ones to those of the less powerful. The chief presupposes the employee, the officer presupposes the soldier, the chief physician presupposes the nursing staff and so on. There is a 'balance of power' (Elias 1978: 15) that is to be considered as a part of the whole.

In all, the term figuration is a 'simple conceptual tool to loosen [the] social constraint to speak and think as if "the individual" and "society" were antagonistic as well as different' (Elias 1978: 130). Instead, the idea is to think of both as one. Figurations are constituted in 'processes of interweaving' (Elias 1978: 130), in which the practices of the people involved are interdependent on and oriented toward each other. With figurations, the 'behavior of many separate people intermeshes to form interwoven structures' (Elias 1978: 132). A figuration is constituted in the continuously changing pattern of interaction between all of those involved.

One specific approach to the concept of figurations is that, as an analytical tool, they transgress the distinction between the levels of micro, meso and macro.[3] The idea of figurations is to have *one* analytical concept that can be applied to dyad or triad relationships as well as larger entities such as communities and organizations or even societies as a whole. For example, a figuration can be a school class being built by pupils and teachers; it can be the service team at a bistro, a company, a city or an entire state. Different figurations overlap with one another but are individually distinct in their members' orientations of practice and their related frames of relevance. To reconstruct figurations analytically, we can begin with the orientation of practice of the individuals from which it is formed and then we can analyze the 'chains of interdependence' (Elias 1978: 131) present between those individuals.

Today, many figurations are constructed around media use. The figurations of collectivities (families, peer groups, communities etc.) and organizations (media companies, churches, schools etc.) are entangled with specific media ensembles that potentially transform the figurations of which they are a part. Deep mediatization also makes new figurations possible, such as online gatherings in chat threads, on various platforms or through apps. Some figurations are even entirely constructed around media technologies. For example, 'collectivities of taste' (Passoth et al. 2014: 282) represent the calculation of groups of individuals brought together because they share product interests on online stores such as Amazon.

From a media and communications research perspective, we can consider each figuration as a *communicative* one: when it comes to the *meaningful* construction of a figuration, communication practices are incredibly relevant. When it comes to their meaning, figurations are typically articulated through practices of communication that take place across a variety of media. Family members, for example, can be separated in space but connected through multimodal communication such as (mobile) phone calls, email and sharing on digital platforms, all maintaining the everyday dynamism of family relationships.[4] Organizations, considered as figurations, are kept together through the use of databases and communication across an intranet, as well as printed flyers and other media for internal and external communication.[5] Individuals are involved in these figurations according to the role and position that they have in their respective actor constellations. Doing media and communications research from a figurational approach, therefore, allows us to connect perspectives on individuals and the social domains they are part of with their entanglement with media in a productive way.

There are three core characteristic features that make up a figuration (see Couldry & Hepp 2017: 66f.; Hepp & Hasebrink 2017):

- First, a figuration contains a certain *constellation of actors* that can be regarded as its structural basis: a network of individuals interrelated and communicating with each other.
- Second, each figuration has dominating *frames of relevance* that serve to guide its constituting practices. These frames define the orientation in practice of the involved individuals and, therefore, the character of the figuration.
- Third, figurations are constantly rearticulated in *communicative practices* that are interwoven with other *social practices*. In their

composition, these practices typically draw on and are entangled with a *media ensemble*.

The figurational approach begins with an understanding of practices as an 'embodied doing'.[6] This 'doing' is based on what Giddens calls 'practical consciousness' (Giddens 1984: xxiii), which is learned in highly contextualized ways as part of our socialization, that is, our "growing into society". Based on this learning process, practices can be realized in a meaningful way *without* being 'discursively' accessible for the involved individuals; that is, they cannot explain what they are doing even though they know how to do it. This stands for communication as much as it does for any other human practice.[7] Practical consciousness as an embodied capacity is generally understood as know-how, skills, tacit knowledge and dispositions and is related to an individual's habits. Most practices are rooted in this 'practical knowledge', which has its own potential for situational creativity. If and when a 'doing' does not require the full mental capacity, this opens up space for creativity.[8] Practices are anchored in the body and cannot be described as a mechanical obedience to rules. In this sense, practices of communication – with media but also without – are also embodied and should be considered in terms of their interrelation with other forms of practice.[9] With deep mediatization social practices turn into a media-entangled and, therefore, object-related practices. It is the change of practices through which media mold figurations.[10]

Following this line of reasoning, we can understand *practices of communication* as complex and highly contextualized patterns of 'doing'. Or, to put it differently: certain forms of communicative action build up complex practices of communication as they are realized in a manifold media environment. Communication involves the use of signs that humans learn and adapt to during their socialization and which, as symbols, are for the most part entirely arbitrary. This means that the meaning of communicative practices largely depends on social conventions. Communicative practices are fundamental to the human construction of reality: we 'create' the meaning of our social world through multiple communicative processes; we are born into a world in which communication already exists; we learn the characteristics of this social world (and its society) through the (communicative) process of learning to speak; and when we proceed to act in this social world, our practices are always also communicative practices.

A FIGURATIONAL PERSPECTIVE ON SOCIETY

When we adopt a figurational approach to an analysis of society, it is insufficient to only consider individual figurations. We have to clarify, then, how different figurations relate to each other and build what we call societies. As Nick Couldry and I have outlined elsewhere (see Couldry & Hepp 2017: 72–76), there are two basic ways in which figurations are interwoven with society: first, through relationships between figurations and, second, by their meaningful arrangements.

A basic interrelation of figurations emerges through the *overlap of actors* who are involved in an actor constellation of more than one figuration. If we take the basic examples that we have already discussed, an individual might be part of a family, a group of friends, a company where he or she might work or the neighborhood where they live. There are various connections between these different figurations, as certain individuals are involved in more than one of them at a time. What we can learn from network analysis is that particular individuals are in a powerful position because of the number and kinds of figurations they are connected to. Manual Castells referred to these actors as 'switchers' (Castells 2009: 45), people that can easily shift from one figuration's actor constellation to another. This is evident in the world of business, where, for example, powerful people are involved in the figurations of different supervisory boards. But we also find this in other domains such as on a local level, where powerful people are part of the inner circle of different associations. Following these connections between figurations provides a starting point for gaining an understanding of how power relations work. Therefore, adopting a figurational approach does not only mean that we are reconstructing the fragile power balances within a figuration; it also means that we are reconstructing the power relations *between* figurations.

A more complex interrelation between figurations occurs when we consider the *figurations of figurations*.[11] A figuration of a figuration emerges when an entire figuration becomes part of an actor constellation of another figuration. This might sound overly abstract, but there are obvious examples. From a political economy perspective, we can consider corporations such as Alphabet (Google) as figurations of figurations: this corporation is a complex figuration in which other companies are part of the overall actor constellation that again have figurations of different departments and so forth.

Speaking of figurations of figurations refers once more back to the idea of 'supra-individual actors' (Schimank 2010: 327–341): Supra-individual actors are figurations such as organizations or communities that have their own agency. When we take a closer look at them, however, they often turn out to be figurations of figurations: a company, for example, is in most cases a figuration of different departments that are figurations of their own. Then there is the possibility that this company is a 'subsidiary' of a 'parent company', which would lead to another level of nesting figurations. Conversely, a figuration of otherwise unconnected individuals *as well as* other figurations can become the figuration of a supra-individual actor when the practices of those involved 'results in an orderly whole and not only occasionally but systematically build upon one another in such a way that an overall objective is pursued' (Schimank 2010: 329, author's translation). This includes corporate actors such as companies and state agencies as well as collective actors such as social movements and communities.

In addition to the relations of overlapping actor constellations, figurations can relate to each other through *meaningful arrangements of figurations*.[12] This means that figurations and figurations of figurations do not just exist – however interlinked – beside each other, but discourse positions the respective figurations within society. Again, this can be best explained with some examples. We cannot understand the power of a state government, for example, as a certain figuration only by analyzing its actor-constellations, practices and frames of relevance as well as how its actors relate to the actor constellations of other figurations. It is just as important to consider society-wide discourses on political decision making and the legal framework that both *position* the government at the center of the state executive. It is discourses like these that make governmental decisions binding. Meanwhile, other figurations are positioned within a society because of overarching discourses: discourses about the nuclear family as the fundamental societal unit (in contrast to the diversity of other forms of living together and raising children); discourses about schools and universities as principal educational institutions (in contrast to self-learning and grassroots approaches to education); discourses about companies and corporations as the main institutions of economic value creation (instead of cooperatives and state agencies) and so on. If we consider particular societies, we find many of these discourses inscribed into legal frameworks. In all of these cases, it is not just about the meaning of a certain figuration as such; it is about the meaning of the *normative* arrangement of figurations within society as a whole.

As far as media are concerned, the meaningful arrangement of figurations also refers to what Nick Couldry (2012: 22) has called the 'myth of the mediated center', that is, the generally shared assumption that the media (as in the totality of mass media) offer privileged access to the society's center: media communicate what is 'going on' in society and in the world. If we follow Roland Barthes (2000: 109), a myth is not an object, a concept or an idea, but a more general form or mode of signification. The myth of the mediated center is related to mechanical and electronic mass media institutions that have positioned themselves at the 'center' of society. In essence, this myth is based on the construction that everything that is of importance in a society takes place in and is represented by mass media. The point here is not to say that the issues, events and matters that are the subject of mass media are not important. The point is that this myth is a powerful principle of discursive construction that excludes other areas of society. With the ideas of a national public and national media systems this myth became well established not only in Europe[13] but also in other regions of the world.[14]

Mass media have for a long time been the space where imaginaries of the meaningful arrangements of figurations have been constructed. But with deep mediatization, 'traditional' mass media radically change when they become digital. This does not mean that mediated discourses about the meaningful arrangement of figurations would cease to exist. However, instead of digital media like social network sites becoming divorced from centrally produced media flows and offering an 'alternative social center' to that offered by mass media, today's platforms and mass media become ever more closely connected (van Dijck et al. 2018: 31–72). For example, Wikipedia became well known because of articles in journals or newspapers, Facebook became a main point of access for single articles from online newspapers and television shows refer to online discussions and YouTube influencers. Deep mediatization does not necessarily work against the articulation of a mediated center but different media become a 'site of a struggle for competing forces' (Couldry 2009: 447) in constructing a mediated center of society.

TRANSFORMATION AS RE-FIGURATION

In sum, figurations are a concept that help us understand the ordered interweaving of humans and the shared meaningful orientation of their practices. With deep mediatization, figurations are entangled with digital media and their infrastructures. The point mediatization research is concerned with is less a reflection on figurations and their interrelatedness as such but on their transformation over time. Transformation at this point refers to a more fundamental, structural shift of human relationships and practices, something more than mere 'change' in the sense that tomorrow is somehow different than today. From a figurational point of view, we are talking here about *re-figuration*.[15] Broadly speaking, re-figuration refers to the transformation of figurations and their interrelatedness to society. Re-figuration is more than a functional adjustment; rather, it is a process that is related to questions of power, tension and conflict. Any re-figuration also refers to the significance of powerful individual and supra-individual actors as well as the power of discursive constructions about what character figurations *should* take. It is not just a question of how, for example, organizations change when digital media are introduced. It is also the question of how they should change – and how they orient themselves to normative discourses when implementing digital media.

As my discussion up to this point exemplifies, in times of deep mediatization we are confronted with a particular form of transformation, which we can call *recursive transformation*. 'Recursivity' indicates that rules are reapplied to the entity that generated them (Couldry & Hepp 2017: 217). In many respects, the social world has always been recursive, at least insofar as it is based on rules and norms: we sustain it, and repair it when problems arise, by replaying once again the rules and norms on which it was previously based.[16] However, and as already argued in the introduction of this book, with deep mediatization recursivity intensifies in tune with its fundamental relation to technology. Many practices are now entangled with digital media, and the algorithms they are based on involve a new kind of recursivity. Human practice, when incorporating digital media and their infrastructures, leads to a continuous processing of data, which in turn is the basis for adapting these media. A continuous technology-based monitoring of social practices takes place, the change of which is inscribed in the further development of these technologies, which, in turn, can stabilize particular practices and question others. We can see this happening in the way platforms like Facebook function: user behavior on these platforms is continuously tracked, which not only leads to friend suggestions but is also the basis for generating new functions. The fact that we are dealing with digital media as a process drives this recursivity. Developers' visions of sociality play an important role here: as discussed in Chapters 2 and 3, implicit ideas of how society *should* be inscribed into algorithms, which are then reapplied to social practices. Through these development loops the transformation of society is in many ways a transformation that occurs through digital media and their infrastructures.

Taking this move into a deeply recursive transformation, non-linear approaches to media-related transformation become more relevant as they are able to grasp these loops. In this way, approaches to 'media evolution'[17] or 'domestication'[18] are widespread. Quite different in their origins, these approaches share the idea of describing media-related transformation not as a 'diffusion of innovations' (Rogers 2003) but as a complex sequence of various circles of change interlinking the production and design of new technologies with their appropriation and use. While the idea of re-figuration as a recursive transformation shares with these approaches a thinking in cycles of development, its emphasis is quite different: approaches of evolution and domestication are primarily focused on transformation in relation to a single medium and the interplay between its production and appropriation. The idea of recursive re-figuration emphasizes the cross-media character and technological anchoring of today's societal transformations (see Figure 4.1).

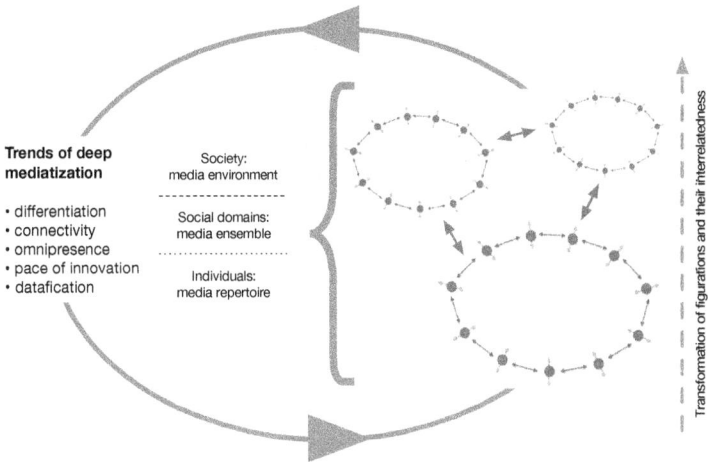

Figure 4.1 Re-figuration as a circle of recursive transformation

Figure 4.1 starts with the considerations set out in Chapter 2, namely the argument that from an actors' point of view the engagement of the large technology companies, state agencies and pioneer communities resulted in five trends of deep mediatization: the differentiation of digital media, their increasing connectivity, media's growing omnipresence through mobile communication technologies, the accelerating pace of media innovation and the rise of datafication. As argued in Chapter 3, these trends are first of all manifested in the media manifold of societies' media environments but become more specific in particular media ensembles of social domains like schools and communities as well as individuals' media repertoires. In all these cases, we must be aware that digital media are a process, institutionalizing and materializing human practices, generating the paradox of a constantly changing sense of stability.

However, as I have argued in this chapter, we cannot conclude that a uniform, linear transformation of society will emerge. Rather, it is always a concrete question of how certain figurations of people change alongside media change. What is decisive – as the right-hand side of Figure 4.1 demonstrates – is the way that figurations transform. Figurations are depicted as dots arranged in circles, with the dots visualizing humans as members of figurations. Their arrangement in circles is intended to illustrate the shared orientation in practice of people in their figurations, their frames of relevance, and show clearly that the actor constellation of figurations is something more than an arrangement of pure networks. The arrows between the actors that form the circle of a figuration represent the practices that are constitutive for each figuration increasingly entangled with digital media and their infrastructures. The arrows pointing inward and outward visualize the power relations between the respective actors in relation to the figuration but also in relation to other figurations of which these actors are also part.

This visualization makes us aware of the complexity we are dealing with when we talk about re-figuration. In order to grasp this complexity, internal and external perspectives on figurations are necessary: the *internal perspective* refers to the question of how individual figurations are transformed by deep mediatization. How do their actor constellations change? How do the underlying practices change? Are there changes in the frames of relevance and in the orientation of practice within the figuration as a whole? Are completely new figurations emerging? The *external perspective* is concerned with the question of the transformation of the interrelationship between figurations. What are the new interrelations between them? Which new figurations of figurations emerge? Are there shifts in the meaningful arrangements of figurations?

If one speaks of a re-figuration, these are the kind of questions that need to be discussed and clarified. Our outlook becomes increasingly complex because we have to be aware that the changes take place not only within a society but also across different societies. And we have to be aware that deep mediatization is only one aspect of the process of re-figuration. Other meta-processes of change – globalization, individualization and commercialization are mentioned here as the main important examples – must also be taken into consideration. It is, therefore, always necessary to question the extent to which the transformation of digital media and their infrastructures are the driving force for change and where other driving forces may be more important (and maybe even the reason why media and their infrastructures themselves transform).

The semicircular arrows at the top and bottom of Figure 4.1 illustrate the overall recursiveness of the process of transformation. We cannot see the transformation of deep mediatization detached from the change of figurations and their interrelationship. To illustrate this, we can use a simple example. When individuals in their various figurations appropriate the already differentiated range of social media platforms, they support their connectivity and omnipresence as they generate data that are continuously processed; this glut of continuous data then stimulates and maintains these platforms' 'innovation cycles'. Therefore, the simple act of appropriating social media platforms can stabilize deep mediatization's core trends. However, the opposite is just as conceivable, at least in theory: perhaps the individuals who form multiple figurations discard certain platforms without moving on to something else. In this scenario, the differentiation of digital media, their connectivity, omnipresence, their pace of innovation and increasing attachment to datafication could taper away.

From this perspective, the left-hand side of Figure 4.1 can also be read as the cumulation of institutionalization and materialization: 'New' media arise and are appropriated in certain figurations, but a more general stability arises when media-related institutionalizations and materializations emerge that then endure across different figurations and come together into overarching trends. And, as I have argued, because of their rootedness in algorithms, the loops of recursiveness tighten as deep mediatization progresses.

Such a figure can, of course, only provide a very rough visualization of the phenomena with which we are dealing. In Chapters 5 and 6, I will therefore deal more concretely with questions of refiguration, first from the perspective of figurations, then from the perspective of looking at the individual. Nevertheless, Figure 4.1 should serve to place what is depicted into the overall context of this book, namely the question of what actually changes with deep mediatization.

NOTES

1 See, Giddens (1984: 180–193), Hahn (2000: 14–24), Schimank (2013: 37–50, 131–149) and Winter & Eckert (1990: 142–151).

2 For this discussion about non-media-centric media studies, see, in addition to others, Couldry (2006), Hepp et al. (2015), Krajina et al. (2014), Moores (2016) and Morley (2009).

3 See, Alexander et al. (1987), Ryan (2005) and Turner (2006b).

4 See, Greschke et al. (2017), Hasebrink (2014), Hepp et al. (2015) and Lohmeier & Böhling (2017).

5 See, Fredriksson et al. (2015) and Fredriksson & Pallas (2017).

6 As far as this idea is concerned, I refer to the discussion on a practice approach in general but also in media and communications research in particular; see, Reckwitz (2002), Schatzki et al. (2001) and Couldry (2012) for this.

7 However, methodologically I do not share the position that we could not gain access to practices and their meaning via interviews. Depending on the interview strategy, we can, in an indirect way, get access to (media related) practices (of communication), for example, by asking questions about specific habits and everyday experiences (Klein et al. 2017).

8 A good example of this is driving a car: as long as a novice driver has to concentrate entirely on shifting gears and using the clutch, driving is barely a part of his or her creative travel practice.

9 See, Bourdieu (1977: 16–22) and Reichertz (2009: 118–120).

10 As the practice theorist Andreas Reckwitz put it, 'writing, printing and electronic media mold social (here, above all, discursive) practices' (Reckwitz 2002: 253).

11 See, Couldry & Hepp (2017: 73).

12 Again, see, Couldry & Hepp (2017: 74–77) for this concept, where it is discussed more in detail.

13 Benedict Anderson (1983) has analyzed this in detail.

14 There are various historical analyses of this process taking place in Europe and beyond, supported by the emergence of mass media institutions and important national media events. See, for example, Martín-Barbero (1993), Scannell (1989) and Thompson (1995).

15 For a further reflection on the idea of 're-figuration', see, Knoblauch (2017: 381–398) and Knoblauch & Löw (2017). While Knoblauch and Löw are interested in the 'spatial re-figuration of the social world' and use the term re-figuration to refer to the whole of society, my focus is the relationship between mediatization and the transformation of specific figurations.

16 This is one of the key arguments of ethnomethodology; see, Garfinkel (1967) and Giddens (1984).

17 See, Neuman (2010), Scolari (2013) and Just & Latzer (2017).

18 See, Berker et al. (2006), Hartmann (2013) and Silverstone & Haddon (1998).

5

DEEP MEDIATIZATION'S RE-FIGURATION OF SOCIETY

The main argument of Chapter 4 was that there is a need to understand social domains as figurations that transform within the process of deep mediatization. But the relationship between these figurations also transforms, representing one more step in the process of re-figuration. Both are, in a way, recursive, as they are tightly entangled with the development of digital media and their infrastructures. Any re-figuration that is institutionalized and materialized by digital media, supports and accelerates or weakens and decelerates deep mediatization's already existing trends. Against this background, re-figuration has a double meaning: on the one hand, re-figuration, from the internal perspective on figurations, means their structural transformation, that is, the permanent change of actor constellations, frames of relevance and practices. On the other hand, from an external perspective re-figuration refers to the transformation of the interrelationships figurations have with one another, which includes the emergence of new figurations and new or shifting meaningful arrangements of figurations.

Based on the arguments made thus far, it should be clear that processes of re-figuration should always be examined contextually. We only can understand re-figuration by analyzing specific examples which I will discuss in what follows. The common lines between these examples are three fundamental patterns of re-figuration which we can consider as characteristic for the present stage of deep mediatization. These are, first, the patterns that arise when figurations interrelate, second, patterns in the transformation of existing figurations and third, patterns that are reveled when new figurations emerge.

At different points in this chapter I discuss some examples that I have already referred to elsewhere in this book. However, based on the figurational approach as developed in Chapter 4, it becomes possible to further contextualize these examples. In addition, new examples will be discussed. We will reflect on the mythical discourses associated with deep mediatization, on processes of data collection and infrastructures across figurations, the changing public debates, the transformation of journalism as well as of family. This diversity of examples from different social domains has been deliberately chosen: it is only through a *contrastive observation* that it is possible to develop an understanding of re-figuration as an overall phenomenon.

THE NEW INTERRELATEDNESS OF FIGURATIONS

In times of deep mediatization we are confronted with a new, globalized relationality of figurations. In part, this relationality arises indirectly through mythical discourses on the capacities of digital media and their infrastructures, discourses that span and work across societies. But we are also dealing with new relations built around digital infrastructures and data. It is this overarching relationality that develops an ordering force across societies. Recent research has shown that these processes of ordering are associated with the expansion of 'surveillance capitalism' (Zuboff 2019b) and 'data colonialism' (Couldry & Mejias 2019b). These patterns of economic transformation are the most evident overarching societal changes stimulated by deep mediatization and I will keep coming back to them several times in this chapter. Nevertheless, analytically speaking, the new relativity of figurations is a far more general and extensive phenomenon than these patterns.

Mythical discourses

Today, there are a number of mythical discourses that surround the character of the (latest) digital media technologies. These discourses are more or less global and are incredibly influential irrespective of whether or not these myths align with the 'real' workings of digital media and their infrastructures. Just as Jesús Martín-Barbero (1993: 150–186) wrote about new media and social development in the 1980s: while it remains an open question in which way these technologies support social development at the level of the everyday, many states in the Global South mainly invested in these media because their availability already symbolized progress.

When electronic broadcasting was the dominant media, the global myth that surrounded them was one of 'keeping' national societies 'together': the aforementioned 'myth of the mediated centre' (Couldry 2012: 22–25). While the 'myth of the mediated centre' – the assumption that everything 'central' for a society is represented in (mass) media – still has a lot of power when it comes to the representation of politics, in times of deep mediatization other myths are established globally: one of them is the *myth of us*.[1] A good example how this myth is represented by media themselves is the celebration of 'You', that is, all of us as demonstrated by TIME magazine in 2006 when their person of the year was, indeed, you the user (see Figure 5.1). The idea of declaring the entirety of individual internet users as person of the year was justified by the fact that on social media platforms 'individuals were wielding power in new and dramatic ways' (Waxman 2016: 1). This statement expresses the essence of the 'myth of us': it is a myth about the collectivity that humans form when they use digital platforms, 'a myth of natural collectivity whose paradigmatic form lies in how we gather on platforms' (Couldry 2014b: 620). This kind of myth positions us as individuals as the decisive players in power and the foundation of social processes: we who network online and build new collectivities. While these platforms – as we already have discussed – are owned by large technology companies and are based on business models of generating revenue from users' data, the myth of us obscures this capitalistic enterprise with an image of digital technology's emancipatory potency.

The *myth of digital purity* is just as popular. For a long time, computer and smartphone operating systems have visualized their default

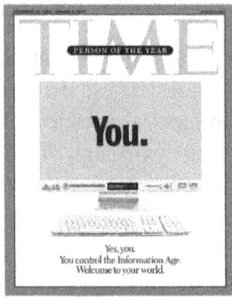

the myth of us

Source: TIME Magazin title page page 2006

the myth of digital purity

Source: Anomaly Google G Suite Campaign 2016

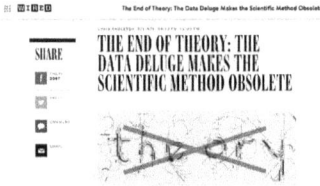

the myth of big data

Source: Wired 23rd of June, 2008

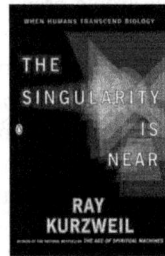

the myth of the singularity

Source: Kurzweil 2005

Figure 5.1 Myths of deep mediatization

home screens with images of nature: hilly meadows, mountainous sil-houettes, clean beaches and starry skies. These images are only part of a wider set of visuals. Even the 'the cloud' evokes an image of purity instead of the reality of vast warehouses acting as data centers. Googles promotional material for its cloud services incorporates the myth of us with the myth of digital purity when, visualized in a cli-part style, a woman plucks a section of a pie chart from a cloud-filled sky (see Figure 5.1). Digital media and their infrastructures are rep-resented as clean and pure, ephemeral and immaterial.[2] However, as we have already seen, this is most definitely not the case. Establishing and maintaining digital media infrastructures is anything but clean. Nevertheless, supported by widespread advertising campaigns the myth of digital purity remains a powerful discourse across very different societies.

The *myth of big data* promises that vast amounts of data will provide rejuvenated access to the social world and make its analysis – and even predictions of the future – achievable without recourse to theory. One of the most prominent expressions of this myth is an article published in 2008 by Chris Anderson in the aforementioned technology magazine *Wired*. With reference to vast data storage capacities in the cloud and the new possibilities of analyzing this 'big data' on the basis of algorithms, Anderson postulated 'the end of theory': the 'massive amounts of data and applied mathematics replace every other tool that might be brought to bear [...] [on] every theory of human behavior, from linguistics to sociology' (Anderson 2008: 1). Faith in scientific models and explanation is dead, 'correlation is enough' (ibid.). According to this myth information on someone's address and income is enough to predict the probabilities of them committing a crime. The idea is to isolate correlations like these to predict possible futures and make (political and societal) decisions. There is plenty of academic criticism of these naïve statements on the nature of big data and the power it is alleged to possess.[3] As a discourse the myth of big data still has far-reaching consequences: it is widely believed that a huge amount of data offers us a new kind of access to the social world and a deeper insight in how social processes take place. The myth of big data encourages business and state agencies to make large investments in the analysis of such data.[4] There also exists a plethora of advisory literature that frames 'using smart big data, analytics and metrics' as a way 'to make better decisions and improve performance' (so says the subtitle of Marr 2015, a practical guide to big data analysis).

One other myth that has risen in prominence over the past fifteen years is the *myth of the singularity*. The myth of the singularity posits a time in the (near) future when machine intelligence will far exceed the capacities of all human intelligence through a process of the exponential growth of technological progress (see Kurzweil 2005). This mythical discourse finds its roots in the early days of cybernetics and computer engineering: the mathematician Stanislaw Ulam assigns the term singularity to John von Neumann, a pioneer of computing, when in his scientific obituary he said that a 'conversation centered on the ever accelerating progress of technology and changes in the mode of human life, which gives the appearance of approaching some essential singularity in the history of the race beyond which human affairs, as we know them, could not continue' (Ulam 1958: 5). Since then, the term has spread across disciplines and has become de facto terminology in the fields of artificial intelligence research (Good 1965), trend analyses (Toffler 1970) and mathematics (Vinge 1993). It is worth looking at Vernor Vinge's ideas on the singularity, if for no other reason than that a version of his paper appeared in the 1993 *Whole Earth Review*, an offshoot of the *Whole Earth Catalogue*, which 'would do for computing what the original had done for the counterculture' (Turner 2006a: 129). Today, the singularity is most commonly associated with Ray Kurzweil's book (2005) *The Singularity is Near*. His main thesis is that Moore's law[5] – which states that the number of transistors in an integrated circuit doubles about every two years – is only the special case of a more general law according to which whole technological evolution proceeds. Kurzweil believes that the exponential growth described by Moore's law will continue in technologies that will replace today's microprocessors bringing us all to the so-called 'singularity', which he defines as a hypothetical point in the future at which humanity is outpaced by technological progress. Transhumanism, a 'loosely defined movement' (Bostrom 2005: 202) that seeks to expand the boundaries of human possibilities, whether intellectual, physical or psychological, through the use of technological techniques is also closely related to the myth of the singularity. Transhumanism is generally concerned with reflecting on being human under the conditions of the singularity. Earlier ideas of the cyborg – which were well-established in the cyberpunk movement – are re-emerging in a new, utopian framing.

These four myths are exemplars for the globalized discourses around media technologies and digital infrastructures. There is one thread of consistency that brings them all together: Technology is constructed as the center of societal change. Through technology – in the form of a clean infrastructure (the myth of digital purity) and artificial intelligence (the myth of the singularity) – society will change for the better by fulfilling every human need and desire (the myth of us) and finding better solutions for our problems (the myth of big data). The main problem with these discourses is that they are reifying and essentializing. The meanings that they represent are typically taken for granted and are rarely questioned. These myths prop up 'practically everything Big Tech stands for' (Mosco 2017: 122): tech companies are the enablers of a brighter future – a future brought about by the benign forces of artificial intelligence, the internet of things and big data.

These myths play a considerable role in the processes of deep mediatization. If we refer back to our arguments on the meaningful arrangements of figurations in Chapter 4, we can understand these myths as orienting discourses across differing societies: they perpetuate the myth of the mediated center at varying scales and form the myths of a deeply mediatized society. This legitimizes a cross-societal consensus towards technology companies which in turn sees them receive a range of state support in the shape of tax breaks and research funding. These myths create a meaningful arrangement of how various figurations *should* relate to new technologies that transcends the most diverse social figurations across societies. To a certain degree, these myths imagine a global vanishing point of technological development creating a cross-societal orientation toward media technological changes.

Digital infrastructures

Looking beyond the overarching myths of our 'bright' technological future, we can see a new relationality of figurations is materially produced through digital infrastructures. It is quite clear that a fundamental characteristic of deep mediatization is that digital infrastructures exist not only across the figurations of one society but across many. The internet in general, as well as the internet of things and the cloud in particular, 'connect' the media ensemble of a wide variety of collectivities and organizations regardless of the societies to which they belong. This results in a new interrelatedness of figurations in which digital infrastructures and their underlying algorithms become globalized molding forces that institutionally and materially influence very different figurations both culturally and socially.

The so-called 'disruptive' platforms, most commonly associated with surveillance capitalism and data colonialism,[6] are creating 'templates' (Scholz 2017: 5) for a society-wide reorganization of work. In a sense, the cross-figurational influence of such platforms is that they institutionalize and materialize these 'templates' using existing digital infrastructure.

These platforms are all based on the idea of directly brokering supply and demand, without having to provide the necessary means of production (workplaces, vehicles and hotels) themselves. This echoes the cybernetic assumptions made by Whole Earth Network that the 'best solutions' are found when people self-organize and interact directly with each other.[7] Platforms such as Airbnb, Uber, Amazon Mechanical Turk and UpWork are attempts to implement processes of market-based 'self-organization' in culturally and socially different figurations. However, the fact that such platforms can have a molding force across the most diverse figurations of human coexistence presupposes a digital infrastructure that makes these overarching institutionalizations and materializations possible. All these platforms rely in various degrees on the internet, its mobile accessibility, the smartphone as a device which makes access to these services through omnipresent apps possible, and highly infrastructure-dependent technologies such as GPS, especially in the case of Uber. The existence of these platforms clearly links back to the current trends of deep mediatization. A crucial point here is that these platforms, to a slight extent, have supported this infrastructure's development. These platforms, in a way, are the commercial beneficiaries of deep mediatization.[8]

Here, the term 'disruptive' takes on a completely new meaning: 'Disruption' is less a 'market innovation', the socially deeper 'disruption' lies in the fundamental molding of very different figurations derived from the use of digital media and overarching digital infrastructures. This does not only take place through these platforms: various other media are part of the equation such as those used for marketing or those that are used by various suppliers and workers that are active on these platforms (van Dijck et al. 2018: 31–48). We cannot necessarily expect this molding to occur across all figurations in the same way: there are opposing forces at work such as the various lawsuits Airbnb and Uber must contend with or the critical discussion on 'crowdwork'. Nevertheless, many local figurations experience pressure from a multitude of directions, pressure that is a direct consequence of existing as 'templates' for this new generation of platforms.

Data

Another fundamental aspect of the interrelatedness of figurations relates to data. Today's data are collected in and across very different figurations but shared and processed centrally. This no longer only concerns the data collected through the digital traces that we leave behind when we communicate online or through our mobile devices, with the advent of the internet of things, centralized data collection and processing is increasingly based on practices like driving smart cars (Sumantran et al. 2017: 158–160) or moving through shopping malls and retail outlets with your mobile phone in your pocket (Turow 2017: 116–142).[9]

We can see here a new emerging kind of surveillance – a shift from 'panoptic surveillance' to 'environmental surveillance' (Andrejevic 2017: 891). Panoptic surveillance, as described by Michel Foucault (1991) through the example of the (early) modern prison which, according to the designs of 18th-century philosopher Jeremy Bentham, affords a sophisticated enclosure for internalized coercion achieved through the knowledge that, as an inmate, you *might* be being watched at all times. By contrast, 'environmental surveillance' refers to a 'total perpetual monitoring and ongoing intervention' (Hintz et al. 2019: 53): all available data from all tangible sources are collected, continuously processed and monitored. The basic idea – and we can connect this to the earlier discussion on the myth of big data – is to be able to predict behavior and subsequently prevent or change it.

In economics, basic forms of the interrelatedness by data are fairly well established, particularly from a users' point of view.[10] Google, as part of Alphabet Inc., for example, stores every user search (even if the search history is deleted locally), tracks websites using cookies and Google Ads, user location (if GPS is activated on the user device), and has access to an individual's YouTube history and every email sent and received by Gmail. The amount of stored data increases when additional Google software is adopted by a user. For example, if someone uses Google Fit, Alphabet Inc. stores information on your daily routine, Google Home stores data from all spoken queries directed at it (and potentially other conversations taking place in the space where it is located). Facebook stores all information users publish on any of its platforms (including posts, photos, friend networks, messages and likes) as well as the time, location and device used for every login.[11] Depending on how the operating system is configured, Facebook also has access to the user's webcam, microphone, contacts and other apps. In both cases, this data congregates into a personal profile on the basis of which individual users can be addressed by targeted advertising.[12] This results in the 'deep personalization' (Couldry & Turow 2014: 1711) of advertising based on data which is collected in the course of an individual's media use across a range of figurations.

Data stored within centralized data centers offer a multitude of new dynamics as they can be used for a variety of purposes that go beyond simple advertising. Google Trends, a real-time index of the volume of queries that users enter into the search engine, has received a lot of attention because of its potential to notice or even predict flu and other epidemics on the basis of an analysis of searches on their symptoms (Carneiro & Mylonakis 2009, Choi & Varian 2012). Another example is the recently highly criticized use of Facebook data for political campaign advertising as was public with the Cambridge Analytica case, which in 2018 sparked widespread outrage when it was revealed that the political consulting firm harvested the data of between 50 million and 80 million Facebook users without their consent and used it to micro-target voters during the UK's EU referendum campaign and the US 2016 presidential campaign.[13] The example of Cambridge Analytica, much like that of Google Trends, illustrates the sheer volume of data collected by the dominant tech firms. Because it is digital in form, and because it is stored centrally, data generated within specific figurations can be singled out and processed in different ways generating highly influential tools for a whole host of different purposes.

While the centralized collection of data was initiated by large tech corporations, state agencies were also involved. This is not only the case through the regulatory and financial enabling of monitoring technologies like those described in Chapter 2. The Edward Snowden leaks in 2013 made it very clear that state agencies have been some of the most prominent supra-individual actors participating in centralized data collection. For informed observers at least, the data collection activities of the US secret services were common knowledge before the Snowden revelations came to light.[14] However, the Snowden leaks 'provided unprecedented insights into the ways in which the mass collection and processing of data have become central to contemporary forms of governance and commercial life' (Hintz et al. 2019: 8). It was revealed that the US National Security Agency (NSA) and the British Government Communications Headquarters (GCHQ) had been surveilling their own citizens and foreign nationals through the analysis of (meta)data for many years.[15] This was made possible because they gained access to data centers belonging to the likes of Apple, Facebook, Google (including YouTube), Microsoft (including Skype) and Yahoo – sometimes with their agreement, sometimes not. Furthermore, these state surveillance agencies were scraping data by tapping the vast network of fiber optic cables that carry all the world's telephone calls and internet traffic. These huge volumes of data were then analyzed by software that facilitated the search of certain types of communications and online activity and was able to profile targets. Furthermore, from their position of power, state agencies installed backdoors into encryption services so that even those who took care to encrypt their communications were vulnerable to compromise through either the breaching of security protocols or by gaining access to services on user devices.[16] What environmental surveillance actually means becomes clear: the goal is no longer to 'map the environment' but to 'redouble it in the form of a model' (Andrejevic 2017: 891). And again, the aim is to model data to such an extent that it affords predictions of the future (terrorist attacks, criminal activity, threats to the state and so on).

The Snowden leaks once again demonstrate what is meant by the new interrelatedness of figurations through data: figurations that until a few years ago were thought of as discrete or only related over long chains of human action have now become intimately enmeshed in data processing. Just as the myth of big data is a considerable driving force in the attempt to model environmental surveillance, monitoring takes place through the processing of centrally stored, accessible data and presupposes the technological connectivity of digital infrastructures.

The crucial point here is that in the course of this new interrelatedness comprehensive patterns of social ordering also shift. As argued at the beginning of this section, these patterns are currently discussed primarily in terms of our arrival at a new stage of capitalism. Shoshana Zuboff (2019b) refers to 'surveillance capitalism', which she connects to value creation around the mass analysis of data. Surveillance capitalism's starting point is the one-sided use of human experience as a resource and its transformation into behavioral data. Initially, companies argued that they used these data simply to improve their products and services,[17] however, the sheer volume of data they have been able to store has led to new products and services, namely those related to behavioral prediction. Assumptions about future developments constructed in this way are in turn traded at the level of financial markets. Nick Couldry and Ulises Mejias (2019b: 3–35) go one step further in their discussion on 'data colonialism' as a result of the increasing interrelatedness of figurations through digital infrastructures and the processing of data. The reason why they speak of data *colonialism* is that, similar to colonialism in the regular sense of the term, they identify a pattern of ordering that structures the entire world with ever-increasing intensity: the new relationality of figurations leads to the commercial handling of data which is primarily concerned with the external appropriation of data on terms that are partly or wholly beyond the control of the person to whom the data relates. These data are then used by the respective technology companies to generate their added value (while at the same time enabling government monitoring). As more facets of everyday life are monitored by digital media the result might be the 'capitalization of human life without limit' (Couldry & Mejias 2019b: 5): through data, capitalism develops new interrelations with every corner of our lives and human practice becomes structured along capitalist principles more intensely than ever before.

This new stage of capitalism is only one example of the transformation initiated by the interrelatedness of figurations through myth, digital infrastructures and data and we must be careful not to reduce deep mediatization to it. However, it works very well to explain the recursive loops related to deep mediatization. The collection and processing of data was designed – driven by the myths of deep mediatization – in the interest of each technology corporation as a means of improving its own services and products. The resulting surplus of data has led to the emergence of new business models based on these data which in turn has led to the investment in appropriate digital infrastructures and software for data processing. A spiral was set in motion through which in just a few years the interrelatedness of figurations intensified to the extent that we are confronted with today.

THE TRANSFORMATION OF EXISTING FIGURATIONS

With deep mediatization we are not only dealing with a new interrelatedness of figurations, we are also confronted with the transformation of existing figurations. Groups, communities and organizations transform alongside media change. In most cases, it is difficult to establish simple causalities associated with the emergence of a certain medium that would, as part of a figuration's media ensemble, result in a specific consequence. The absence of simple linear causality is mostly related to the complex dynamics that take place in the appropriation of (digital) media and their infrastructures, but just as relevant is the fact that media change is not the only driving force behind the transformation of figurations. Today's figurations are also subject to change because of other meta-processes such as globalization, individualization and commercialization. The opportunity and the obligation to lead an individualized life, for example, has much to do with the fact that 'post-traditional communities' such as fan cultures and subcultural scenes are becoming more prominent among the communities in which we live.[18]

With these complexities in mind, a comprehensive shift of the media ensembles within many figurations can be discerned as a consequence of deep mediatization, namely a shift towards a (more) activated media ensemble. By *activated media ensemble*, I mean those media ensembles that include communicative robots as discussed in Chapter 3. The reason why I call them 'activated' is that communicative robots do not only mediate human communication but they themselves became 'quasi-communicative partners'.

There are many general statements about what change might come about due to artificial intelligence and robots. However, large parts of the public discourse on the subject are driven by science fiction discourses and the visions of pioneer communities.[19] Such imaginaries are maintained by the myths described above, in particular the myth of big data that argues that the mass processing of data would give rise to a new form of machine intelligence and the coming of the singularity. Pop-cultural products are full to the brim with these stories like the film *Her* (2013), in which a man falls in love with his artificial companion, Samantha. When dealing with communicative robots, there are two things worth avoiding: on the one hand, the mystification of artificial intelligence through imaginaries such as those described above. On the other, it is most likely analytically healthy to avoid trivializing transformation according to the principle that communicative robots are merely objectifications of human action to which one cannot ascribe any independent agency. The actual potential of communicative robots lies somewhere in between the two extremes.

To adequately grasp this potential, it is necessary to further contextualize the phenomenon of communicative robots. Communicative robots are not an isolated phenomenon; if we want to take them seriously, we must see them as part of a broader media ensemble with which the practices of different figurations are interwoven. But this media ensemble is different when communicative robots are involved; it is activated in a new way. This does not mean, as I have already argued, that communicative robots have the same agency as humans, however, we must remain mindful of the fact that communicative robots stimulate new forms of agency in and across different media ensembles.

In the following, I want to discuss three examples for the transformation of existing figurations: figurations of public discourse, of journalistic news production and of the family. This is obviously only a very limited selection in view of the diversity of possible figurations but the selection addresses characteristic contexts that are relevant for mediatization research: in the first case the dynamics of change in discourse, in the second case the dynamics of change in organizations and in the third case the dynamics of change in communities.

Public debate

We can see these new forms of agency play out in the figurations of mediated public debate.[20] Public debates are formed within a constellation of actors through communicative practices that are entangled with a particular media ensemble. When it comes to the media involved, until the 1990s mediated debates were comparatively stable in their character, at least in most Western countries. The principal corporate actors in this mix were news and media organizations as well as public service broadcasting which, as gatekeepers, provided external actors with access to a debate: politicians, members of associations and companies, social movements and in some cases private individuals (who were primarily understood as the audience).

With deep mediatization the media ensemble of public debate has fundamentally changed. Online and mobile editions of established news publishers emerged, as did Facebook and Twitter, as new access points for consuming news. Reflecting on the role platforms play in this transformation process José van Dijck, Thomas Poell and Martijn de Wall describe this process as the 'platformization of news' (van Dijck et al. 2018: 51–56): the initial steps towards platformization was when search engines started to establish themselves as critical access points for online news; individual news articles were extracted from their original media outlets and became, therefore, 'a separate product [...] [that] lives or dies on its own economic merits' (Carr 2009: 154). This focus on the single published entity was further strengthened by news aggregators such as Apple, Google and Yahoo News, who compile news from different sources on a website or in an app. In the US, Facebook and Google are 'by far and away the most important external referral sites for news traffic' (Bell et al. 2017: 25) and comparable developments can also be identified in Europe (Newman et al. 2018).

As advertising has shifted toward digital platforms and a younger readership has begun to access most of their news online, regional news providers experienced a great deal of financial pressure and publishing houses have had to close or merge.[21] Furthermore, with the emergence of online platforms, news companies had their gatekeeper role taken away from them and politicians, businesses, other actors in civil society and ordinary people were able to engage in the actor constellation of public debate in a more direct way.[22]

These developments demonstrate how the emergence of communicative robots in the media ensembles of public debate was but just one other step in a much longer process. We can see the platformization of public debate as a first step in this process, creating the infrastructure in which social bots have become possible. The implementation of bots on social media platforms has proven to be a fairly simple task as instructions are provided online.[23] The Bot Traffic Report in 2016 reported that a total of 51.8 percent of online traffic was generated by bots, of which 22.9 percent were 'good bots' and 28.9 percent were 'bad bots'.[24] Even if one moves within the framework of statistics like these, the numbers need to be put into perspective since a large proportion of bots are not designed to interact directly with people. For example, these statistics also include bots that collect data for search engines (according to these figures, these alone account for 6.6 percent of online traffic). The number of social bots that are 'active' in public debate is, therefore, much lower.

In their analysis of over 20 million tweets generated between 16 September and 21 October 2016 by approximately 2.8 million distinct users as part of the online debate on the US elections, Alessandro Bessi and Emilio Ferrara (2016) came to the conclusion that 15 percent of the total population of their study were bots and 'most importantly that they are responsible for roughly 3.8 million tweets (nearly 19 percent of the total conversation)'.[25] The most significant results they arrived at were that 'bots produce systematically more positive content in support of a candidate' and that 'that bots become more and more central in the rebroadcasting network' (Bessi & Ferrara 2016: 9–10). Bessi and Ferrara's interpretation suggests that, with the inclusion of social bots, the public debate becomes more polarized and the spread of misinformation is increased.

Bessi and Ferrera's study is but one of many looking at the role bots play in online political debate.[26] However, it is worth our attention as it stands as a prime example of all that is problematic in capturing social bot activity. First, it is no simple task to identify which Twitter accounts are bots and which are regular accounts by simply looking at their activity. Indicators include tweets that are not geo-located, large numbers of retweets and also that bots tend to tweet news headlines without links to the original source (Stukal et al. 2017). Due to these (and other) indirect deductions, the exact number of active bots and the ratio between different types of bots vary considerably depending on of the methods used for data generation and analysis. As it is stated in a recent *Science* paper, 'in the absence of methods to derive representative samples of bots and humans on a given platform, any point estimates of bot prevalence must be interpreted cautiously' (Lazer et al. 2018: 1095). In other words, on the basis of existing research, it is not possible to know exactly how many bots are part of a public debate, nor what dynamics of transformation are associated with them.

In addition, with social bots we are only dealing with a minor part of the media ensemble that is going through a process of change. Most research on social bots refers to Twitter, because bots for the platform are comparably easy to create and because a fair degree of access to data is permitted by Twitter. Far fewer studies deal with Facebook, for example. And we must bear in mind that the media ensemble of public debate encompasses many more sites that just online social media platforms (Newman et al. 2018: 8–31): television still has a place, whether online, terrestrial or via cable. Newspapers are still relevant online and in print, as is the communication of politicians, representatives of public institutions and civil society and ordinary citizens through a range of platforms. We have to contextualize social bots within the dynamic of the media ensemble's changing nature if we want to make statements about the transformation of the figuration of public debate. Nevertheless, the discussion so far demonstrates how enduring the transformation of the public debate is in regard to deep mediatization. The changing media ensemble makes new dynamics of communication possible. Which dynamics these are in detail is an open empirical question. The task of future mediatization research is to describe exactly what these dynamics look like and what patterns will emerge in the long term.

Journalistic news production

Another example for the transformation of existing figurations are the figurations of news production in journalism. Again, it is possible to begin the analysis with a focus on communicative robots, specifically work bots that operate in the field of robot journalism as discussed in Chapter 3. Here, too, this example has to be considered in the broader context of long-term change in news production. Traditionally, research into the practices of journalistic production has focused on the newsroom.[27] Initially, this research was mainly concerned with 'the daily negotiations through which structure is produced and reproduced in everyday workplace settings' (Lounsbury & Kaghan 2001: 28). How the practices of journalistic production themselves changed with the underlying media ensemble became an issue when digital tools arose in the field. A broader interest in questions around these tools emerged as online journalism also started to change journalists' production practices as a whole. How innovation in journalism is related to new media technologies has become an issue of moderate urgency.[28] This has been researched as part of the general processes of reducing costs and implementing a new managerial culture of news production (Born 2005), as a tension between non-technological organizational factors and new technology (Boczkowski 2004), or as a fear of discontinuity in reinvention (Carlson 2007). With the spread of digital media in journalistic production, the 'newsroom-centricity' of research became problematic as more decentralized 'electronically based forms of editorial organization' (Wilke 2003: 474) emerged and new technologies began 'challenging the centralization of news work in the physical site of the newsroom' (Wahl-Jorgensen 2009: 33). The figuration of journalistic production moved towards a 'post-industrial' (Anderson et al. 2012) model for news-work transgressing the 'borders' of the newsroom and stimulating various new forms of journalism.

Subsequently, the transformation of journalistic production has been examined from a range of perspectives as the actor constellation of news production has fundamentally changed. The role played by freelance journalists as a 'flexible workforce in media industries' (Edstrom & Ladendorf 2012: 711) has increased due to job cuts in editorial offices and the job profiles of professionals have been shaken up alongside processes of media change. The role of the entrepreneur journalist has emerged, journalists who act independently, focus on their individual skills and develop new formats and business models that are focused on individual engagement in a changing media environment.[29] With the establishment of tools for analyzing and visualizing large datasets, freelance data journalists and data analysts have seen themselves become an important part of the professional news making environment.[30] The new pioneer journalists as described in Chapter 2, have emerged, whose work is delimited by various technology-centered communities such as the hacker and open source movements. Beyond the newsroom, start-ups have gained in importance especially for the development of new forms of journalistic production.[31] With all these changes, our understanding of what journalism is has shifted, as demonstrated by the more reflexive discourses in the field.[32] So, journalism is not (only) dealing with a simple crisis, but with a fundamental transformation of journalistic news production in terms of its actor constellation, practices and its frames of relevance.

It is in the context of this comprehensive transformation of the figuration of journalistic production in which the so-called robot journalism must be considered. Here work bots are software tools that serve to automate journalistic tasks which were originally carried out by humans. We cannot understand work bots' potential for change if we see them in isolation or simply as a replacement for human labor. Rather, they become part of the media ensemble of journalistic production as a whole.

This has already been demonstrated by research on robot journalism dealing with automated text production. Interviews with journalists who use work bots show that these applications cannot be considered in isolation, not only because they are based on scripts written by journalists themselves and rooted in their existing everyday practices, but also because it remains a journalistic task to contextualize and personalize the content automatically generated by bots (Thurman et al. 2017: 1254). A closer look at work bots, such as those from the Structured Stories Project, reveals the extent to which they are also entangled with journalistic practice. These bots are based on platforms which enable journalists to enter events and narratives into a 'story database'. In so doing, the news stories are entirely represented as structured data which can then be used to automatically generate event-driven narratives using automated writing tools (Caswell & Dörr 2018: 479).[33] Apart from content that is automatically accessible via existing sensors or that has already taken the form of database entries (such as sports results, stock market trades or earthquake information), journalists need to feed data, design the narrative scripts and maintain the databases. For this reason alone, we cannot see robot journalism detached from other journalistic practices.[34]

We can substantiate this in other working examples of robot journalism. The Homicide Report by the *Los Angeles Times*[35] had the original goal of recording all homicides in the LA area in blog form as an addendum to the detailed reporting on selected cases in the newspaper. Initially this blog was realized by a journalist who wrote the individual entries by hand. In a second iteration it is now realized with the help of a work bot, that is, an automation script using data from the coroner's office. If a death is listed as a homicide the bot automatically writes up a short blog entry based on this data and the homicide becomes added to an interactive map. In addition to this automated documentation, longer journalistic articles on selected homicides are written in the same blog. In their detailed study on the entanglement of different technologies and practices in the making of this report, Mary Lynn Young and Alfred Hermida (2015) show the extent to which this is an example of the general transformation of journalistic production at the *Los Angeles Times*. The implementation of work bots is part of the general establishment of journalistic practice in which content available from the internet is automatically fed and processed. This automated reporting gains importance because of the fact that it is embedded in an intensified reporting on the subject: journalists conduct in-depth research and publish based on this more detailed information. These changes in reporting practice go hand-in-hand with changes to the editorial office as a whole, a process in which external pioneers with data journalism and programming expertise became part of the core team. This relates to the change of the organizational culture to one of more openness toward technological innovations.

Local and translocal families

One more example of the transformation of existing figurations worth considering is that of the family.[36] The family is particularly interesting because of the long tradition of investigating its media-related transformations. It was research on media use in the family from which the argument arose that it would be best practice to less investigate the appropriation of individual media in isolation but, rather, to focus instead on the families' media ensemble.[37] Various studies on media appropriation in the family have been carried out, and one result has been that media play an important role in the construction of family life particularly in regard to gender roles and power relations.[38] Television is of particular importance, but has to be seen in the context of ensembles of other media such as video recorders, telephones and newspapers. Overall, these studies demonstrate that the construction of the family cannot be seen in isolation from the media appropriated in the family.

In this case, too, the spread of digital media stimulated new research in the field. While digital media were widely appropriated by families, mediatization research shows that this did not lead to turmoil in families' media use, but, rather, that there is an inertia of existing practices.

For example, watching television together is maintained to 'enable and synchronize' (Röser et al. 2017: 142) relations within families while watching can also mean watching Netflix or another purely digital television channel. We can see an expansion of families' media ensemble, just with different dynamics. Computer and video games do not just lead to a divide between the generations in families, but can also be a resource for building intergenerational relationships through different competences.[39] With the spread of platforms such as Facebook, the question came up as to what extent social media can be used for social control by parents. This issue arises when parents become 'friends' with their children on social media platforms and gain insight into their online activities.[40] Another dynamic is to negotiate communication rules within the family, for example, who in the family can make a pregnancy and birth public online (the parents or other family members?) or are parents allowed to communicate online about their children and post pictures?[41] A further dynamic relates to the construction of a shared memory in families, for which digital media are becoming an important resource.[42]

Besides the shifts in family relationships, digital media and their infrastructures supported new forms of articulating family life and this is made clear in the example of translocally widespread, transnational families. The rise of today's transnational families refers not only to mediatization but also to globalization when precarious working conditions in one's original place of residence and increasing labor and mobility opportunities in other countries become the motivation for economic migration. Research demonstrates how transnational families are kept together by a complex media ensemble, consisting of telephone and internet calls, email, social media, text messages, letters and the joint use of produced media content.[43] In today's media environment, transnational families can 'create a particular configuration of media that works best for their particular communicative needs' (Madianou & Miller 2013: 179). Migrant women, for example, not only have the opportunity to maintain their maternal role by 'mothering at a distance' (Madianou & Miller 2012: 70) through the combined use of internet telephony, email, phone calls and text messaging to help children with their daily tasks (schoolwork, for example), but to also have a disciplinary insight into their lives by observing the activities of their children online. Digital media create possibilities for fathers to establish special situations of childcare, as well, such as learning support (Greschke et al. 2017: 68). For children, these mediated forms of relationship mean that they have to express themselves to their parents in new ways while also allowing them to avoid contact totally by postponing responses to emails and other messages. We can see here a remarkable re-figuration of family life: through a digital media ensemble it is possible to maintain transnational family relations even when dispersed across space and time. As a consequence of these families' communicative constructions, their character changes compared to families who live together: the definition of family shifts into a transnational actor constellation as do the definitions of family roles such as in the example of 'mothering at a distance'.[44]

Even within the family unit, communicative robots such as the artificial companions embedded in the Amazon Echo and Google Home can become part of the media ensemble. As these devices are only in their early iterations, there is still little research on the subject.[45] Nevertheless, it is apparent that previously existing family dynamics continue to exist. Market research into early adopters in the US shows that Amazon's Echo, with over 80 percent market share, is typically appropriated in multi-person households and that around 50 percent of users use the device in the kitchen and 33 percent in the living room. From this point of view the 'Echo's standalone speaker design encourages family, friends and children alike to interact with Alexa' (Ong & Suplizio 2016: 1). The most widespread interactions, at over 50 percent, include 'set a timer', 'play a song', 'read the news', 'set an alarm', 'check the time', 'tell a joke' and 'control the lights'.[46] These results are confirmed in a diary study on the use of Alexa by Irene Lopatovska and colleagues, where they found that the most frequent uses were quick information searches (weather, facts, news), entertainment (play music, tell a joke) and the control of external devices (Lopatovska et al. 2018: 5–7). Furthermore, this study shows that the Echo device was mainly positioned in three rooms: the living room, the kitchen and the bedroom, while most tasks were performed in the living room.[47] It seems that the domestication of the Echo takes place primarily in spaces that accommodate family interaction and the dominant ways of handling it are those that are either purely functional, stimulate family communication, or provide access to other media content such as music or news. There exists a considerable gap in the discussion on Amazon Alexa in critical media and communications research,[48] in which the infrastructures that undergird the device, the centralized storage of data and the associated possibility of continuously recording interactions at home are discussed.[49] While there are many reasons for skepticism,[50] it is an open question as to what extent or in what ways families will change when their homes become 'smart' and are permeated with the types of technologies such as those currently offered by Amazon and Google.

At this point, we could continue the descriptions of the transformation of existing figurations with a changing media ensemble by taking a closer look at different organizations such as schools or private companies, different communities such as diasporas or circles of friends, or different actors in civil society such as social movements or associations.[51] Contextual research is necessary because deep mediatization is not a homogeneous process, but one that differs from one social domain to another. However, beyond these differences, some more general statements can be made on the basis of the examples discussed so far.

First of all, we saw in all three examples – the figurations of public debate, of journalistic news production and of the family – that the decisive transforming factor was not simply a new medium, but how digital media and their infrastructures were integrated into the media ensemble. Secondly, we are not dealing with the simple effects of change, but with complex interactions. Media ensemble and practices are entangled with one another and, therefore, transform together. Thirdly, these examples have also shown that we have to consider media-related changes in relation to other types of change: the increasing commercialization of certain practices (e.g. in journalistic production), the individualization of public connection (e.g. in public debate) or the globalization of communities (e.g. in family relations). If one wants to grasp the transformation of figurations associated with deep mediatization it is necessary to focus on the relation to other meta-processes of change rather than looking for simple causalities. Fourth, we are able to grasp slightly more rigorously what recursiveness means. In all these cases, it can be said that the appropriation of digital media in each figuration supports the trends of change in the media environment: the differentiation of media through a willingness to appropriate them for public debate, journalism and the family; through the continued use of these media the maintenance of their omnipresence; an albeit hesitant acceptance of the pace of innovation; and encouraging datafication by making digital media part of each figuration. The quantitative trends of deep mediatization are, therefore, not external at all. Rather, they refer back to the recursive transformation of various human figurations – through which these trends are rearticulated and sustained in the first place.

THE EMERGENCE OF NEW FIGURATIONS

The idea that all social relationships will take on the form of networks has been a popular topic in media and communications research, particularly in relation to digital media. The argument is that instead of being part of static groups and neighborhoods, people are embedded within open networks which represent the 'new social operating system' (Rainie & Wellman 2012: 3) of the 'network society' (Castells 1996: 6). Looking at it today, after the initial hype of the early internet and network metaphors, it is clear that not every social relationship has become a network or that networks dominate our relations. Rather, these kinds of statements are associated with the problem that a descriptive language used to characterize society finds itself mistaken with the diagnosis of this society.[52] But these exaggerated statements have roots. These can be found when considering that deep mediatization is associated not only with the transformation of existing figurations but also with the emergence of new ones. These are multifaceted in nature and the language we use to describe them is still in its infancy. Nevertheless, some general tendencies can be identified: on the one hand, emerging new figurations are often more fluid as far as their actor constellations are concerned while at the same time they extend to greater lengths. On the other hand, digital media are constitutive of these figurations. While this has some parallels with network thinking, we need more specific language to describe these phenomena instead of simply referring to them as networks. In the following, I want to substantiate this by discussing the examples of platform collectivities, connective action and financial markets.

Platform collectivities

Platform collectivities are figurations that group around digital platforms. In a way, we adopt a slightly different perspective from the previous section. Instead of asking how platforms contribute to a media ensemble and the transformation of existing figurations, why not examine which new figurations of humans group around platforms? Here, we can identify processes of numeric inclusion.[53] This means that the digital traces users leave on these platforms are processed and grouped into different collectivities, which are then addressed by these platforms as a single entity. One simple example is the categorization of people along the lines of their tastes. On platforms such as the Amazon Online Store or Apple Music collectivities of taste are calculated on the basis of previous online purchases which are then harnessed as criteria for further purchase or listening suggestions. These collectivities are constructed in human practice – the practice of buying online or online media use –, they are based on common frames of relevance (taste) and are mediated by the platforms into particular constellations of actors. It is in this sense that they constitute a figuration. However, the individual users who form the basis of these figurations are typically not aware of their entirety and do not develop a shared 'we'.

Such figurations are formed technologically, more often than not as a result of data processing. Nick Couldry and I have described these figurations elsewhere as 'collectivities without communitization' (Couldry & Hepp 2017: 183). They are articulated through a process of 'recursive inclusion' (Lury & Day 2019: 25): The likes, purchase decisions and selections on which the formation of these collectivities are based represent a continuous data flow along which algorithmic collectivity formation takes place. This results in narrow loops of recursiveness in which both the individual and the collectivity 'are repeatedly specified anew' (Lury & Day 2019: 25).

Currently, these kinds of collectivities are primarily related to just one platform. They are created in the Amazon Online Store, at Apple Music, on Facebook and so on. Looking at technological change as it is occurring now, we may soon be confronted with platform collectivities that are processed through an ensemble of different digital media. It is already the case that, depending on the platform, collectivity can include not only the pure data tracks on the online platform but other processed information such as the geodata shared by mobile phones and web browsers. If one follows current developments in data collection and processing across different companies,[54] one can expect that in the future even more complex forms of generating platform collectivities may emerge.

Once one has developed just such a view on platform collectivities, the previously discussed surveillance capitalism and data colonialism appear in a different light. For example, we can now describe Uber as a platform collectivity produced by 'algorithmic management' (Rosenblat 2018: 199): the app provides to the company a deep, quantifying insight into the working practices of drivers by processing mobility data. The drivers are monitored by a rating system (and may be excluded from work by deactivation) and controlled by promises of lucrative jobs (or possibly misinformation such as fake drivers). It is a collectivity of isolated workers held together by a platform only – a collectivity without communitization.

A central characteristic of platform collectivities is that social inequality is created in and through them. Uber's drivers, for example, are, to a large extent, people who do not have access to other professions due to their personal situation or their level of education. Furthermore, this platform also reproduces racist discourses and social exclusion through its rating system as 'consumers can directly input their biases into worker evaluation systems in ways that companies cannot do on their behalf' (Rosenblat 2018: 155). We can see here another form of 'automating inequality' (Eubanks 2017), an oft noted characteristic of digital data processing, only that here it is directly connected with the construction of a certain collectivity.[55] Platform collectivities are, therefore, no less shaped by power relations and social exclusion than other figurations.

However, the Uber example also illustrates how platform collectivities can trigger an array of social processes once their participants recognize themselves as part of them and their relative positions to other members of the group. This takes place when Uber drivers – often together with drivers of other platforms such as Lyft – gather on online forums, exchange their experiences with 'algorithmic management', provide to other drivers hints on how to handle the app or even organize protests against the company. These processes of mutual exchange can be seen as an example of how a collectivity created by a platform can become, through the use of an ensemble of other digital media, a different kind of figuration – a community of the exploited that begins to articulate its interests.

Connective action

We can also detect emerging new figurations in other areas. In the field of political communication, they tend to be discussed around the concept of 'connective action' (Bennett & Segerberg 2013). Examples include the protests that sparked up around the year 2011: the Put People First campaign in the UK, the Arab Spring, the Indignados in Spain and the Occupy Wall Street protests in the US. The background for these forms of protest is the overarching shift towards individualization through which engagement with politics became more 'an expression of personal hopes, lifestyles and grievances' (Bennett & Segerberg 2012: 743) than an engagement with the aim of structural change as was the case for 'collective action' of labor unions, for example. The individualization of political engagement is matched with the opportunity to organize protests in a new way through the use of digital platforms – Facebook, Twitter, YouTube, messenger services and so on – where the ideas and mechanisms for organizing action are more personalized than in cases of collective action where 'action is organized on the basis of social group identity, membership, or ideology' (Bennett & Segerberg 2012: 744). Protesters, for example, become collected through memes, that is, iconographic visualizations of the respective protest that spread across platforms. Therefore, 'the starting point for connective action is the self-motivated (though not necessarily self-centered) sharing of already internalized or personalized ideas, plans, images and resources with networks of others'. (Bennett & Segerberg 2012: 753). This 'sharing' takes place across various platforms but it also is the subject of general media coverage which further intensifies perspectives on and engagement with the protests.

Bennett and Segerberg are at pains to stress that connective action and collective action are types of mobilization that can also occur in hybrid forms. Connective action, therefore, did not simply displace collective action (there are still different forms of political protest strongly coordinated by social organizations) but both forms can exist side by side. By looking in more detail, we can understand both forms grounded in different figurations of political protest. Collective action is oriented around formalized figurations whose actor constellation is typically characterized by formal memberships such as trade unions or NGOs. The figurations of connective action are less fixed, they can arise more situationally from individual protest moments, but are able to integrate different people rapidly thanks to having a more flexible actor constellation. Digital media and their infrastructures play a role at both ends of the spectrum of protest figurations albeit in different ways: in the case of figurations of collective action, the question is more about how figurations of existing political organizations are transformed by deep mediatization. In the case of connective action, the question refers to which new types of figurations – protest smart mobs, politically engaged scenes, spontaneous yet coordinated demonstrations – emerge.

Situational figurations of connective action can, in turn, develop into organized figurations of collective action. It is the dynamics between connective and collective action, therefore, that have become the subject of research on digital media and social movements which has demonstrated that more stable shared political identities can be articulated in connective action.[56] Beyond these differentiations we can see the Bennett and Segerberg's argument as evidence of the emergence of new figurations for political protest. These figuration's practices refer to digital media and infrastructures, their frames of relevance are articulated through online communication, and they have a much more fluid actor constellation than campaigns conducted by traditional protest organizations. These figurations of political protest can be seen as an articulation of skepticism towards existing forms of institutionalized politics including established civil society organizations and trade unions.

Financial markets

Another example of emerging figurations are financial markets or more specifically foreign exchange trading markets which are grouped around what Karin Knorr Cetina (2014: 39) calls 'scopic media'.[57] At the traders' desks these scopic media are the various screens from which they follow the financial market. Through these screens they have access to foreign exchange trading systems (for example, the Reuters 3000), which are the platforms for global electronic trading and include various subsystems that continuously represent the data from various markets. We can understand these platforms as an ensemble of scopic media that are at the same time a 'mechanism of observation and projection' (Knorr Cetina & Reichmann 2015: 151): they construct the respective markets by observing them. With these scopic media, a 'synthetic situation' of locally dispersed actors is created and enables the figuration of the financial market: 'When a "scoped" reality is projected to everyone connected simultaneously, the scope acts as an integration and communication device that places all those observing it (as professional traders must) instantly into an identical world'. (Knorr Cetina & Reichmann 2015: 152) Scopic media deliver data that the traders perceive as information. In this way the scopic media used in financial markets brings together events, phenomena and actors that would otherwise be separated by distance.[58] In so doing, scopic media present content in a sequential, streamed, constantly updated, fluid form. Embedded within these scopic media are communicative robots, that is, algorithms that 'learn' to 'make' decisions. This results in a figuration that can no longer be described as the 'network' of relationship markets.[59] – it is a new figuration of scopic markets: 'the screens contain the referential whole of everything relevant and actionable in a fully electronic market' (Knorr Cetina & Reichmann 2015: 154).

We see yet another emerging figuration which depends entirely on an ensemble of digital media beyond which it has no existence. The market requires speed and efficiency that is only made possible by digital media because people alone are unable to anticipate and make decisions so speedily. A fundamental argument for delegating trade decisions to algorithms is the idea of being able to utilize the (transmission) time advantages of digital infrastructures. Investment firms upgrade their data connections to the highest speeds possible to facilitate them just to gain milliseconds worth of advantage or even to make these speed advantages the basis of their profit model, as in high-frequency trading.[60] But there is a second argument, that algorithms are used to make 'rational' decisions instead of those influenced by human frailties and passion (MacKenzie 2019: 39). At the same time the construction of meaning in automated data processing and automated trading remains in traders' own narratives. Financial analysts, for example, construct narratives that are not simply extracted from data but, rather, assemble a 'plausible story' of the automated trading activities, often after discussions with contacts and colleagues

(Reichmann 2013). We cannot, therefore, simply reduce figurations of foreign exchange trading markets to automation; scopic media and human practice constantly refer to one another.

The examples discussed so far – platform collectivities, connective action and financial markets – represent the emergence of new figurations that come about as a consequence of deep mediatization. If one compares these figurations, we can see how diverse the new figurations are that emerge with deep mediatization. The scientific discussion on the vast assortment of these figurations is certainly not complete. This is demonstrated not least in the number of different concepts to describe their specificities. New concepts come under consideration such as 'swarms' or 'smart mobs'.[61] Legacy concepts from media and communications research are being reinterpreted, as exemplified by the idea of 'crowds'.[62] In sum, we can understand this discussion on a new kind of descriptive language as an exploration of the character of the emerging new figurations.

The observations made so far in this chapter have made clear what it means to understand the transformation of deep mediatization as a re-figuration: today we are dealing with a new interrelatedness of figurations that arises from globalized myths about digital media from globalized digital infrastructures and data processing. Re-figuration also refers to the transformation of existing figurations, whether they be those that are part of communities such as families or organizations such as media corporations. It also refers to the emergence of new figurations, as we have just discussed. These different examples also show what is meant by the recursive loops that are present in this process: data is continuously generated which, in turn, forms the basis for the further development of digital media and their infrastructures. In this process existing trends are stabilized more than they are questioned. The re-figuration of deep mediatization is certainly not automatic, since responsibility for this process entirely lies at the door of humans. However, it is a process that is, to a considerable degree, stable and potent.

NOTES

1   See, Couldry (2014b): 619 and Couldry (2014a: 885). David Morley discussed the 'mythical we' of media more generally in Morley (2000: 105–127).

2 In this sense, the myth of digital purity also relates to what Trebor Scholz has called the 'myth of immateriality': a discourse which frames digital work in spite of all the necessary infrastructures required for 'immaterial work' (Scholz 2017: 97–99).

3 See, for example, boyd & Crawford (2012), Crawford et al. (2014), Elmer et al. (2015b) or Puschmann & Burgess (2014).

4 See, for a detailed analysis, Beer (2019), who carried out an ethnographic study on the data analytics industry and how this industry facilitates the spread and intensification of datafication.

5 As James Bridle (2018: 80) argues, we must be careful with the self-description of statements such as 'Moore's law' and considering them as 'laws'; in essence they are instead 'self-fulfilling technological prophecies': As quasi-natural statements they act as an orientation for technological development and sometimes stimulate billions in (often public) investment, a process through which they become part of social reality.

6 Trebor Schulz (2017: 42) highlights that the widespread term 'sharing economy' (Zervas et al. 2014) is somehow misleading as 'these businesses are not genuine about sharing: they are dedicated to the renting out of assets such as rooms, labor, tools, and, importantly, time'.

7 This refers back to considerations of cybernetics and general systems theory of the 1950s and 1960s, which was transferred to human relations (see, Turner 2006a: 41–68).

8 Trebor Scholz expresses this in very clear words when he writes about the platform ecosystem: 'This ecosystem would not be possible without the human effort of computer engineers and the hardware – satellites, cables, Wi-Fi routers, and mobile phones that makes online communication possible in the first place. Labour companies like Mechanical Turk, Uber, or UpWork did not contribute a dime to this spadework' (Scholz 2017: 31).

9 Even Wi-Fi connected digital scales are used to collect personal data. For example, the Withings body scale which measures the temperature in each room where it is located – users are not informed on why this data is collected and what it is used for.

10 A well-researched newspaper article on this was published in *The Guardian*. See: https://www.theguardian.com/commentisfree/2018/mar/28/all-the-data-fac ebook-google-has-on-you-privacy (accessed: May 1st, 2019).

11 For Alphabet/Google's data collection, see, Schmidt (2018) and https://ww w.bbc.com/news/technology-45952466 (accessed: May 1st, 2019).

12 See, Joseph Turow's analysis in (2011) and Couldry & Turow (2014). The phenomenon of 'data doubles' is discussed from an individual perspective in Chapter 6.

13 This part of the scandal is well documented in the press, see, for example, Halpern (2018) and Weissman (2018).

14 For example, in 2005 the *New York Times* reported that in the aftermath of 9/11 the NSA had been granted extensive secret powers by President George W. Bush to spy on US communications as part of a project called Stellar Wind. Court ordered warrants were unnecessary and *Wired* magazine published a report in

2012 on the NSA's construction of a data center in Utah, which suggested that Stellar Wind was still active (cf. Bridle 2018: 176).

15 For a (scientific) review of the Snowden revelations, see, Fidler (2015), Greenwald (2014), Lyon (2014) and (2017).

16 The NSA has access to GPS location data with which they 'can attempt to track individuals to private homes and can also retrace earlier journeys, whenever the phone is on' (Lyon 2014: 3).

17 Shoshana Zuboff (2019b: Chapter 3) sees Google in particular as a pioneer, but one must be careful not to lose sight of the fact that the construction of corresponding infrastructures in China took place almost simultaneously.

18 See, in more detail, Hepp & Hitzler (2016) on the relationship between individualization and mediatization in the transformation of communitization.

19 Meredith Broussard (2018, especially 67–86) has very clearly dealt with this, also discussing the role of the Whole Earth Network for the development of such fantasies.

20 Here I use the more open concept of the 'mediated public debate' (Hintz et al. 2019: 85) in order to avoid the narrower and more normative concept of Jürgen Habermas' 'public sphere' (1989). In contrast to Habermas, I understand 'mediated public debate' first of all as descriptive, that is, I am less concerned with the question of what a deliberative public sphere should look like than I am with describing what changes we are currently confronted with.

21 This is discussed in detail and in a US context by Joseph Turow (2011). See, also, Couldry & Turow (2014).

22 See, again, Newman et al. (2018).

23 See, regarding Twitter bots, https://readwrite.com/2014/06/20/random-non-s equitur-twitter-bot-instructions/ and http://www.pygaze.org/2016/03/how-to-code-twitter-bot/ (accessed: May 1st, 2019).

24 See, Zelfman (2017) and https://www.incapsula.com/blog/bot-traffic-report-2016. html (accessed: May 1st, 2019).

25 Their tool for isolating bots can be found on the following web page: https://botometer.iuni.iu.edu (accessed: May 1st, 2019).

26 For more work on the role bots play in public debate, see, Ferrara et al. (2016), Nimmo (2018), Stukal et al. (2019) and Tsvetkova et al. (2017).

27 See, Wahl-Jorgensen (2009: 22–25) and Deuze & Witschge (2018).

28 Early studies include, Boczkowski (2004), Cottle & Ashton (1999), Deuze (2007) and Quandt (2005).

29 See, Briggs (2012), Mensing & Ryfe (2013), Vázquez Schaich & Klein (2013) and Wagemans et al. (2019).

30 For research on data journalism, see, Anderson (2013), Fink & Anderson (2015), Flew et al. (2012), Lewis (2014), Loosen (2018b) and Parasie & Dagiral (2013).

31 The role of start-ups in journalistic production has been studied by, Carlson and Usher (2016), Chadha (2016), Hess et al. (2014), Usher (2017) and Wagemans et al. (2016).

32 See, Carlson (2016), Loosen et al. (2017) and Vos & Singer (2016).

33 This database can be accessed via the following web page: http://www.struc-turedstories.com (accessed: May 1st, 2019).

34 We must remain aware that these particular transformations are accompanied by media discourses on robot journalism in which journalists themselves reflect on such changes (Dalen 2012). As Matt Carlson shows in an analysis of the media coverage on Narrative Science, a provider of a tool for automated journalism, during the period January 1, 2010 to March 1, 2014, dominant themes at the positive end of the spectrum included insights into how the growth of automated journalism expands the amount of available news and frees up journalists to pursue less mechanical stories, on a more negative note, the idea that it stimulates an environment of increased layoffs, polarizes personalization and news writing becomes more commercialized (Carlson 2015: 429). A negotiation on the significance of communicative robots in journalistic production is still ongoing.

35 See, https://homicide.latimes.com (accessed: May 1st, 2019). This script was also the basis for the work bot used for the documentation of earthquakes described in Chapter 3.

36 For this example, see also, Couldry & Hepp (2017: 70–71).

37 This argument has been articulated by (Hermann Bausinger 1984).

38 See, Bryce & Leichter (1983), Goodman (1983), Lindlof et al. (1988), Lull (1988), Lull (1990), Morley (1986), Morley & Silverstone (1990) and Silverstone & Hirsch (1992).

39 See, Aarsand (2007) and more recently, focusing the internet, Correa et al. (2015).

40 See, Child & Westermann (2013).

41 See, Clark (2012); Livingstone (2014), Mascheroni (2018), Schmidt (2019) and Thornham (2019).

42 See, Lohmeier & Böhling (2017).

43 See, Madianou (2014), Madianou & Miller (2012), (2013) and Greschke et al. (2017). While Mirca Madianou and Daniel Miller mainly focused on transnational families from the Philippines, Heike Greschke, Diana Dreßler and Konrad Hierasimowicz have researched families from Hungary, Poland, Spain and Ukraine.

44 As other studies have shown, relationships in families of co-presence are more closely related to media use and the expectation of a more intensified communicative connectivity is the inevitable result. See, Jansson (2015b) and Linke (2011).

45 A main problem for any reflection on these technologies is that '[d]ue to the novelty of the IPA technology, most of the information about Alexa's adoption comes from industry reports' (Lopatovska et al. 2018: 2).

46 However, we must be very careful when generalizing this kind of information as it is based on a survey of 1,300 American users, 180 of whom were 'early adopters' of the Amazon Echo, https://www.experian.com/innovation/thought-leadership/amazon-echo-consumer-survey.jsp (accessed: May 1st, 2019).

47 These results are also supported by an analysis of the user comments at the Amazon online store (Purington et al. 2017: 2857) and the study by Sciuto et al. (2018).

48 See, Crawford & Joler (2018), Stark & Levy (2018) and Zuboff (2019a): 15–16.

49 The latter is increasingly the subject of media coverage of the two devices, see, for example, https://www.theguardian.com/technology/2019/apr/11/amazon-st aff-listen-to-customers-alexa-recordings-report-says (accessed: May 1st, 2019).

50 Remarkably, the early academic developments in smart home technologies began with a completely different structural modelling than Amazon and Google currently do. The considerations at that time were that the resulting data were so private that their centralized processing at locally remote servers was ruled out. Such data should be available in the household of the persons concerned.

51 See, (in order of the examples mentioned above) Breiter (2014), Øyvind & Pallas (2014), Hepp et al. (2012, 2014) and Mattoni & Treré (2014).

52 See, for more detail, Couldry & Hepp (2017: 60–63).

53 See, for the concept of numeric inclusion, Passoth et al. (2014) and Wehner (2010).

54 See, Turow (2017).

55 Safiya Umoja Noble (2018) has shown in her detailed study 'Algorithms of Oppression' how such inequalities and racism are re-articulated by search engines.

56 See, Kavada (2015, 2016) and Dahlberg-Grundberg et al. (2016).

57 As she puts it, '[e]xchange trade markets have moved only in the last decade from their open outcry system to embracing scopic media and to transnational arrangements' (Knorr Cetina & Reichmann 2015: 152).

58 See, Knorr Cetina (2014): 43–45 and Knorr Cetina & Reichmann (2015: 154–156).

59 Knorr Cetina & Preda (2007).

60 See, the illustrative examples in Bridle (2018: 106–108).

61 See, Brejzek (2010), Kaulingfreks & Warren (2010) and Rheingold (2003).

62 There is a broad discussion in media and communications research related to how far this concept contributes to the description of new, media-based collectivities; cf. Baker (2011), Dolata & Schrape (2015), Schnapp & Tiews (2006), Stage (2013) and Torres & Mateus (2015).

6

THE INDIVIDUAL IN TIMES
OF DEEP MEDIATIZATION

In this chapter, I would like to switch to the perspective to the individual and his or her embedding within figurations. As mentioned at the beginning of Chapter 4, one key point in Norbert Elias' sociology of processes is not to pit the individual against society but, instead, to focus on the interplay between the individual and the social by thinking in terms of figurations. He argues that the problem with large sections of the social sciences comes from thinking in terms of the individual as a discrete entity – either as a material actor or in terms of their ego – and to position society, in the shape of common institutions such as school, the workplace and the family, *around* that individual.[1] For Elias, there is no 'absolute individual' (Elias 1978: 117). From birth, we are implicated within figurations – the parental relationship, the family, circles of friends, health care institutions and so on – and, detached from these figurations, we could not develop as human beings at all. Individuals are never completely independent but hold a position (of power) in these figurations even at a young age. In this line of argument one important concern for process sociology is to overcome the distinction between the individual and society.

In concrete terms, this means that when one speaks of the individual or of society, one is just taking different *perspectives* on the same phenomenon: the figurations of individuals. One can either take the perspective of the individual actor or one looks at figurations in their entirety, the two perspectives complement each other to form an overall picture.

These perspectives may well contradict one another, for example, when it comes to the function of particular figurations. The social function of a figuration in relation to other figurations might be completely different from the point of view of the individuals who make up its actor constellation. An example of this is the editorial department in journalism whose function as a whole (the production of a particular media product, the construction of public debates and so on) may differ from its function for the individual employee, the freelancer and the data analyst (to make ones living, to advance one's career and so on). Ultimately, these differential perspectives go some way to explain the multiple tensions that arise within and between figurations, tensions that are often overlooked in functional sociology in which the focus is on overarching questions of function (Elias 1978: 126–128).

In not positioning the individual in opposition to society a different view of what the individual is opens up. For Elias, what we call the individual is an ongoing process of constructing individuality at the intersection of different figurations, or as he puts it: 'a person [...] not only goes through a process, he [or she] *is* a process' (Elias 1978: 118). This does not simply mean the process of his or her personal development, as discussed in psychology, rather, it refers to the process of continuous interaction between the individual and his or her figurations resulting in a dual articulation of each analytical object. The practices, frames of relevance and tension-laden power relations within the actor constellation are always part of constructing the individual.

This view coincides with some other approaches in the social sciences. Erving Goffman (1974, 1978), for example, has spoken of the self and personal identity as something that is continuously created in and through the situations in which people find themselves and, accordingly, is neither static nor coherent. Stuart Hall (1992) also emphasized the processual character of identity which he understands as an ongoing articulation, a continuous process of identification. Bernard Lahire (2011) has employed one of the most differentiated reflections on this topic, arguing that each human is a 'plural actor' being characterized by contextual habits. He also opposes the idea that humans have coherent and, therefore, a unified habitus, in Bourdieu's words.[2]

If we follow Lahire, the plural actor is, from birth, embedded within numerous figurations. Media and especially digital media have to be seen in the context of the differentiation of figurations individuals are involved in. We meet online, are part of platform collectivities and are involved in the transforming figurations of friends for whom the open-ended use of platforms becomes characteristic. This results in a plurality which is the reason why in today's differentiated societies even schools are incapable of producing uniform habitus. What we are dealing with is a 'plurality of social contexts and repertories of habits' (Lahire 2011: 26). There is a diversity of figurational contexts in which humans are involved, in which they form their habits, which go on to characterize them as a person. Individuals have repertories of habits which – depending on context – can contradict one another in many ways and do not necessarily constitute a coherent habitus in and of themselves. One characteristic of today's highly differentiated and deeply mediatized societies is, therefore, that no particular habitus or limited set of habitus can develop. Rather, their characteristic feature is the contradictory, power-shaped variety of different repertoires of individuals' habits to which one can gain access by examining contradictions and the power relations of the figurations of which these individuals are part of.

It is to these arguments about the individual that I would like to use as a starting point for my reflections in this chapter. I will switch perspective from one of an overall view of particular figurations and their transformation to the one of the individuals implicated in them. In a certain sense, we are moving towards what has been increasingly demanded of mediatization research, namely a closer examination of audiences.[3] The need to consider ordinary people as actors when analyzing mediatization has been stressed for a long time. In her criticism of research into the mediatization of politics, Tamara Witschge points out that '[m]ore often than not the audience remains an implicit actor, or better yet, a non-actor' (Witschge 2014: 345). She argued that the

audience can also take the role of an 'active disruptor' in mediatization processes. With this is mind, Knut Lundby has put forward the
critique that 'mediatization research is more or less blind to the role
of audiences' (Lundby 2016: 1) while Kim Schrøder has argued that
the role of audience dynamics has been underestimated and under-
investigated. While audiences are discussed in mediatization research,
the point being made here is that there has not enough recognition of
the ways in which 'individual practices may aggregate into a cumulative collective force, which shapes media institutions and the media
landscape as such, as well as their interrelations with other societal
domains' (Schrøder 2017: 88). Recently, Sonia Livingstone made
a comparable argument when she said that 'the lived experience of
audiences is largely invisible' (Livingstone 2019: 175) in mediatization research.

In this chapter I would like to take these criticisms seriously.
What I refer to as an individual perspective does not necessarily
accord one to one with the call for greater consideration of the audience in mediatization research. But to deal with the individual in
mediatization processes means to incorporate this criticism. First,
I will discuss individual media repertoires and how they contribute
to the dynamics of deep mediatization. Then I want to reflect on
the role digital traces and data doubles play in our perspective of
the individual. Finally, I will deal with the question of individual
interveillance and the re-orientation of the self in times of deep
mediatization. In all these cases I take, first and foremost, the perspective of the individual; the relevant dynamics, however, are only
ever revealed through understanding them as unfolding through
multiple figurations.

MEDIA REPERTOIRES AND THE MULTIPLICITY
OF FIGURATIONS

We have already introduced the concept of the media repertoire when
it came to what today's media manifold means for the individual: his
or her practices are not entangled with a single medium but with a
variety of different media, a repertoire of them. Following Lahire's
argument, it can be said that this media repertoire also solidifies a certain repertoire of habits of media use. In other words, many practices

of dealing with media are habitualized to such a degree that the individual is, at best, 'practically conscious' of them (Giddens 1984: 41–45). In their everyday lives, individuals deal meaningfully with the media, but more often than not, they would be unable to discursively express the dynamics involved.

Taking a figurational approach, a person's media repertoire no longer appears as an unstructured totality of all the media he or she uses. Rather, the structure of the media repertoire results from the various figurations in which a person is implicated: in every grouping an ensemble of different media is used and the individual selection of them then accumulates in the media repertoire of the individual.

This structuring of a media repertoire along different figurations and their media ensembles also explains how the concept of media repertoire is differentially scaled within mediatization research, something that was already discussed in Chapter 5. For example, research exists on 'couple specific communicative repertoires' (Linke 2011: 101) that, is the section of the media repertoire that refers to the figuration of the romantic couple. Other research already discussed in this volume addresses various 'information repertoires' (Hasebrink & Domeyer 2010: 49), the section of the media repertoire that serves to provide information on the interests of certain figurations. 'News media repertoires' (Adoni et al. 2017: 226) and the 'repertoire of public connection' (Hasebrink 2019: 1) refer to the section of the media repertoire that is centered around relating with public discourse. As previously mentioned, the term 'communication repertoire' is often preferred[4] to emphasize that in the respective figurations it is not only mediated communication that is relevant but direct communication as well.

The idea of the media repertoire provides easy access to the individual perspective on deep mediatization. The five trends of deep mediatization – the differentiation of digital media, their increasing connectivity, omnipresence, pace of innovation and datafication – are accompanied by a diversification of individual media repertoires. However, individuals are not simply exposed to these trends, but adapt to and appropriate the changing media environment based on their already existing everyday practices. In the following, I would like to illustrate these dynamics by means of two examples, news media repertoires and demarcation.

News media repertoires

Christian Kobbernagel and Kim Schrøder (2016: 18–20) distinguished in their qualitative study a total of six *news media repertoires* through which people in Denmark establish a 'public connection' (Couldry & Markham 2006: 251).[5] These were online quality omnivores, hybrid public service lovers, (light) news snackers, mainstream networkers, professional networkers and print addicts. Online quality omnivores prefer legacy media online, social media online and news aggregators, email alerts and blogs, while television and radio news are assigned a low priority. Hybrid public service lovers find their public connection mostly through broadcast and online public service media. The news snackers achieve a public connection by harnessing frequent news updates in brief and light genres, while television formats and online news outlets dominate. Mainstream networkers' repertoire is characterized by receiving news through one's online networks and searching for news through relatively mainstream national and international news providers, among them lean-forward news aggregators. The professional networkers primarily find their news through online networks (Facebook, Twitter), current affairs programs (radio and television) and professional or party-political magazines. Print addicts' news media repertoire is dominated by printed newspapers – national and local, paid and free – and national public service television news as well as some online news services.

These news media repertoires also correlate with different social positions, milieus and classes. For example, the print addicts indicate a strong upper middle-class orientation as do the professional networkers. Depending on cultural background, the repertories vary further.[6] While these are important points, I want to highlight one more: all six types of media repertoires are about connecting to the figuration of public political discourse which is achieved with a varying media repertoire depending on the individual's media habits. The principal diversity of the public debate's media ensemble does not, therefore, correspond to an equally diverse individual media repertoire; depending on habits, the latter may lessen in diversity and only represent part of an overall ensemble. These habits refer in considerable part to the figurations of families, friends and groups in which the individuals are involved and which also determine the repertoire through which public connection is formed. As Kim Schroder (2017: 100) puts it, 'patterned repertoires represent a ground-level snapshot of the media audience dynamics that are played out across the intersecting communicative figurations in which people live their everyday lives'. It is also a matter of seeing news repertoires in reference to the dynamic tensions brought about by the diversity of figurations in which individuals are involved: The figuration of public debate as well as the figurations comprising a circle of friends, the family and acquaintances which not only shape an interest in public topics but also different habits of media use. At this point, a holistic view of repertoire research is required.

This emphasis on the other figurations in which individuals live should not be misinterpreted to suggest that general transformations would not emerge across various media repertoires. From an overarching, aggregated position, changing news repertoires reflect the general transformation of political discourse whose media ensemble is shifting towards digital media, and to platforms in particular. We can see this in the figures published in the Reuters News Report, where platforms such as Facebook in general are becoming important for public access to news information.[7] News repertoires with an overall digital orientation gain relevance and are especially popular among younger people. But, at the same time, we should be aware that a differentiation of news media repertoires will remain, and this differentiation is related to differences in the figurations people are typically involved in.

Demarcation

While the trends of deep mediatization manifest themselves in various changing media repertoires, we should not assume that individuals are simply at the mercy of this process. Rather, such changes go hand-in-hand with comprehensive communicative demarcations. Cindy Roitsch (2017) has dealt with this issue in a detailed study that investigates young people in Germany.[8] Communicative demarcation refers to the various practices through which individuals attempt to develop a certain resilience to the changes in their everyday lives associated with deep mediatization. The initial consideration of the study is that young people make up part of diverse figurations of communities. Some examples, in addition to their family circle, include the partnerships in which they live, cliques and circles of friends, sports clubs, fan groups, and work or business colleagues. For each of these figurations, a specific media ensemble can be identified. Circles of friends, for example, prefer certain social media for group communication, watch soaps together or play computer games. In sports clubs there is an online information bulletin, instant messenger services or mailing lists as well as a club magazine. Within the family, certain programs are watched together on television, local radio is listened to in the morning, pictures are exchanged via chat and social platforms and so on. If young people want to be part of these communities, they have to insinuate themselves into the respective media ensemble – the social need for communitization shapes the media repertoire of young people more than the media repertoire shapes their aspirations towards social bonding.

From that perspective, young people often experience mediated involvement in different communities as an acceleration of communication, an increasing immediacy in their relations and a differentiation of communicative involvements to which they react by drawing communicative boundaries (Roitsch 2017: 56). Acceleration results in a shortage of time, excessive demands on time and pressure to be constantly available. Their practices of communicative demarcation resist these burdens by reducing the use of certain media, dividing the use of media over time and actively withdrawing from mediated communication. A sense of and need for immediacy means that through the differentiation of media, the reach of relevant figurations is extended. In communicative terms, cliques and young person's circles of friends can be locally dispersed, as long as the platforms on which the corresponding communication takes place are available. Here, too, young people respond with communicative demarcation practices: they focus on certain communities through the use of specific media, restrain themselves in relation to others, or shield themselves by not using certain media at all. The differentiation of communities in which young people are involved means that for them a variety of constraints and forms of social constraint manifest themselves. This becomes a problem when circles of friends are not socially compatible with each other. They react by excluding certain communicative relationships, separating individual communities from one another and concealing relationships with one community from another.

At its core, Cindy Roitsch's study demonstrates how young people, through their broad media repertoire, are communicatively connected to the figurations of communities to which they belong. On the one hand, this creates the potential for community building, but on the other, it is also experienced as a challenge – this is reflected in the acceleration, immediacy and differentiation of community communication. Young people are not simply exposed to these challenges, they react to them with a variety of communicative demarcation practices.

We can see the two examples discussed so far as indications of the dynamic relationship between individual media repertoires and the figurations in which those individuals are implicated. The structure of a media repertoire is shaped by the figurations in which the individual is involved. At the same time, however, people are not simply at the mercy of the media ensemble of public political discourse, the communities of which they are a part of or other figurations. They acquire these practices, they create repertoires of public connection drawn from their overall lifeworlds and sedimented experiences and they draw communicative boundaries. This all represents a complex interplay between the changes in the media environment that solidify themselves within media ensembles of particular figurations and their appropriation in individual media repertoires and practices. It is in the context of this interplay through which deep mediatization has be seen if we are looking at it from the individual's point of view.

We can see also the extent to which individual media practices are part of recursive transformation: Only when media are integrated into people's everyday lives can they exhibit their molding capabilities. Although individuals are not always resistant to change, it is, nevertheless, possible to discern a degree of resilience in everyday practices, something that is evident in the demarcation of communicative boundaries. Or as Kim Schrøder put it: 'it is essential that the individual and collective agency of audiences be kept in sight and that audiences not be relegated to the role of merely adapting to and conforming with media logics' (Schrøder 2017: 110).

EVERYDAY AMBIVALENCES OF THE DATA DOUBLE

The reflections on media repertoires have shown that humans appropriate media in an active process and, in part, productively integrate them into their everyday lives. Such research positions itself within the tradition of investigating media use as appropriation.[9] In times of deep mediatization, the validity of this approach has been questioned, especially with regard to the progress of datafication. The argument is that the digital traces people leave behind during their media use leads to data being processed, the significance of which can no longer be grasped with existing approaches to media research. This results in a general shift of attention in audience research. As Sonia Livingstone argued: 'attention to empirical audiences is easily displaced by a fascination with the data traces they leave' (Livingstone 2019: 176).

With Livingstone's critical intervention in mind, I would like to adopt in what follows a more intermediary position which acknowledges the agency of individual media users as well as the opacity of datafication. I want to look at how digital traces accumulate into a data double that is, on the one hand, a point of reference for surveillance capitalism and data colonialism, but on the other, also opens up spaces of individual agency and self-reflection. These ambivalences of the data double become particularly tangible through the self-tracking phenomenon as it can be realized in both a pragmatic and enthusiastic orientation. Overall, we can speak of an individual 'everyday ambivalence' in relation to the data double: practices of generating data involve people in an all-encompassing digital infrastructure over which they have very limited influence. At the same time such practices open up a wide range of other possibilities for agency related to everyday life.

From digital traces to the data double

As detailed in Chapter 3, digital media are not only media of communication but are at the same time media that continuously generate and process data. They form the basis of a datafied life. This means that 'our data, produced in accelerating quantities and with increasing intimacy, is not just data but constitutive material for interpretative, structuring, and ultimately modulatory classifications' (Cheney-Lippold 2017: 27). The aggregation of data is grounded in the traces that individuals (and their devices) leave behind through their practices as they become entangled with digital media and their infrastructures. To some degree individuals do this consciously; when we upload photographs to or write comments on the timelines of the digital platforms we use, we leave an enduring imprint of our presence there. But more often this is done without any awareness as an (unintended) side consequence of our media practices. Digital traces are left, for example, when using a search engine, when reading newspapers online, or when posting on Facebook or Twitter.

We can extend the notion of digital traces to the figurations individuals are embedded within: An individual's digital traces are also produced by others; when friends, family, or colleagues interact online with reference to a certain person, by synchronizing address books with individual addresses, or by tagging pictures, texts, or other digital artifacts with handles, they inadvertently contribute to an individual archive of digitally rendered echoes. As Louise Merzeau argues, 'we cannot not leave digital traces' (2009: 4) in times of deep mediatization.

Digital traces form the basis for constructing a *data double* that has a dual link to the individual.[10] On the one hand, the data double is built from individual digital traces, it is grounded in the traces that individuals leave behind through the use of digital media and their infrastructures. The individual body and individual practices are observed by algorithms and become a hybrid construction: First, they are 'broken down by being abstracted from [their] territorial setting [and] then reassembled in different settings through a series of data flows' (Haggerty & Ericson 2000: 611). The resulting data double is 'decorporealised'. The algorithms that process the data double are based on the idea of constructing a new, second 'virtual individual'. This corresponds to technology companies' general interest in information on individuals as customers and as the addressees of online advertising. As Evelyn Ruppert (2011: 220) put it: 'Biographical data are the basic identifiers and locators of subjects and include name, date and place of birth, gender and address' (Ruppert 2011: 220). It is through this relationship between individuals and their data doubles that the interest in capturing our data for companies and state agencies arises.[11] But it is precisely because of such commercial interests that data doubles cannot be equated with particular individuals. They are 'not real persons but abstract operations enacted through the aggregation of singular data-points' (Couldry & Kallinikos 2017: 153).

The productivity that the data double can develop is highly contradictory because of its dual character. For state agencies and companies, it opens up the possibility of the comprehensive monitoring of an individual, be it for political interests ('combating terrorism', 'preventing crime') or economic interests ('recording user wishes', 'targeted advertising'). This is where diverse research comes in, warning us of the risks engendered by constant monitoring that the global digital infrastructure makes possible.[12] The most prescient arguments here are those related to surveillance capitalism and data colonialism. The surveillance capitalism critique argues that digital traces enable the accumulation of knowledge to serve the economic interests of a few oligopolistic companies (Zuboff 2019b). Data colonialism assumes that, based on the continuous tracking of individual digital traces, individuals are exploited by integrating them more comprehensively into capitalist structures than before: 'capitalism affirms the uniquely identifiable *reference-point* on which all notions of the self-rest; it is this 'self' whose market potential gets traded in proxy form' (Couldry & Mejias 2019a: 10). This raises the question of not only the potential of representing digital traces in a data double for individual agency but also the limitations as well as the ambivalences in between. These dynamics will become comprehensible through an examination of a concrete example, in this case I will take a closer look at self-tracking.

Self-tracking between pragmatism and enthusiasm

In Chapter 2, we have already taken a closer look at the Quantified Self movement as a pioneer community and the role it plays in the making of deep mediatization. The main argument was that this community's visions of self-measurement and personality development, its experimental practices and techniques paved the way to self-measurement as an everyday phenomenon. With the spread of appropriate wearables such as smart watches and fitness trackers, self-measurement became widespread.[13] As such, it is, to a large extent, highly ambivalent. On the one hand, individuals generate a data double that cannot be surpassed in terms of its scale and intensity: they offer the companies that process their fitness and health data highly detailed information on their everyday routines, practices and well-being in a way that means that these companies can relate individuals' data to their 'identity' on digital platforms. This has been criticized as the colonization of everyday life by an advanced digital economy as well as the spread of the dominant neoliberal discourse on self-improvement and self-surveillance.[14] On the other hand, self-tracking and the collection of the appropriate data serves processes of individual personality development.

We cannot understand self-tracking beyond the other practices of which it is part such as, for example, participating in a certain sport or following a particular diet regime. Self-tracking is a threefold communication practice that involves the software, the self and the figurations of which they are part (Lomborg & Frandsen 2015: 1025). It constitutes virtualized communication with a software system because the digital traces produced and analyzed are presented to the individual as singular communication acts with a data double being represented by means of software. Communication with the self takes place as these systems provide opportunities for self-communication regarding one's own practices. Communication within figurations is typically communication with others about tracked data, related practices and a user's own reflections. All these practices are entangled with various media: digital devices, apps and platforms that we can understand as a repertoire of self-measurement.

Self-tracking is fundamentally embedded within and dependent on figurations that include others – mainly collectivities (groups and communities) and organizations (companies and associations). We can look to communities of practice such as sports clubs or self-help groups that integrate self-tracking into their activities as well as friends and family members with whom self-tracking is discussed.

Furthermore, to really understand self-tracking it is necessary to contextualize the practice as part of other societal discourses. First of all, this is a discourse about quantification according to which apparently 'neutral' and 'objective' data contribute to a deeper insight into the world.[15] These discourses are rearticulated in the assumption that a data double provides a certain access to the self that affords deeper insights into one's own lifestyle thereby echoing the myth of big data. The case of self-quantification in the health domain is particularly illuminating. People increasingly use tracking devices to generate continuous data flows about themselves through which they position themselves into discourses on the 'ordinary' and 'normal' (for example, the average heart and metabolic rates). As Deborah Lupton (2016) points out, this is more than just another 'technology of the self' (Foucault 1988); it is a way of embedding the self and its data practices within a much wider discursive frame that relates to infrastructures of data generation, aggregation and processing.

Having this threefold contextualization of self-tracking in mind – with other practices, figurations and discourses – we can take a closer look at the 'mundane experience' (Didžiokaitė et al. 2018: 1470) of self-tracking. Not all self-tracking is the same and different forms must be seen. In a qualitative study on self-tracking, we distinguished two basic orientations in practice: a 'pragmatic' and an 'enthusiastic' one (Gerhard & Hepp 2018: 683).[16] Orientation in practice means that the overall alignment of self-tracking is part of the individuals' everyday practices, needs and the purposes they attach to them. Pragmatists are more concerned with achieving certain goals in the course of their self-tracking, while enthusiasts are more oriented toward the overall excitement of self-tracking practices.

Pragmatists use self-tracking for particular reasons such as weight control or to manage an illness. They share a distanced, instrumentalist relation to self-tracking, are goal-oriented and have little pleasure for tracking as such. For pragmatists, self-tracking is a means to an end, it refers only to its direct purpose, and the (imagined) endpoint of their self-tracking activities is the achievement of this purpose. The pragmatists are rather ordinary in their lifestyle in the sense that they have no extreme orientation toward health or fitness. Their repertoire of self-measurement is limited, consisting of a smartphone and one or two apps dedicated to their tracking. Self-tracking practices are only slightly supported by the figurations of the pragmatists. However, the goals that they are trying to achieve are deeply embedded within their particular social contexts. With their friends and partners, they share, for example, the aspiration to actively shape their bodies according to certain dominant ideals of beauty and productivity, that correspond with the expectations of health professionals and educational institutions. Sociologically, pragmatists' self-tracking is driven by a 'motivational relevance' (Schütz & Luckmann 1973: 208) to achieve something that is contextualized in the figurations within which they are implicated.[17] Pragmatists engage in self-tracking not because they understand it as a relevant practice in and of itself but, rather, for them, self-tracking becomes incorporated into other essential practices: weight control and maintaining sleep and work routines.

Enthusiasts also understand the technologies of self-tracking as a means of constructing a kind of external authority through which they can apply discipline. But for enthusiasts, self-tracking is not a necessary evil that is merely one component in other practices; rather, it relates to various other kinds of practices such as adopting a healthy lifestyle. Their repertoire of self-measurement is much more comprehensive than that of the pragmatists. Besides apps, it includes various devices (smartphones, smart watches, shoe sensors and other devices), data analysis software and digital platforms for discussing their practice. Discourses about sports and a healthy lifestyle are connected to the enthusiasts' identity, and related practices are integrated into their daily routines. Enjoying sports is an important part of their life that is closely related to health and self-care. For enthusiasts, the reason for self-tracking is to support a lifestyle. Their tracking is not solely self-centered; it also forms part of others' figurations who share similar interests. This could be a football team operating as a community of practice, circles of teammates who enjoy intensive sports training. In these figurations, the exchange of sporting digital traces is common. But as our research has revealed,[18] within other figurations, such as the family and among friends and colleagues, this kind of exchange also plays an important role in the lives of enthusiastic self-trackers. For enthusiasts tracking as a process of collecting, recording and comparing the results has long been an integrative part of competitive sport practices and their related figurations. Using the digital traces of sports activities is not entirely new; rather, it is the execution of the noting and calculating of activities by hand to software-based systems. There is an unproblematic fit between older and newer elements of practice here that serves as a corrective to the novelty associated with tracking devices. This is, in part, the reason why enthusiasts find self-tracking 'unproblematic' and a 'natural part' of doing sports and living a healthy lifestyle.

Our empirical analyses reveal the ambivalences associated with phenomena such as self-tracking and the data double from an individual perspective. There emerges a certain naturalness in self measurement for both pragmatists and enthusiasts, albeit in different ways. For pragmatists, it is clear that self-tracking is an adequate tool for their purposes. While they remain distanced from and somewhat skeptical about self-tracking, self-measurement is fairly unproblematic to them because it clearly helps them to use these technologies to achieve certain aims. And while they are aware that they produce data which are used by tech companies for various purposes, they accept this as a side consequence of their practices. This applies even more so to enthusiasts who integrate these technologies with their lifestyle in a comprehensive way. We can understand both positions as an expression of the increasing self-evidence of self-measurement in everyday life.

The implicit adaptation to societal models of the self under the guise of control is particularly striking here. As our research demonstrates, self-tracking is primarily about exercising personal control over self-development. But this becomes more complex when we examine the character of this formation of the self. The process of self-development addresses social expectations of particular ideas around beauty, physical appearance, professional and personal productivity and health. In Western societies, these types of social expectations dominate popular discourse and these expectations, when addressed in relation to self-tracking, directly refer to the available software tools and the ways in which they are appropriated: from the ways in which norms about healthy bodyweight are institutionalized and materialized as sums of calories within the software, the ways in which appropriate activity is defined as an achievement, the ways in which hours and phases of sleep are measured, to the ways in which ongoing feedback operates as a guide for self-improvement. Self-tracking becomes an instrument the user harnesses as a tool to guide them toward conforming to dominant discourses about the body and mind.

All this relates to self-trackers' attitude to data, commercial data processing and data security. Pragmatists have, as the name suggests, a pragmatic attitude to technology; their primary concern is that technology performs its primary functions and helps them achieve their goals; our interviewees discussed the technology they used purely in terms of its practical utility. Their attitudes towards technology are at times contradictory: on the one hand, pragmatists are characterized by a distrust of and doubts concerning the technical characteristics of the equipment and applications that they use and they express concerns about the social compatibility of their use. They deal with their skepticism toward tracking technologies by emphasizing their independence from the devices and applications and applications they use. Enthusiasts place more trust in the applications they use as well as unquestionably trusting the companies that collect their personal data. Enthusiasts deal with the opaqueness of data processing by assuming that their tracking data is of no interest to anyone other than themselves. They overlook the ways in which their data can be exploited for commercial purposes so that they may appropriate their data doubles as a source of information for personal development.

Everyday ambivalences

Our results point to a general discussion about 'surveillance realism' (Dencik 2018: 31) and 'digital resignation' (Draper & Turow 2019: 1), which both argue that, from an individual perspective, the normalization of surveillance infrastructures – as it characterizes surveillance capitalism and data colonialism – limits the possibilities of even imagining alternatives to data processing and analysis by companies and state agencies. As a consequence, there is a 'common sense' acceptance of data collection, which means that the ongoing analysis of data is taken for granted as data-driven surveillance is justified and normalized in public discourse. This is true not only when discussed in terms of national security and crime prevention, but also at a commercial level where the processing and analysis of user data has become a generally accepted business model. Nora Draper and Joseph Turow – referring to their own work and other empirical studies[19] – describe this acceptance as 'digital resignation': Ongoing data surveillance and a public discourse that buttresses it leads users to a certain resignation of 'inaction, limited actions or inconsistent actions [...] in relation to their privacy concerns' (Draper & Turow 2019: 2).[20] This acquiescence, in turn, grants private companies and government agencies the freedom to continue their data collection and analysis which again reinforces the feelings of individual resignation among users.

This everyday realism and resignation can also be found in our self-tracking example: if people want to use these technologies they are confronted with the fact that the tech companies that provide them will almost certainly be processing their personal data; they are forced to manage this realization with the knowledge that without this data their goals toward self-measurement would not be possible. This ends up in the expression of an ambivalent attitude towards these technologies. Ambivalences arise when one is confronted with a range of options for practice, with different evaluations or frameworks of values that cannot be easily resolved but between which one has to decide.[21] The conflicts emerge between the desire to use certain digital media while at the same time being aware of what is problematic about them. For the individual, these conflicts are not easy to resolve. The managing strategy for many users is to adopt an attitude of ambivalence: even if one is skeptical, uncertain, or does not have confidence in certain media technologies, one still uses them – either because its use provides a range of benefits or because of pressure exerted by others within an individual's figuration.

We can understand such everyday ambivalences as a more general phenomenon by referring back to what was said in the last section about media repertoires. It can be argued that the plural actor Lahire refers to (Lahire 2011: 11) corresponds to what Rössler calls the 'ambivalent self' (Rössler 2017: 84). Because of the necessity to act in a variety of very different figurations each individual is confronted with a multitude of media ensembles through which he or she forms his or her own media repertoire. Dealing with particular digital media then becomes a process of ambivalence management. Ambivalences can then be 'integrated, tolerated, accepted, compartmentalized, they can be reconciled with each other, compromises can be made and attempts made to switch between identities' (Rössler 2017: 92, translation A.H). However, the hallmark of individual life within a media environment characterized by deep mediatization remains as a fundamental ambivalence towards digital media and their infrastructures. This ambivalence is unlikely to go away because these media are not simply neutral tools but must always be considered in light of the power relations of which they are a part.

THE RE-ORIENTATION OF THE SELF

One important transformation that individuals experience as a consequence of deep mediatization are the various forms of communicative embeddedness within figurations. With digital media, ongoing communication can take place with and within them – and in many cases this is expected. To conclude this chapter, I would like to take a brief look at what this ongoing communication means for the construction of the self.

The discussion about the self and its changing construction operating in line with media change has been an enduring research tradition in the social sciences. Following Norbert Elias (1978: 18) we can assume that the self is not a static phenomenon, but is to be understood as a process. The processuality does not only concern the person themselves, but also the figurations within which they are embedded and which are to be understood as part of the construction of the self. As Nick Couldry and I (2017: 145–161) have argued, with deep mediatization the socialization in which the self develops, and existing resources that exist for the construction of the self in the progression of their life course change. Such changes accumulate – as I would like to argue here – into what we can call the 're-orientation of the self'. This generally means that the alignment of the self in and toward the figurations in which an individual is involved are part of the construction of the respective self. So, the question I am concerned with here is: How exactly does the orientation of the self change in light of deep mediatization?

Interveillance or monitoring one's own figurations

To look at the ongoing communication within figurations more broadly, the embeddedness of the individual in many figurations is accompanied by forms of an everyday, mutual observation. Mediatization research refers to this intimate form of surveillance as 'interveillance' (Christensen & Jansson 2015: 1474). This term has its origins in surveillance studies which, as time went by, began to focus on everyday practices. When platforms became part of many figurations' media ensembles, the possibility arose to monitor one's own (future) partners, friends and acquaintances on the basis of their digital traces. Various concepts have been established to describe this process. Mark Andrejevic (2004: 1477), for example, refers to 'lateral interveillance' to describe the use of surveillance tools by individuals for gaining information on friends, family members and potential love interests.[22] Anders Albrechtslund (2008: 1) has dealt with the horizontal practice of mutual observation on digital platforms as a type of 'participatory surveillance', which is not necessarily as sinister as it sounds because it can also take on playful characteristics. Alice Marwick (2012: 378) shines a more critical light on 'social surveillance'; this is when users generate contact but approach its creation by viewing it through the eyes of others to strategically create connections with an imagined audience. All these practices embody a kind of monitoring of individuals that reciprocates the kinds of surveillance carried out by private companies and state agencies. Against this background, the term interveillance makes more sense, especially if we are to grasp the ambivalences and contradictions present in the everyday, mutual observation through digital media.[23]

Interveillance refers to all of the mutual monitoring practices that have been made possible by digital media and their infrastructures. The range of related practices is broad. While it might begin with investigations into a person's digital traces through search engines, interveillance can take on other forms such as the continuous observation of partners, friends and acquaintances on online platforms resulting in reflections on self-presentation and the optimization of data traces against the background of knowing that you are being observed by others. In sum, the foci of interveillance are the data doubles of online connections and one's own data double, a double that is optimized in the knowledge that it is being monitored. However, we cannot see this interveillance as detached from its organizational contexts. Interveillance practices are 'inseparable from societal surveillance processes, foremost algorithmically based commercial surveillance' (Jansson 2015a: 85): Without the collection and processing of digital traces by private companies, that is, without datafication, everyday interveillance would not be possible.

Miyase Christensen and André Jansson (2015) investigated interveillance by means of four ethnographic case studies: one on Kurdish-Turkish transnational migrants in the Stockholm area, one on a Scandinavian expatriate community in Managua (Nicaragua), one on inhabitants of Stockholm and one on inhabitants of a small town in Sweden. They demonstrated that interveillance refers to three modes of routinized social monitoring: first, watching and judging networked others (morally and aesthetically), second, observing others observing oneself (anticipating the gazes of strangers as well as fellow group members) and third, observing one's own data double. The interviewees discussed a range of personal examples of 'how the routinized 'checking' of others is bound up with self-monitoring and social discipline' (Christensen & Jansson 2015: 1481). This includes the monitoring of how one is exposed by friends through tags and images as well as a reflexive stance toward the 'moral premises of social integration'. Interveillance is not simply about controlling those close to you, rather, it is a matter of 'self-making' (Christensen & Jansson 2015: 1485) in the figurations within which an individual is embedded. Interveillance practices became an integral part of the negotiation of belonging and identity in times of deep mediatization.

If we understand the internet of things as part of deep mediatization's ongoing progress (Miller 2019), forms of interveillance do not only refer to observation via social media platforms. The use of everyday objects leaves behind traces of data that make mutual observation a mounting possibility. Especially within the domestic space, figurations can become the object of interveillance: With the convergence of mobile communication technologies and the internet of things, new models of data management can generate 'new forms of observability to fellow members of settings, in the form of what we term interpersonal data, in which the "data subject" is the group' (Goulden et al. 2018: 1580). A shared router at home, for example, makes it possible to observe whose device had been online when and where. This can become a topic in a family or relationships, discussing individual practices and collective expectations. Interveillance then becomes a negotiation process within the figuration itself: It is about drawing boundaries between observability and discretion, about defining a moral order, about dealing with breaches of the rules and the ambiguity of erroneous data logging.

Interveillance does not only need to be considered in relation to deep mediatization, we can also consider it in relation to the flourishing individualization of society.[24] Individualization is not used here to discuss the isolation of the individual, but to describe the shift in responsibility for one's own life course from social institutions to the individual:[25] this opens up certain possibilities; individuals are relieved from the inherited identity-forming structures such as kinship relations, the church and class. But individualization is not a harmonious process, especially when it comes to struggles over resources (Bauman 1998, Beck 1987). It is hard to ignore the ways in which, while traditional and direct distributional struggles lose force, all kinds of other post-traditional and more indirect distributional struggles emerge around material goods, conceptions of the world, collective identities, ways of living and quality of life and social spaces. Many of these struggles no longer fit easily into established analytical frameworks of left and right, progressive and conservative, revolutionary and reactionary. There is a new fragmentation in which ever newer, localized and specific conflicts over meaning erupt; new, unstable interpretative coalitions successively form and reform.

Individualization makes completely new demands of orientation for the figurations in which an individual is embedded. We can *also* understand interveillance as a way of responding to these demands. It is about gaining orientation and recognition. In this sense, André Jansson has argued, relying on Axel Honneth's theory of recognition, that a deficit of recognition through individualization is an important driving force for interveillance. If one follows the argument that 'groups should be understood […] as a social mechanism that serves the interests or needs of the individual by helping him or her to achieve personal stability and growth' (Honneth 2012: 203), mutual observation through digital media is also about seeking the recognition of others, expressing recognition to others and developing the self along these lines. Dominant platforms 'build their success upon the promises of providing solutions to recognition deficit, but contribute at the same time to the reinforcement of interveillance culture through the circulation of simulated forms of recognition' (Jansson 2015a: 87).

From being other-directed to the pluralization of the self

The close interrelation of interveillance and individualization has stimulated a discussion on the change of 'social character' (Fromm 1941: 305) or 'habitus' (Bourdieu 2010: 165) through (deep) mediatization.[26] Stig Hjarvard has developed an argument on 'soft individualism'. His starting point is the book *The Lonely Crowd* by David Riesman (1950), in which the sociologist distinguished three ideal types of social character: the traditional, the inner-directed and the other-directed. The traditional character is linked to agrarian societies, governed by shame and exercised by the extended family and local community. The inner-directed character relates to industrial society, regulated by feelings of guilt. Finally, the other-directed character refers to the expanding middle class in modern societies, less regulated by guilt but by a diffuse anxiety of not being recognized and loved by his or her contemporaries. If we follow Stig Hjarvard, it is this other-directedness, which characterizes the habitus of today's deeply mediatized and individualized societies. Hjarvard (2013: 147) sees three reasons for this: First, the formation of habitus is, to a great extent, shaped through interactions with contemporary society. Second, habitus is reproduced through intensified practices of monitoring of the extended social environment and third, recognition becomes an important regulatory mechanism for the development of self-esteem and behavior. From this point of view, widespread practices of interveillance correspond to the transformation of habitus as mediatization progresses. It is this other-directed character in today's deeply mediatized societies that engenders a type of soft individualism. One of soft individualism's primary characteristics is the predominance of 'weak ties' (Granovetter 1983: 203), weak social relationships that are also produced by digital media. Accordingly, soft individualism is neither a strong, self-dependent type of individualism nor is it a type of strong collectivism, but the result of a 'paradoxical combination of individualism and sensibility toward the outside world [that] has gained ground, while strong social ties toward family, school, and workplace are subject to increased competition from weaker social ties enabled via media networks' (Hjarvard 2013: 137).

Hjarvard's argument somewhat echoes writings that assume the 'network' would become the new 'social operating system' (Rainie & Wellman 2012) of deeply mediatized societies. However, as we have seen in Chapter 4 it is not just networks that matter but the diversity of different figurations in which people are embedded, and which – especially when one considers organizations and state agencies – still wield power over the individual. In this light, reducing the transformations of deep mediatization in regard to the individual to the idea of *one* emerging new social character or habitus thus appears simplistic.

At this point, it look again to Bernard Lahire's plural actor and extend it to an understanding of the pluralization of the self. As we have already seen, the argument goes that in today's deeply mediatized and individualized societies we cannot assume that individuals have a coherent habitus, not even one that embodies an outward orientation. Rather, we are confronted with a variety of habits which we need to consider in relation to the respective figurations in which they are rooted. Practices of interveillance can be understood as part of these habits: it becomes a habit to monitor others in certain figurations and these observations then form one of the bases for personal and mutual recognition and the development of the self. There exists many other habitualized media practices, only a few of which we have discussed in this chapter: practices of self-measurement, practices of communicative demarcation and practices of public connection. These practices contribute to a change in the construction of the self, but not necessarily in a straightforward way. Through practices of communicative demarcation, for example, individuals create the space for their own self-development to define themselves in a mediatized world. Tracking, as we have seen, can also open up spaces for self-development while at the same time embedding the individual via his or her data double into the institutionalizations and materializations of digital infrastructures that depend on discourses of normalization. Deep mediatization from an individual perspective remains much more ambivalent and contradictory than the linear narratives of an emerging new social character or the idea of habitus suggest. Keeping the more general discussion about individualization in mind, deep mediatization is closely related to the pluralization of the self as well as its life course.

The example of interveillance remains of interest for one other reason; it is once again a demonstration of the recursive character of deep mediatization, in this case, from an individual point of view. We have already seen how the collection of data by private companies is intertwined with people's interveillance practices because it is digital traces and data doubles which make interveillance possible after all. Interveillance practices create additional data that can be exploited by the companies concerned: observing partners, friends and acquaintances, clicking, reading, looking and liking create new flows of digital traces that represent intimacy with and interest in other individuals. These data provide the foundations for the platforms' services and business models. The myths that digital platforms would serve 'us', that big data analysis would open up a neutral perspective on each individual in his or her relationships constantly maintain this process.

Therefore, interveillance can be channeled to better understand how the process of deep mediatization is a recursive transformation: deep mediatization is not a uniform process, we have to examine it in detail according to every social domain and the individuals within them. What does exist across these figurations is a recursive dynamic. Supported by the myths of media-related change, the emergence of new figurations as well as the transformation of existing figurations contribute to the stabilization of deep mediatization, the differentiation of digital devices, their connectivity and omnipresence, their pace of innovation and increases in datafication processes. Individual practices are inescapably involved. And as part of this recursive transformation they support a pluralization of different forms of the self. But as we have seen in this chapter, such a pluralization is never random nor unrelated to power. Because of the individuals' embeddedness in figurations we can discern certain patterns, such as patterns made visible in people's different news repertoires or self-tracking orientations. Therefore, we should not confuse the pluralization of the self with the argument that it might result in pure idiosyncratism. As we have seen a deeply mediatized society is a highly differentiated one. But there are patterns within each process of differentiation which we can describe analytically by looking at figurations in their entirety as well as adopting the perspective of the individual.

NOTES

1 See, this discussion in Elias (1978: 13–16, 116–120).
2 The concept of habitus was historically developed on the basis of tribal societies in which differentiation is low. But habitus cannot simply be transferred to today's highly differentiated societies. See, for a detailed discussion, Lahire (2011: 18–26).
3 Referring back to the work by Kim Schrøder, we can define 'audience' here as 'as the people who, in their capacity as social actors, are attending to, negotiating the meaning of, and sometimes participating in the multi-modal processes initiated or carried out by institutional media' (Schrøder 2017: 89). See also, for a similar position, Livingstone (2005) and Schrøder & Gulbrandsen (2018).
4 See, for example, Hasebrink (2015) and Linke (2011).
5 The qualitative study was based on a total of 36 in-depth interviews in which the media used were sorted according to the Q-Sort method (Davis & Michelle 2011 and Schrøder 2016) in order to reconstruct the participants' news media repertoires.
6 Research on media repertoires has shown that the specific media used by migrants differ according to their overall social orientation which can be an orientation to their origin, their current place of residence, or the diaspora community. See, Hepp et al. (2012), where we describe the media appropriation in the Turkish, Moroccan and Russian diaspora in Germany, depending on the

questions of whether migrants are 'origin-', 'ethno-' or 'world-oriented'. In addition, migrant repertories are generally structured differently than those of non-migrants because of their language skills and interests.

7   See, *Reuters Digital News Report*, published annually by The Reuters Institute for the Study of Journalism, University of Oxford. http://reutersinstitute.politics.ox .ac.uk/ (accessed: May 1, 2019).

8   The study is realized in the context of a larger project on the mediatization of communitization in a comparison of different media generations; see, in particular, Hepp et al. (2014a, b) and Hepp et al. (2017). Cindy Roitsch's argument refers to an evaluation of 60 young people aged between 16 and 30 years. For further results from this project, see, Chapter 7.

9   See, Berker et al. (2006), Butsch & Livingstone (2014), Gillespie (2005), Hasebrink (2003) and Livingstone (2004).

10 For a discussion on this term, see, Haggerty & Ericson (2000), Lupton (2012), Lyon (2014) and Ruckenstein (2014).

11 As Haggerty and Ericson wrote: 'The monetary value of this surplus derives from how it can be used to construct data doubles which are then used to create consumer profiles, refine service delivery and target specific markets' (Haggerty & Ericson 2000: 616).

12 See, for an overview, Hintz et al. (2019) and the discussion in Chapters 3 and 5.

13 See, Ajana (2013), Lupton (2014), Reigeluth (2014) and Strübing et al. (2016).

14 This is one of the Nick Couldry and Ulises Mejias' main points of criticism (2019a: 9). See, also Crawford et al. (2015: 493).

15 See, on the development of this discourse, Hall & Link (2004), Crawford et al. (2015) and Mau (2017).

16 The following arguments are based on Gerhard & Hepp (2018).

17 Referring to Schutz, originally German terminology, the motivation to track is rather an *Um-zu-Motiv* than a *Weil-Motiv*.

18 See, Gerhard & Hepp (2018: 694).

19 See, L. et al. (2016), Draper (2017), Hargittai & Marwick (2016), Hoffmann et al. (2016) and Dencik et al. (2016).

20 Such feelings of resignation are a 'typical emotional response in the face of undesirable situations that individuals believe they cannot combat' (Draper & Turow 2019: 5).

21 See, Rössler (2017: 63–93).

22 Andrejevic is particularly interested in the use of professional services such as DateSmart.com, Check-Mate.com and DateDetectives.com, as well as the surveillance capabilities of home computers.

23 As André Jansson puts it, '[w]hen applying the term surveillance to the analysis and understanding of more horizontal processes of information gathering and disclosure one runs the risk of misnaming and simplifying aspects of social life that are dense with social and cultural ambivalences' (Jansson 2015a: 84).

24 See, Christensen & Jansson, (2015: 1481), Jansson (2015a: 85–88 and 2016).

25 For the concept of individualization in an individual perspective, see, Beck (1987), Beck & Beck-Gernsheim (2001), Beck et al. (1994), Giddens (1990) and Hepp & Hitzler (2016: 135–138).

26 See, Hjarvard (2013: 137–152; 2009), Krotz (2017: 360–362) and Gentzel et al. (2019).

7

DEEP MEDIATIZATION AND THE GOOD LIFE

As I explained in the introduction, my aim with this book was to introduce into an already complex field the idea of researching deep mediatization. In the following chapters, we first dealt with the making of deep mediatization and saw how companies, state agencies and pioneer communities in their role as supra-individual actors were decisive for this process. Their practices cumulated in five trends that represent the current change of the media environment: the increasing differentiation of digital media, their connectivity, their omnipresence, pace of innovation and datafication. On this basis, we turned to the question of what this means for our understanding of media. The core argument was that digital media have become even more processual than media in general, but that a single medium's influence is not a decisive factor in the phenomenon of deep mediatization. Rather, it is the manifold character of the media environment, the media ensembles of organizations and collectives and the media repertoires of individuals that should be the focus of our attention. Accordingly, we need an approach when describing deep mediatization that does not aim at the single medium, but starts from the various social domains that make up society. In order to achieve this, I have presented a figurational approach which focuses on the various human figurations and their entanglement with media. The recursive transformation of deep mediatization can be described in how these figurations change and their interrelationship to one another. We discussed deep mediatization's new relatedness with figurations through global myths, infrastructures and data, the emergence of new figurations as well as the transformation of existing ones. Finally, we reflected on what this all means for the individual and their embeddedness within society. While these reflections were largely analytical and descriptive, in this concluding chapter, I have set another goal, switching to the normative question: What would deep mediatization look like if it was to promote a good life for as many people as possible?

If we raise this question, it breaks with the kind of thinking that is common to many Silicon Valley technology visionaries. For example, Kevin Kelly – a technology visionary, founding executive editor of the *Wired* magazine and former publisher of the Whole Earth Review – called one of his books *The Inevitable*. The title is intended to express that our future will be steered in a certain direction by current media technologies. As Kelly puts it: 'There is bias in the nature of technology that tilts it in certain directions and not others' (Kelly 2016: 3). Kelly envisages twelve 'meta-trends' in future development that are 'inevitable', because 'they are rooted in the nature of technology, rather in the nature of society' (Kelly 2016: 7). From this angle, the possibilities for shaping the future are limited by the fact that once developed, technologies define the course of social transformation. One of his examples is 'sharing'; if one understands 'sharing' as a 'meta-trend', a certain attitude towards platforms and their regulation persists while particular ways of sharing might not. Kelly illustrates this with the example of Uber: 'We can and should regulate Uber-like taxi-services, as an example, but we can't and shouldn't attempt to prohibit the inevitable decentralization of services' (Kelly 2016: 5). For Kelly, the 'inevitability' of today's platforms is actually the 'decentralization' of society.

Kelly's arguments fundamentally contradict the figurational approach on deep mediatization that I have developed so far. It would be short-sighted to deduce a linear development of the future from an analysis of the past as it is wrong to position technology against society. The future – including the future of technological development and the ways technology shapes the world – is, in principle, wide open. Here it is helpful to recall Norbert Elias' (1978: 158–167) argument regarding how problematic it is to discuss the 'inevitability' of social developments. If we understand history as a sequence of figurations there are two possible perspectives on how they connect: early figurations connect to later figurations and later figurations connect to early ones. From the viewpoint of the early figurations, later ones are in most, if not all, cases only one of *various possibilities*. From the viewpoint of the later figurations, the earlier ones constitute the *necessary conditions* for their realization.[1]

These arguments shed another light on the 'inevitability' of technological transformations: When one refers to 'inevitability', one adopts the perspective of the later figurations, looking back at their historical development to explain the specificity of today's figurations relative to the early ones. Such an observation should not, however, make us forget that today's figurations allow for a multitude of different future developments. This remains the case even if today's figurations are tightly interwoven with digital media and their infrastructures. Future developments are at the same time not random but, nevertheless, flexible, as media technologies constitute a part of *societal* change.

Against the background of the fundamental openness of future developments, I would like to conclude – as I have already mentioned – with a different take on deep mediatization than in previous chapters. This chapter is less concerned with explaining existing dynamics than it is with the normative question of what kind of deep mediatization we want in our search for the good life. If we understand deep mediatization as a process that, going forward, is flexible in nature, the main challenge is to see it formed in a way which is 'good' for as many people as possible. Such a statement may sound off-hand, but it has two complex implications, namely, what does a 'good life' even mean? And, what does 'form' represent in this context?

The expression of the 'good life' is a puzzling term.[2] What the good life *actually is* can vary according to one's own values, cultural background and the variety of contexts in which one's life may take place. The ways of leading a good life are correspondingly diverse – and one almost tends to say that a part of a good life lies in this plurality and diversity of living. But, if we follow the idea of an Aristotelian virtue ethic, more detailed statements about the good life are revealed. One way to approach the good life is to consider a person's various needs. Adopting a conception of needs based on general 'human capabilities' (Sen 1992, 1999), we see needs as socially constructed and shaped by the common pressures of material and historical conditions. Nick Couldry (2012: 163–179) offers the example of seven fundamental needs based on these assumptions: economic needs (which are related to economic security), ethnic needs (togetherness in ethnic groups), political needs (political inclusion and participation), recognition needs (reflecting social acceptance within various contexts), belief needs (concerning the field of religion), social needs (those of social connection) and leisure needs (recreation). While these needs intersect and the list is open to expansion, it offers a point of departure from which to reflect on the ways in which deep mediatization might enable or constrain the satisfaction of such needs by affording relevant capabilities. But fostering a good life means – also from an individual point of view – more than just addressing our basic needs. It is about leading an autonomous life, characterized by the chance of realizing meaningful projects.[3] Accordingly, we can specify the question of this chapter about deep mediatization and the good life as follows: How should we act in relation to deep mediatization so that we contribute to lives that, both individually and together, we can value at all levels?[4]

This brings us to the point of discussing how to 'form' deep mediatization in order to do justice to such a normative goal. In German there is a better expression for this than the English 'form', *Gestaltung*.[5] *Gestaltung* expresses the process of giving something a Gestalt, a word that is often harnessed in English prose, at least in academic discourse. It does not just mean 'designing', 'making' or 'crafting', it also implies forming something in a positive way. The *Gestaltung* of one's own life, for example, refers to leading the best and most productive life possible. We are, therefore, dealing with a broad field of implications which is why it seems sensible to me to use the expression of *Gestaltung* when discussing the normative expectations against the formation of deep mediatization.

In order to address the normative challenges of deep mediatization, I would like to draw the following lines in this concluding chapter: First, I will go back to the technology pioneers who imagined what we today call digital media as the 'tools' of a generational 'project' for changing society. Questions of *Gestaltung* were also important for them but as we will see in a naïve expectation against the idea that with well-designed technologies everything would automatically change for the better. A criticism of this automatism serves as the basis for my argument to focus on two main issues when it comes to the *Gestaltung* of deep mediatization that could make a good life feasible: first, the necessity of developing new forms of organization; second, a stronger consideration of individual autonomy. Ultimately, these two issues echo the basic idea of a figurational approach, namely, to interweave the perspective of society with that of the individual and to think in terms of processes.

A DEEP GENERATIONAL CHANGE?

There is a plethora of popular writing on the generational shift in relation to the latest media technologies. An incomplete list would contain book titles such as 'Generation X' (Coupland 1992), 'Net Generation' (Tapscott 1998), 'App Generation' (Gardner & Davis 2013) or 'Generation AI' (Hoffman 2019). The most recent discussion concerns 'Generation Z' (Dimock 2019) that is, the 'cohort that follows the "millennials", growing up in a world of smartphones, mobile internet, and the emerging internet of things'. For journalists the enthusiasm to coin myriad terms to describe different generations in relation to emerging media is even greater. The 'Facebook Generation' is here replaced by the 'WhatsApp Generation', quickly succeeded by the 'Instagram Generation' and the 'Snapchat Generation'.

We could dismiss the explosion of these different media generations which represent the profound change stimulated by deep mediatization as superficial generalizations. But that would be too easy: If we follow sociological analyses, the acceleration of social change in general can be seen in the relationship between generations. Popular writing about media generations represents a public negotiation of the relationship between generations in regard to the relevance and position of digital media and their infrastructures in society. Such negotiations are largely about the perception of change: Looking back historically, more comprehensive social changes occurred over three or four generations than took place during the generations they followed. In the last century this 'intergenerational' tempo of change has, as Hartmut Rosa suggests, become an 'intragenerational' one

(Rosa 2013: 109f.). Profound transformations no longer last from one generation to the next but are contained within the lifetime of one single generation. This is especially true for the processes of deep mediatization: driven by digitization, the media environment of entire generations is changing before their eyes.

This alone reveals how questions of the *Gestaltung* of deep mediatization refer, to a considerable extent, to generation. But 'generation' is, in a broader sense, an important starting point from which to begin thinking about the *Gestaltung* of deep mediatization. From the perspective of the digital media pioneers the changes we connect to deep mediatization began as a 'generational project'. As Fred Turner has argued, we cannot understand the emergence of digital media and their underlying infrastructures without taking into consideration the influence of American counterculture from which the pioneer communities of the Whole Earth Network – as well as today's makers, quantified-selfers and technology visionaries like Kevin Kelly – emerged. The counterculture represented a generational project that criticized the mainstream way of life while seeking new forms of community beyond what they understood as an American post-war society in stasis. It was about the 'felt sense of generational togetherness' (Turner 2006a: 54). When the hoped-for community failed, media technologies offered a chance to transfer this feeling of a generational awakening to a new terrain. Here, media theorists such as Marshall McLuhan were vital as their writing 'allowed young people to imagine the local communities they built around these media not simply as communities built around consumption of industrial products, but as model communities of a new society' (Turner 2006a: 54).

The narrative of a generation building a 'new society' through media technologies runs through the entire process of deep mediatization. Since the 1960s, Stewart Brand, the pioneer of the Whole Earth Network discussed in more detail in Chapter 2, has repeatedly referred to the idea of generational change, as has Louis Rossetto in his first editorial for *Wired* magazine in his role as co-founder, editor-in-chief and publisher of the technology periodical:

> '*Wired* is about the most powerful people on the planet today – the Digital Generation [...]. These are the people who not only foresaw how the merger of computers, telecommunications, and the media is

transforming life at the cusp of the new millennium, they are making it happen'.

(Rossetto 1993: 1)

The transformation of the world through new media technologies became represented as the project of a *digital* generation. From here it was only a small step to contrast a generation of 'digital natives' (those born after 1980 who grew up with digital media) with a generation of 'digital immigrants' (those who learned to use digital media at an advanced age and, so we might assume, would never interact with them as seamlessly as the 'digital natives') (Prensky 2001, Palfrey & Gasser 2008).

We can see here a remarkable discursive construction: the generation of those who wanted to change society with digital media technologies imagined the next as the children of this grand project, those who would actually be the ones to carry it out: the digital generation. If one wants to deal with the *Gestaltung* of deep mediatization, it is necessary to be cautious of premature grand narratives of generational change. We need at the same time a broader sociological understanding of generation as well as a more concrete one of media generation if we are to capture the generational dynamics of deep mediatization.

An appropriate point of departure for a sociological understanding of generation is the work of Karl Mannheim.[6] According to him, it is necessary to distinguish concepts of *generation* from an age-group construct based on cohorts. As he points out, every generation is marked by a 'social location' (Mannheim 1952: 291) within a historical context. This 'social location' tends to accord with generation-specific 'experiences' and 'events' (Mannheim 1952: 297) that take place during certain phases of an individual's biography. In this respect, Mannheim assumes that a generation is influenced by the experiences and events that occur in the formative phase of its members' younger years. However, one should not neglect the life events that take place later, especially when these are connected with decisive, generation-specific turning points in individuals' biographies (Mannheim 1952: 282).

Taking this discussion to another level, in light of the figurational approach it is possible to grasp *media generation* in a processual way. One can then define media generation as a thickening of one or more age groups of people who, in their media appropriation, share the experience of a specific media environment and subsequently, based on their personal media biographies, develop a shared self-perception as exactly that, a media generation.

In concrete terms, this means that we cannot assume that a media generation, for example, a generation of digital natives, would share ways of dealing with digital media, would have the same degree of media literacy, or would try out the same forms of new participation through digital media. This would be a naïve understanding of media generations. Media generations are highly diverse, contradictory and multifaceted. What its members share is not the homogeneity of media use, what they do share is their mutual growth into a certain media environment. This conveys what they regard as 'normal' forms of communication; which media technologies and infrastructures are 'naturally' available, which content and media events were 'widespread' in a certain phase in life which all, therefore, represent a common point of reference. The appropriation of a media environment in the respective individual media repertoires and in the media ensembles of the various figurations of which one is a part is highly diverse and stands for the variances within a media generation. Nevertheless, the defining reference point to a particular media environment remains shared and this has considerable consequences. To provide an example: while for older media generations it was especially 'meaningful' when individuals *had* a mobile phone as part of their own media repertoire at a young age, for the current media generation it is just as 'meaningful' when individuals do *not* have a mobile phone as part of their own media repertoire at a young age.

On the basis of this understanding of media generations, we can assume that the different waves of mediatization signify relevant tipping points between generations. Therefore, it is not simply the arrival of a 'new' medium in the process of mediatization which marks the difference between media generations, and it makes no sense to speak of a Facebook, WhatsApp or Instagram generation. Rather, as outlined in the introduction to this book, a wave of mediatization means the emergence of a qualitatively new media environment. The most recent wave of mediatization we can identify is digitalization which entails – as we have seen across this whole book – much more than the mere emergence of 'new' media such as social networks it also shapes 'old' media such as television, cinema, radio and their interrelatedness. By the same token, digitalization does not affect *one* specific media generation – it affects the media environment of different media generations albeit in different phases of their media biography and life course. At this point, we can see the acceleration of change as the 'intragenerational experience' of which Hartmut Rosa spoke: digitalization does not mark a shift from one media generation to another, it is experienced *within* different media generations and at different stages of the generations' life course.

It is here where we can refer to all the reflections developed so far on what distinguishes a media generation back to the original promise of the digitization pioneers. In popular publications a certain picture of the digital natives was painted:[7] digital natives would have a high level of digital literacy, would spend much of their lives online and make no distinction between online and offline. Digital natives would be reachable everywhere and at any time and would exchange ideas openly with people all over the world. Digital natives are enormously creative with digital media giving their creativity a very different expression than the generations that came before them. For the information they need digital natives rely entirely on that available from the internet. Digitally oriented, they build new forms of community and at the same time new forms of political activism. In short, through digital media and their infrastructures this generation would be different and at the same time change the world for the better.

If we argue on a more empirical basis, we must draw another picture of the current spectrum of media generations as my own research shows.[8] First of all, there is not one sole generation confronted with digitalization but at least three different ones. First, the *mass media generation* that experienced the radio, cinema, print, post and the landline telephone in their formative phases and later on became familiar with television, and in old age are confronted with digitalization. At the other extreme, there is what we can call the *digital media generation* that grew up after the emergence of digital media and for whom the change brought about by digitalization is a natural component of their overall media environment. Finally, between these two – a quasi-'sandwich generation' – the *secondary digital media generation* that also grew up with the television, cinema, radio, print, post and the landline telephone, but then more or less comprehensively embraced digital media in the course of their (vocational) life and made it an integral part of their individual media repertoires.

Of interest here are findings concerning the creation of (new) communities by means of digital media. As my research has shown, many members of the digital media generation have a much more diverse repertoire of digital media used for community building than most members of the mass media generation. However, if we then turn our attention to the types of communities that are most relevant, the different media generations vary much less than expected with regard to the discussion on digital natives. As my colleagues and I were able to show, five overall 'mediatized horizons of communitization' – that is the totality of relevant communities in which a person positions themselves – can be distinguished *across* the three media generations: minimalism, localism, centrism, multilocalism and pluralism. These differ in relation to the types of relevant communities, in relation to communicative networking and in relation to the dominance of individual topics of community building.

For simplicity's sake, the horizon of communitization is reduced to very few people and themes. Accordingly, community-based communicative networking is severely restricted in both local and translocal terms. Localism is characterized by a primarily local form of communicative networking. When it comes to community building, the horizon is dominated by (local) mediatized communities such as families, the local circle of friends or the neighborhood. All in all, this horizon focuses on the local experience of community in the city, district or village. Centrism is characterized by a pronounced thematic focus and equally communicative networking. This refers to the dominance of a particular community on the horizon, for example, a particular cultural scene or religious community. The prominent community superimposes a coexistence of further communities. The fourth type is called multilocalism. Its decisive factor is the existence of a translocal communicative network in relation to certain persons or themes at individually defined locations (for example, two cities). We are dealing with the locally related coexistence of different communities. Pluralism, finally, is characterized by very strong local and translocal communicative networking. People within this horizon of communitization are interested in communities related to a variety of issues which is reflected in a scattering of thematic orientations and in the diversity of communities they are involved in.

Across the three media generations there exists a great stability of these types. It becomes quite clear that while with deep mediatization the ways of communicatively creating a community have changed considerably, *the overall orientations toward community are much more stable over generations*. Put simply, we can say that as deep mediatization progresses not everyone becomes a pluralist even if a variety of different communities are accessible through digital media. Or, put differently, as a *media* generation, the changing media environment brought forth by deep mediatization is a matter of course for today's young people. But this does not mean that as a *cultural* generation they are completely different from previous generations in terms of community building – more cosmopolitan, more pluralistic, more open.[9] If one looks at more fundamental aspects of life, many statements made regarding the digital media generation are put into a more accurate perspective.

This does not mean that the new digital infrastructure discussed in this book would not also make a generational difference. But again, we must be careful to not relate this difference to the idea of *media* generations only. If we look at the platform economy again, as operationalized by Uber and Lyft, the generational ambivalence of these offerings is clear. On the one hand, these services operate under the 'myth of glamorized millennial labor' (Rosenblat 2018: 34). As a platform, Uber, for example, addresses an archetypal image of 'millennials', that is, a generation of 'digital natives' as 'active technology users' (Rosenblat 2018: 35) who know how to use these services as employees (and passengers) as part of a flexible lifestyle. This is a construction that we can connect with the pluralistic horizon of community described above. Through this kind of generational discourse, platforms and the work carried out through them, are framed as having higher social value: they represent the positive side of the digital generation – the very well-educated pluralists – while the reality of many working practices is excluded from the discussion, namely that working through these platforms is not the lucrative dream they are endorsed as but merely a means of survival.[10]

As a *cultural* generation, US 'millennials' were and still are highly affected by the Great Recession of 2007–2008, which resulted from the dramatic bursting of the American real estate market bubble. Practically speaking, this means for many, especially those from lower income groups, that the salary of one job does not suffice to earn a living. There is a need, therefore, for additional sources of income which can be found by working for platforms such as Uber, Lyft or Mechanical Turk or by monetizing (rented) property through Airbnb. We can argue that 'the "need" for extra work has been reframed by the gig economy as a positive opportunity for "extra" income' (Rosenblat 2018: 38).

This example illustrates the contradiction of the generational promise associated with deep mediatization: digital media technologies and their infrastructures saturate the life of a digital media generation like no other. The figurations in which their members live are comprehensively interwoven with media technologies; a digital infrastructure exists across these figurations, offering opportunities for communicative networking but also online platforms and other services. However, the idea that this generation would be one of digital natives that would necessarily realize a new and better society through these technologies has proved to be merely utopian. In many areas, 'new' digital media technologies are used to re-articulate 'old' patterns and inequalities. Inequalities spread globally through the digital infrastructures that enable digital platforms. The problem here is that, based on the general myths of deep mediatization, the discourses about a generation of digital natives continue to be served in order to cover up the risks and harms associated with digital media and their infrastructures.

NEW FORMS OF ORGANIZING

The *Gestaltung* of deep mediatization is, therefore, first of all a matter of replacing transfiguring myths of a generation of digital natives with a serious interpretation of what deep mediatization means for different generations, understood here as both media generations and as cultural generations. A first step towards this goal is to accept the extent to which deep mediatization represents a generational tipping-point: for people who are currently growing up, the 'natural' media environment is completely different than for previous media generations. But we cannot conclude that there are linear consequences. In the best-case scenario, this opens up a variety of possibilities exemplified by the potential of globalized communicative networking. But there are many other scenarios such as that of 'surveillance capitalism' (Zuboff 2019b) and 'data colonialism' (Couldry & Mejias 2019b) described in Chapter 5.

But how should deep mediatization then be structured in definite terms? How should we imagine the *Gestaltung* of deep mediatization? To answer this question, it is necessary to think about what the idea of the good life means in practice. It seems as though 'no life can be *good* for a person that is not his own, *self-determined* one' (Rössler 2017: 237, emphasis in original, author's translation). The point is that people can live their lives autonomously regardless of what generation they inhabit. Autonomy does not simply mean the individual freedom to do what comes to mind. Autonomy in one's own everyday practice means being able to 'independently weigh up reasons – namely one's *own* reasons – against one another and take responsibility for the results' (Rössler 2017: 164, emphasis in original, author's translation). An autonomy understood in this way is always a social phenomenon not only because the 'reasons' at issue here refer to needs that are developed in socialization and negotiated in societal discourses. Autonomy is a social phenomenon as a person experiences themselves as autonomous *in* social relationships – in the figurations he or she is part of. If one relates this to the *Gestaltung* of deep mediatization, it is a matter of shaping figurations in such a way that enables as many people as possible to live an autonomous life, one which reflects each person's needs.

This is the normative argument behind the critique of surveillance capitalism and data colonialism: as more and more figurations are saturated by digital media, human lives are permeated with value creation in the interest of technology companies limiting the potential for an autonomous way of life. The *Gestaltung* of deep mediatization should mean organizing digital media and their infrastructures so that they foster figurations that support the greatest possible sense of personal autonomy. Organizing becomes an open sense-making process[11] which must be critically examined and constantly questioned. It is about organizing as a social practice, or to be more precise, it is about new forms of organizing deep mediatization.

The political regulation of digital media and their infrastructures play a critical role in the organization of deep mediatization. In this discussion it is important to remember the horizons of possibilities:

we have become accustomed to thinking of digital media and their infrastructures as something that is primarily organized in the private sector. But this path of thinking refers to a special historical situation, namely the fact that the spread of digital media coincided with the time when media across the globe were being deregulated as part of various mainstream political projects. A thought experiment demonstrates how other possibilities for organizing digital media might just be possible: if one imagines that platforms such as Facebook or Twitter were not invented in the 2000s, but in the 1960s and the 1970s, not one person in most European countries would have had the idea of organizing such important media – which now claim a status as infrastructures (Plantin & Punathambekar 2019) – privately. Can it be that a platform that connects billions of people, collects comprehensive data about them and that is the backbone of public discourse as well as many businesses, is in the hands of a private company? It is highly probable that in the 1960s and the 1970s 'public service platforms' would have been chosen as an organizational model, based on the long tradition of public service broadcasting in Europe (Lunt & Livingstone 2012). Public service platforms should be independent from the state but remain in public hands and, therefore, would not serve private economic interests. The history is a different one, but this thought experiment makes clear what is possible.

This thought experiment also refers to an important opposition, namely, that between 'public value and private interest' (van Dijck et al. 2018: 22). Particularly in Europe, there is a long tradition of considering public value as an organizational principle, not least because it is about enabling as many people as possible to lead an autonomous life. It is about public goods, which are protected and maintained accordingly. But online platforms as they currently exist are built according to a different set of principles. They are not platforms of communities where shared responsibility is at stake, but platforms that address individuals, that offer them services in order to monetize their use and the data they leave behind. As addressed several times in this book, this implies a particular model of society – institutionalized and materialized within these platforms – that finds its roots in the ideas of early cybernetics and the Whole Earth Network, namely, that the best 'solutions' to social problems are found through the 'self-organization' of individuals, a model of society that also becomes manifest in the myth of 'us': platforms serve to make life better for 'us' through their organizational principles.

The regulation of digital media and their infrastructures are not simply about the protection of individual rights. As important as the General Data Protection Regulation (GDPR) act in the European Union is for the extensive protection of citizens' personal data (Hintz et al. 2019: 68–74), regulation should also enable other forms of organization and a *Gestaltung* of deep mediatization to a greater degree. The principle of 'cooperative responsibility' (Helberger et al. 2018: 1) is fundamental here and needs to be considered when questioning platform regulation. With platforms key public values such as transparency, diversity and civility can only be secured through the involvement of various stakeholders such as the companies that operate the platform, its users and public institutions. For a 'cooperative responsibility' four key steps of organizing the (re)distribution of responsibilities are useful (Helberger et al. 2018: 10): first, to collectively define the essential public values that play a role in the particular modes of public exchange a platform addresses; second, each stakeholder has to accept that they have a role to play in the realization of these values; third, a (multi-stakeholder) process of public deliberation and exchange has to be established, one in which agreement on the implementation of important public values can be reached between platforms, users and public institutions; and fourth, this has to be translated into regulations, codes of conduct, terms of use and built into the design of the platforms themselves. We are, therefore, dealing with a proposal that not only focuses on the adoption of certain laws regulating individual rights, but on social processes to establish a shared understanding of what platforms people want in regard to their dominant public values. However, if one looks at the current situation, with Airbnb, Facebook, Uber and others, we are still a long way off from this scenario becoming reality. Even if Mark Zuckerberg was to suddenly declare that a company like Facebook needs tighter state regulation or global governance and that Facebook will in the future focus on 'private communication',[12] the form of regulation outlined above is much broader and at odds with what he imagines.

A great challenge in realizing ideas like these is that many of the institutionalizations and materializations that come about through the design of digital media and their infrastructures remain 'invisible' to the majority of people – which is why we live, so to speak, in 'black box societies' (Pasquale 2015). To break open these black boxes the need for new actors in civil society is greater than ever. As described in more detail in Chapter 2, one consequence of deep mediatization is that social movements find themselves oriented toward 'acting on media': as digital media and their infrastructures become fundamental to an ever-growing number of social domains, civil society actors tend to make them an object of their engagement. This is, for example, an engagement in more sustainable ways of dealing with media technologies, for example, through practices of repairing or fair production (Kannengießer 2019). We also can see this taking place in acts of 'data activism' (Milan 2017: 151), which uses the accessibility of digital data to reveal the risks and harms associated with datafication and make them the subject of critical public discourse.[13] Maps, graphs and visualizations of digital traces are used to publicize the ways in which datafication affects contemporary society. But many forms of data activism are in the paradoxical situation that they leave behind in the course of their political acts the same digital traces and use the same datafied technologies that are the object of their criticism (Hintz et al. 2019: 134).

There are forms of activism that break this cycle. AlgorithmWatch,[14] for example, is a Berlin-based non-profit organization whose goal is to make the processes of algorithmic decision making comprehensible. To make the algorithms used by the German credit check company Schufa understandable to the layperson, AlgorithmWatch created a crowdfunding campaign: interested persons could donate their own Schufa credit information and other core data to AlgorithmWatch. The donation of data by around 3,000 individuals allowed AlgorithmWatch to reconstruct Schufa's data processing techniques leading to a broad public discussion on the subject. We can see this as an example of the breaking open of the digital black box by a civil society actor through which it became possible for others to negotiate what forms of regulation are considered meaningful. Similar considerations are important to The Markup, a New York City-based nonprofit organization that supports investigative data journalism that addresses the ethics and impact of technology on society.[15] The kinds of data collection and analysis are typically so extensive that most news organizations don't have the resources to do so. This gap can be filled by The Markup which aims to secure and support the monitoring of technology companies such as Google and Facebook. We can conceive of these kinds of engagement as activism that seeks to break up the isolated work of data analysts and integrate them more closely into a general negotiation of the implicit societal models underlying data analysis. The 'support [of] new kinds of organizational arrangements to foster a culture of ethical data science practice' (Neff et al. 2017: 96) is one of the starting points for improving the practice of data analysis.

All these are examples of a vital public discourse on how to organize the regulation of technology companies. However, with reference to the demand for a better *Gestaltung* of deep mediatization it is also possible to imagine new forms of organizing in an even more tangible way. Are there completely different ways of organizing digital media and infrastructures than those that currently exist?

If one raises the question and refers to online platforms, one ends up at 'platform cooperativism' (Scholz & Schneider 2017).[16] The core idea of platform cooperativism is ownership of online platforms by the people who produce the content and services they rely on or by the users themselves. A form of organization like this one would relate to income security, transparency in data handling, acknowledgment of the work carried out, co-determined work and a protective legal framework. There already exists various examples of this type of organization. Fairmondo is a Berlin start-up that sells goods online, mainly books, domestic appliances, clothing and food. Fairmondo refer to themselves as a 'cooperative 2.0', which in practice means that it is owned by around 2,000 individuals and commercial dealers who want to trade on the basis of an online platform in a fair way and for fair prices.[17] Loconomics is a cooperative owned by service professionals located in San Francisco 'who want to find clients, help clients find them, and support local business'.[18] The idea is to offer these services predominantly in the fields of care, homework and minimal office support in a fair way without the involvement of brokers or distant investors. Stocksy is located in Victoria, Canada, and is a cooperative of around 980 photographers from 65 countries who offer their pictures directly and for fair prices.[19] The platform operates as a cooperative with three classes of cooperation members, Class A is made up of advisors, Class B is made up of staff and Class C is the artists who contribute content (Marshall 2017).[20]

Journalism has a longer tradition of cooperatives,[21] but here too the idea has received a new boost with the spread of digital media (not least because many jobs in traditional journalism have been lost as a result).[22] The Bristol Cable, for example, is a local journalism coop based in Bristol, UK. It was founded in 2014 and owned by over 2,000 members who each have an equal share of the organization. While local news stories are regularly published online, the main outcome is a free quarterly magazine with a circulation of 30,000 copies. To support new forms of local journalism, the Cable offers free media training with professional journalists.[23] The German *Krautreporter* is a cooperative of more than 400 members who want to support independent journalism.[24] Originally crowd-funded, they have since 2014 published an online magazine to which users can subscribe for a monthly fee. A comparable model is the Swiss online magazine Republik, which was originally funded by a crowdfunding campaign in 2017 and is now owned by the Project R Genossenschaft, a corporative of its readers whose aim is to support democracy with independent journalism.[25] Data journalism itself can also make a contribution to these developments if it includes collaboration, crowdsourcing and co-creation (Loosen 2018a).

These forms of organizing platform- and digital-journalism coops demonstrate that surveillance capitalism and data colonialism are not the *necessary* outcomes of deep mediatization. If we relate the idea of platform coops with the idea of regulating platforms with a cooperative responsibility, the main connection between the two is to bring digital media closer to the figurations of the people who produce and use their content. An increase in autonomy is the result when collectives own the platforms through which they offer their products and services, as well as the data that their products generate. They mark a promising opportunity to break the cycle of expropriation of individual data- and surveillance-based practices which characterize the business models of many of the platforms we use today.

The notions of platform- and digital-journalism cooperatives, cooperative responsibility and a stronger orientation towards producing public goods through digital media certainly leave a utopian taste in the mouth, particularly in relation to the current oligopoly of just a few technology companies. But as examples, they show that a different kind of *Gestaltung* is possible. We can view these examples as an invitation to think more openly about existing path dependencies and about how we want to organize the spread of digital media in our lives. Deep mediatization is not on automatic pilot; it is made possible by human beings and thus remains shapeable by them.

THE NEED FOR INDIVIDUAL AUTONOMY

When we speak of a better *Gestaltung* of deep mediatization, it is also necessary to adopt an individual perspective. As stated at the beginning of this chapter, the focus here is on how digital media and their infrastructures should be structured in order to enable the good life from an individual point of view. This requires some further clarification of the relationship between individual autonomy and the good life. If we follow Beate Rössler (2017: 27) autonomy is a necessary prerequisite for a good life, but not yet sufficient. From an individual point of view, we can refer to the good life as if it is autonomous, meaningful and filled with contentment.[26] As we have already seen, autonomy does not simply imply individual freedom (Pauen & Welzer 2015: 33–36), but the ability to take part in the differentiation of the rules according to which we act. These rules are always social rules, we experience them as part of and alongside others, that is, the ability to choose rules is always a relative one in a set of social rules. Autonomy does not mean freedom *from* the figurations in which people live, but self-determination *in* the figurations in which they do.[27]

The good life is about being able to choose 'projects that give sense to our lives' (Rössler 2017: 114, author's translation). These meaningful projects can vary: specific relationships, professional undertakings, political engagements and involvement in popular cultures. It is crucial that the decision to pursue a project is made autonomously – however the meaningfulness of these projects is never a question of the individual but is conveyed through the figurations in which a person lives. Personality development occurs through the figurations within which a person is implicated and through the projects developed in these figurations. Consequently, the good life is more than a life that meets one's own needs. It is about a life which, in the relationality of the figurations in which a person stands, opens up spaces for the meaningful conduct of life that relates back to individual needs.

If one now applies these considerations to the transformations inherent in deep mediatization, its ambivalences for the individual become manifest. Deep mediatization in its current form can be seen as a considerable restriction to individual autonomy. Examples of these restrictions, as discussed earlier, are diverse and go far beyond the limitation of autonomy imposed by constant accessibility to digital media: there is a restriction through global discourses and myths that position us as human beings in relation to digital technologies; through globalized digital infrastructures and data processing that disseminate implicit models of society in which the individual is paramount, they are a customer and a source of data through platforms that manage new collectivities in which the individual is an isolated worker and consumer. In all these cases, the restriction is that individuals are positioned in a particular way through as well as in relation to digital media and their infrastructures.

At the same time, digital media and their infrastructures – at least in principle – open up new possibilities for achieving individual autonomy. Digital media bring to light new possibilities for (self-)organization, protest, community, learning and self-development. Looking historically at the 'generational project' located behind the phenomenon of deep mediatization, it was these ideas that drove those pioneer communities at the time and they're still doing it today. We can see this taking place in relation to the idea of personality development in the Quantified Self movement, on self-determined manufacturing that supports creativity and learning in the Maker movement, or in the new investigative journalism strategies of the Hacks/Hacker movement. Despite all the ambivalences that also characterize these pioneer communities, their ideas can be interpreted as a call for autonomy.

From an individual perspective, the *Gestaltung* of deep mediatization requires the structuring of digital media and their infrastructures in such a way that they ensure the greatest possible degree of individual autonomy, take individual needs into account and aid in fostering projects aiming to promote the good life. If we take our seven basic needs as a starting point – economic needs, ethnic needs, political needs, recognition needs, belief needs, social needs and leisure needs – digital media would then have to be structured in such a way that they work to secure these needs for as many people as possible without positioning one group of people against another. Digital media and their infrastructures should then help provide access to economic security; to promote the communitization of individuals with different ethnicities (and common understandings between them); they should help support political decision-making in and across different communities, and the participation of individuals in this process; individuals in all their diversity should find recognition in digital media; different forms of faith, religiosity and spirituality should have their place without being exclusionary; digital media should offer possibilities to establish and maintain social relations; and finally they should also make individual recreation and leisure accessible.

A *Gestaltung* that takes these individual needs into account is an important first step. However, the good life means more than that: it is also about individual autonomy and the possibility of realizing meaningful projects. Against this background, at least four demands on digital media and their infrastructures can be formulated from an individual perspective: self-determination, formability, supportiveness and the promotion of knowledge. All four can be understood as basic requirements for a productive *Gestaltung* of deep mediatization, which must be considered while addressing each of these various needs.

The good life requires opportunities for *self-determination* and if digital media help propagate this idea then all the better. Self-determination works on various levels of scale in terms of deep mediatization. It is about individuals being able to decide for themselves what data they disclose, to whom and what benefit they derive from it. It is also about being able to shape one's own social relationships with and through digital media. It is a matter of self-determination, who has access to one's own produced content and how it can be exploited or appropriated. If one considers how current platforms, apps and the various devices that make up the internet of things are designed, it is clear the extent to which they question the principle of self-determination. Popular business models in the field derive from the fact that they utilize user data without considering the perspective of users. The latter must just accept it as long as they want to use these services and devices. Users are constantly confronted with the processes of data-based creation by platform collectivities, part of which they may never see or even be aware of. 'Suggestions' are made for new 'friends' or others to 'follow'. 'Recommendations' are made for purposeful behavior. Surely it is ultimately the individual who should decide whether or not to accept these proposals. In the underlying processes of curating and moderation, questions of self-determination have so far only played a subordinate role.

Formability refers to the user's ability to shape the digital media – especially platforms – they use. In our current digital media environment individuals are confronted with institutionalizations and materializations over which they have no formative influence. The roles as driver and passenger at Uber, for example, are defined by the platform as are the roles as host and tenant at Airbnb. A social negotiation of different role models does not take place at the level of the platform. This is not particularly notable at first glance; other social organizations also impose transactional roles in similar ways. There are two main differences between traditional organizations and digital platforms: on the one hand, there are few other organizations that structure social processes to such an extent and across such different contexts. On the other, principles of operational co-determination – which are more widespread in other areas – are rarely established in larger technology companies. Online platforms' creation of their added value is based on their users' practices and they should, therefore, be afforded the opportunity to participate in the decision-making process. We can consider how drivers for Uber, Lyft and other transport platforms find each other online and articulate their interests as a move toward empowerment.[28] It is then a matter of turning platform collectivities into communities – in this case, a community of drivers that recognizes a common 'we' and articulates their interests.

Supportiveness refers to the opportunity for digital media and their infrastructures to make a concerted effort toward empowering users to realize their own projects to add a sense of meaningfulness to their lives. The earlier discussion on pioneer communities demonstrated the extent to which this is important from an individual point of view. A platform's supportiveness, for example, relates to the development of 'platforms for creativity' (Gauntlett 2018: 231), platforms that help individuals develop their own creativity and support their meaningful life. Smaller, less-established offerings exist on some current platforms – but this should become a general development principle.

Support is also about individual personality development, a point that has rarely been addressed empirically nor from a normative point of view in mediatization research. Individuals develop at the intersection of varying, transforming figurations, 'sociogenesis' (the transformation of figurations) and 'psychogenesis' (the transformation of individual practice, habits and affect) interrelate.[29] If one begins from the fact that with deep mediatization new figurations such as platform collectivities emerge and existing figurations transform, one is inevitably confronted with the question of how this relates to individuals' personality development.

Finally, the *Gestaltung* of deep mediatization is about *promoting knowledge*, knowledge that will empower individuals to access the information they need to develop their own position on public concerns as well their own sense-making projects. This idea is addressed in a variety of traditional theories of the public sphere, where it has been a question of the media making sufficient information available for a conflicting formation of public opinion.[30] In times of deep mediatization we need to develop a broader perspective. Despite the dependency of any mediated communication, deliberate misinformation is problematic. This has been demonstrated not least by the growing discussion about fake news, which has prompted various platforms to apply greater weight to the curation of content and to no longer simply see themselves as distribution platforms only.[31] When we look at the variety of digital media and the relevant information they provide so that citizens may make informed decisions about the political process it becomes clear just how comprehensive this question is. Think also of the trackers and apps that people use to gather information on their activity and health, in so doing, depending on the model of data processing, one and the same activity can lead to different information outputs. It is, therefore, also a question of making adequate and relevant information accessible. The way in which digital media operate partly defines the possibilities for generating knowledge.

These points make it clear that the demands on digital media and their infrastructures to advocate the autonomy necessary for the good life are incredibly far-reaching. If one generalizes these principles and contrast them with the digital media that exist today, the need for a better *Gestaltung* of deep mediatization is quite clear. Questions of autonomy may only play a very small role in the lives of many, per-haps because their social situation makes it difficult for them to make choices about the life they want. People might feel like putty in life's hands instead of feeling like they are on the road to an autonomous life. But we can also adopt another perspective: the very fact that many in this world have little access to the possibility of an autono-mous life demonstrates how important the issue is and how urgent the need is to address it. Digital media and infrastructures can – at least in principle – also advocate for this scenario. Critical mediatization research should not only investigate media-related transformations, it also should reflect upon what alternatives to what already exists might be possible so that space is provided for an alternative approach to its future development.

NOTES

1 As Michael Pauen and Harald Welzer (2015: 280, author's translation) put it, 'Elias' theory is not an optimistic sequence of steps towards a more and more peaceful and freer world. Achieved standards are always endangered because the world is constantly changing [...]'.

2 See, in terms of media and communications research, the discussion in Wang (2015).

3 For this idea, I will refer several times in the following to arguments of Beate Rössler (2017), who published the book *Autonomie. Ein Versuch über ein gelungenes Leben*.

4 Here, I develop further the question along which Nick Couldry has discussed the requirements for a general media ethics: 'How should we act in relation to media so that we contribute to lives that, both individually and together, we would value on all scales, up to and including the global?' (Couldry, 2012: 189).

5 For example, Gestalt psychology is an approach to psychology which argues that 'Gestalt' (a whole form) is perceptually primary, defining the parts it was com-posed from rather than being a secondary quality that emerges from them. Just as widespread is the term 'Gestalt therapy', a method of awareness practice. Along these lines, the term 'Gestalt' in English refers to a collection of physical, biological, psychological or symbolic elements that creates a whole, which is more than the sum of its parts.

6 See, for example, Bolin (2016), Siibak et al. (2014), Vittadini et al. (2013), Volkmer (2006) and Wachelder (2019), who all base their reflections on media generations by referring back to the sociological concepts of Karl Mannheim.

7 See, in particular, Palfrey and Gasser (2008: ii–xv) and Prensky (2001).

8 See, Hepp et al. (2014a, b) and Hepp et al. (2017), the results of which are similar to Bolin (2017), Opermann (2014), Siibak et al. (2014) and Vittadini et al. (2013).

9   I am referring here to the concept of the 'cultural generation', as used by Monika Wohlrab-Sahr, who defines these generations by their 'generation-specific upheavals of the world view' (Wohlrab-Sahr 2002: 209).

10 As Rosenblat puts it, 'by using the image of a millennial to identify who workers are in the gig economy, Uber and other on-demand platforms project a higher social status onto work that has long been associated with lower-status workers' (Rosenblat 2018: 37).

11 For just such an understanding of 'organizing' see, in particular, Weick (1979) and Weick et al. (2005).

12 See, Zuckerberg (2019). As Carys Afoko (2019) put it, it 'is not whether to regulate social media companies such as Facebook, but how to'. For all of Zuckerberg's statements, see, www.zuckerbergfiles.org/ (accessed: May 1, 2019).

13 See also, Milan & Velden (2016) and Hintz et al. (2019: 131–134).

14 For further information on the following, see, https://algorithmwatch.org/black box-schufa-auswertung-von-openschufa-veroeffentlicht/ (accessed: May 1, 2019).

15 See, https://themarkup.org and www.taz.de/!5538173 (accessed: May 1, 2019). Started with a donation of $ 20 million by Craig Newman, the nonprofit organization is in a crisis in spring 2019 after a part of the founding team left The Markup.

16 More about this initiative on 'platform corporatism' established by the Platform Cooperativism Consortium of The New School, can be found here: https://platform.coop (accessed: May 1, 2019).

17 See, for more information, https://info.fairmondo.de/geno20/ (accessed: May 1, 2019).

18 For more information about this platform, see, https://loconomics.com/#!about/us (accessed: May 1, 2019).

19 See, for more information, www.stocksy.com/service/about/ (accessed: May 1, 2019).

20 These examples are discussed by Scholz (2017: 175–179) and Scholz & Schneider (2017: 75–90).

21 One good example is the German taz, which is a printed and online newspaper founded in 1978 (www.taz.de). Another example is the community-based, and now employee-owned, *West Highland Free Press*, which was founded in 1972 (www.whfp.com).

22 See, Fenton et al. (2010).

23 See, https://thebristolcable.org (accessed: May 1, 2019).

24 Details can be found on their web page: http://genossenschaft.krautreporter.de (accessed: May 1, 2019).

25 See, www.republik.ch/statuten and https://project-r.construction (accessed: May 1, 2019).

26 In the German original, Rössler makes the distinction between the 'good life' ('gutes Leben') and a 'successful life' ('gelungenes Leben'), since philosophical literature discusses forms of the 'good life' that are not self-determined (cf. Rössler 2017: 27, 231–279). In the following, I have not adopted this distinction, on the one hand, because the concept of the 'good life' is firmly established in

media and communications research, and, on the other, because the concept of 'gelungenes Leben' can only be insufficiently translated as a 'successful life'.

27 In this sense, autonomy does not contradict dependency (Jansson 2018: 7). Individuals can only experience autonomy in relation to their dependence on other people, that is, in the figurations in which they stand. Michael Pauen and Harald Welzer call this the 'dialectic of autonomy'. Among others, with reference to Elias, they state that 'humans do not occur in the singular, but only in relationships with others, and a human brain does not develop alone, but organizes itself in its synaptic architecture according to the social and cultural contexts mediated by the relationships of which it is a part' (Pauen & Welzer 2015 265f., author's translation).

28 See, Rosenblat (2018: 199–202).

29 See, Elias (2000 and 1991).

30 One can think, for example, of Habermas' (1989) criticism of the 'structural change of the public sphere', in which he criticized the traditional mass media for reporting less and less on public concerns. For further discussion, see, Lunt and Livingstone (2013).

31 The challenges posed by this issue has prompted Facebook to consider becoming a 'privacy focused' platform for communication in groups of people who know each other. Whether these ideas will ever be implemented is another question, especially as they contradict Facebook's primary business model (Hern 2019).

REFERENCES

Aarsand, P.A. (2007) Computer and video games in family life. The digital divide as a resource in intergenerational interactions. *Childhood*, 14, pp. 235–256.

Abbate, J. (1999) *Inventing the internet*. MIT Press, Cambridge, MA.

Abend, P. & Fuchs, M. (Eds.) (2016) *Quantified selves and statistical bodies*. transcript, Bielefeld.

Adoni, H. et al. (2017) Introduction: News consumption as a democratic resource - news media repertoires across Europe. *Participations*, 14, pp. 226–252.

Afoko, C. (2019) Government can't regulate Facebook - it's up to all of us. *The Guardian*, April 1st, retrieved from: https://www.theguardian.com/commentisfre e/2019/apr/01/government-regulate-facebook-mark-zuckerberg-social-media (Last accessed: 15th August 2019).

Agar, J. (2003) *Constant touch: A brief history of the mobile phone*. Icon Books Ltd, Cambridge.

Ajana, B. (2013) *Governing through biometrics: The biopolitics of identity*. Palgrave Macmillan, Basingstoke.

Ajana, B. (2017) Digital health and the biopolitics of the quantified self. *Digital Health*, 3, pp. 1–18.

Albrechtslund, A. (2008) Online social networking as participatory surveillance. *First Monday*, 13, March 3rd, retrieved from: https://firstmonday.org/article/view/214 2/1949 (Last accessed: 15th August 2019).

Alexander, C.P. (1983) The new economy. *Time Magazine*, May 30th, retrieved from: http://content.time.com/time/magazine/article/0,9171,926013,00.html (Last accessed: 15th August 2019).

Alexander, J.C. et al. (Eds.) (1987) *The micro-macro link*. University of California Press, Berkeley, Los Angeles.

Altheide, D.L. (2018) The media syndrome and reflexive mediation. In *Media logic(s) revisited: Modelling the interplay between media institutions, media technology and societal change* (Eds, Thimm, C., Anastasiadis, M. & Einspänner-Pflock, J.) Palgrave Macmillan, London, pp. 11–39.

Altheide, D.L. & Snow, R.P. (1979) *Media logic*. Sage, Beverly Hills.

Amoore, L. & Piotukuh, V. (Eds.) (2016) *Algorithmic life: Calculative devices in the age of big data*. Routledge, London.

Andersen, J. (2018) Archiving, ordering, and searching: Search engines, algorithms, databases, and deep mediatization. *Media, Culture & Society*, 40, pp. 1135–1150.

Anderson, B. (1983) *Imagined communities: Reflections on the origins and spread of nationalism*. Verso, New York.

Anderson, C. (2008) The end of theory: The data deluge makes the scientific method obsolete. *Wired Magazine*, June 23rd, retrieved from: https://www.wired. com/2008/06/pb-theory/ (Last accessed: 15th August 2019).

Anderson, C. (2012) *Makers: The new industrial revolution.* Random House, New York, London.

Anderson, C.W. (2013) Towards a sociology of computational and algorithmic journalism. *New Media & Society*, 15, pp. 1005–1021.

Anderson, C.W., Bell, E. & Shirky, C. (2012) *Post-industrial journalism: Adapting to the present.* Tow Center for Digital Journalism, New York.

Andrejevic, M. (2004) The work of watching one another: Lateral surveillance, risk, and governance. *Surveillance & Society*, 2, pp. 479–497.

Andrejevic, M. (2017) Digital citizenship and surveillance: To pre-empt a thief. *International Journal of Communication*, 11, pp. 879–896.

Appelgren, E. & Nygren, G. (2014) Data journalism in Sweden. Introducing new methods and genres of journalism into "old" organizations. *Digital Journalism*, 2, pp. 394–405.

Arora, P. (2019) *The next billion users: Digital life beyond the west.* Harvard University Press, Cambridge, MA.

Asp, K. (1990) Medialization, media logic and mediarchy. *Nordicom Review*, 11, pp. 47–50.

Astheimer, J., Neumann-Braun, K. & Schmidt, A. (2011) MyFace: Die Portraitfotografie im Social Web. In *Freundschaft und Gemeinschaft im Social Web: Bildbezogenes Handeln und Peergroup-Kommunikation auf Facebook & Co* (Eds, Neumann-Braun, K. & Autenrieth, U.P.) Nomos, Baden-Baden, pp. 79–122.

Atkinson, P. (2006) Do it yourself: Democracy and design. *Journal of Design History*, 19, pp. 1–10.

Baack, S. (2015) Datafication and empowerment: How the open data movement re-articulates notions of democracy, participation, and journalism. *Big Data & Society*, pp. 1–11. doi: 2053951715594634.

Bakardjieva, M. (2015) Rationalizing sociality: An unfinished script for socialbots. *The Information Society*, 31, pp. 244–256.

Baker, S.A. (2011) The mediated crowd: New social media and new forms of rioting. *Sociological Research Online*, 16, pp. 1–5.

Barbrook, R. & Cameron, A. (1996) The Californian ideology. *Science as Culture*, 6, pp. 44–72.

Barile, N. & Sugiyama, S. (2015) The automation of taste: A theoretical exploration of mobile ICTs and social robots in the context of music consumption. *International Journal of Social Robotics*, 7, pp. 407–416.

Barthes, R. (2000) *Mythologies.* Vintage Books, London.

Bauman, Z. (1998) *Work, consumerism and the new poor.* Open University Press, London.

Bauman, Z. (2000) *Liquid modernity.* Polity Press, Cambridge, Oxford.

Bauman, Z. (2005) *Liquid life.* Polity Press, Cambridge.

Bausinger, H. (1984) Media, technology and daily life. *Media, Culture & Society*, 6, pp. 343–351.

Beck, U. (1987) Beyond status and class: Will there be an individualized class society? In *Modern German sociology* (Eds, Meja, V., Misgeld, D. & Stehr, N.) Columbia University Press, New York, pp. 340–355.

Beck, U. & Beck-Gernsheim, E. (2001) *Individualization: Institutionalized individualism and its social and political consequences*. Sage, London, New Delhi.

Beck, U., Giddens, A. & Lash, S. (1994) *Reflexive modernization: Politics, tradition and aesthetics in the modern social order*. Polity Press, Cambridge.

Beer, D. (2016) *Metric power*. Palgrave, London.

Beer, D. (2017) The social power of algorithms. *Information, Communication & Society*, 20, pp. 1–13.

Beer, D. (2019) *The data gaze: Capitalism, power, perception*. Sage, London.

Bell, E.J. et al. (2017) *The platform press: How Silicon Valley reengineered journalism*. Tow Center for Digital Journalism, New York.

Benjamin, W. (1977) The work of art in the age of mechanical reproduction. In *Mass communication and society* (Eds, Curran, J., Gurevitch, M. & Woollacott, J.) Edward Arnold, London, pp. 384–408.

Bennett, W.L. & Segerberg, A. (2012) The logic of connective action: Digital media and the personalization of contentious politics. *Information, Communication & Society*, 15, pp. 739–768.

Bennett, W.L. & Segerberg, A. (2013) *The logic of connective action: Digital media and the personalization of contentious politics*. Cambridge University Press, Cambridge.

Bentley, R.A. & O'Brien, M.J. (2017) *The acceleration of cultural change: From ancestors to algorithms*. MIT Press, Cambridge, MA.

Berg, M. & Hepp, A. (2018) A qualitative network approach to transmedia communication. In *The Routledge companion to transmedia studies* (Eds, Freeman, M. & Gambarato, R.R.) Routledge, London, pp. 455–463.

Berger, P.L. & Luckmann, T. (1966) *The social construction of reality: A treatise in the sociology of knowledge*. Penguin, London.

Berker, T. et al. (Eds.) (2006) *Domestication of media and technology*. Open University Press, London.

Bessi, A. & Ferrara, E. (2016) Social bots distort the 2016 U.S. presidential election online discussion. *First Monday*, 21, November 7th, retrieved from: https://firstmonday.org/article/view/7090/5653 (Last accessed: 15th August 2019).

Bird, S.E. (2011) Are we all produsers now? *Cultural Studies*, 25, pp. 502–516.

Bjur, J. et al. (2014) Cross-media use: Unfolding complexities in contemporary audiencehood. In *Audience transformations: Shifting audience positions in late modernity* (Eds, Carpentier, N., Schrøder, K.C. & Hallet, L.) Routledge, London, pp. 15–29.

Blöbaum, B. (1994) *Journalismus als soziales System: Geschichte, Ausdifferenzierung und Verselbständigung*. Westdeutscher Verlag, Opladen.

Bloom, T., Cleary, J. & North, M. (2016) Traversing the "twittersphere". Social media policies in international news operations. *Journalism Practice*, 10, pp. 343–357.

Blumer, H. (1954) What is wrong with social theory? *American Sociological Review*, 19, pp. 3–10.

Boase, J. (2008) Personal networks and the personal communication system. *Information, Communication & Society*, 11, pp. 490–508.

Boczkowski, P.J. (2004) *Digitizing the news: Innovation in online newspapers*. MIT Press, Cambridge, MA.

Böhle, K. & Bopp, K. (2014) What a vision: The artificial companion. A piece of vision assessment including an expert survey. *Science, Technology & Innovation Studies*, 10, pp. 155–186.

Böhle, K. & Pfadenhauer, M. (2014) Social robots call for social sciences. *Science, Technology & Innovation Studies*, 10, pp. 3–10.

Böhlen, M. & Karppi, T. (2017) The making of robot care. *Transformations*, 29, pp. 1–22.

Bolin, G. (2011) *Value and the media: Cultural production and consumption in digital markets*. Ashgate, Farnham.

Bolin, G. (2014) Institution, technology, world: Relationships between the media, culture and society. In *Mediatization of communication* (Ed, Lundby, K.) de Gruyter, Berlin, pp. 175–197.

Bolin, G. (2016) Passion and nostalgia in generational media experiences. *European Journal of Cultural Studies*, 19, pp. 250–264.

Bolin, G. (2017) *Media generations: Experience, identity and mediatised social change*. Routledge, London.

Bolin, G. & Hepp, A. (2017) The complexities of mediatization: Charting the road ahead. In *Dynamics of mediatization* (Eds, Driessens, O. et al.) Palgrave, London, pp. 315–331.

Boltanski, L. & Thévenot, L. (2006) *On justification: Economies of worth*. Princeton University Press, Princeton.

Bolter, J.D. & Grusin, R. (2000) *Remediation: Understanding new media*. MIT Press, Cambridge, MA, London.

Borges-Rey, E. (2016) Unravelling data journalism. A study of data journalism practice in British newsrooms. *Journalism Practice*, 10, pp. 833–843.

Born, G. (2005) *Uncertain vision: Birt, Dyke and the reinvention of the BBC*. Random House, London, New York.

Bostrom, N. (2005) In defense of posthuman dignity. *Bioethics*, 19, pp. 202–214.

Bourdieu, P. (1977) *Outline of a theory of practice*. Cambridge University Press, Cambridge.

Bourdieu, P. (1992) *The logic of practice*. Polity Press, Cambridge.

Bourdieu, P. (1993) *The field of cultural production: Essays on art and literature*. Polity Press, Cambridge.

Bourdieu, P. (2010) *Distinction: A social critique of the judgement of taste*. Routledge, London, New York.

Bowker, G.C. et al. (2010) Toward information infrastructure studies: Ways of knowing in a networked environment. In *International handbook of internet research* (Eds, Hunsinger, J., Klastrup, L. & Allen, M.) Springer Netherlands, Dordrecht, pp. 97–117.

boyd, d. (2010) Social network sites as networked publics: Affordances, dynamics, and implications. In *Networked self: Identity, community, and culture on social network sites* (Ed, Papacharissi, Z.) Routledge, London, pp. 39–58.

boyd, d. & Crawford, K. (2012) Critical questions for big data: Provocations for a cultural, technological, and scholarly phenomenon. *Information, Communication & Society*, 15, pp. 662–679.

Brand, S. (1987) *The media lab: Inventing the future at MIT*. Viking, New York.

Breiter, A. (2014) Schools as mediatized organizations from a cross-cultural perspective. In *Mediatized worlds* (Eds, Hepp, A. & Krotz, F.) Palgrave, London, pp. 288–303.

Breiter, A. & Hepp, A. (2017) The complexity of datafication: Putting digital traces in context. In *Communicative figurations: Rethinking mediatized transformations* (Eds, Hepp, A., Breiter, A. & Hasebrink, U.) Palgrave Macmillan, London, pp. 387–406.

Brejzek, T. (2010) From social network to urban intervention: On the scenographies of flash mobs and urban swarms. *International Journal of Performance Arts & Digital Media*, 6, pp. 109–122.

Bridle, J. (2018) *New dark age: Technology and the end of the future*. Verso, London.

Briggs, A. & Burke, P. (2009) *A social history of the media: From Gutenberg to the Internet. Third edition*. Polity Press, Cambridge.

Briggs, M. (2012) *Entrepreneurial journalism: How to build what's next for news*. CQ Press, London.

Broussard, M. (2015) Artificial intelligence for investigative reporting: Using an expert system to enhance journalists' ability to discover original public affairs stories. *Digital Journalism*, 3, pp. 814–831.

Broussard, M. (2018) *Artificial unintelligence: How computers misunderstand the world*. MIT Press, Cambridge, MA, London.

Bruns, A. & Schmidt, J. (2011) Produsage: A closer look at continuing developments. *New Review of Hypermedia and Multimedia*, 17, pp. 3–7.

Bryce, J.W. & Leichter, H.J. (1983) The family and television. Forms of mediation. *Journal of Family Issues*, 2, 4, pp. 309–328.

Bucher, T. (2012) The friendship assemblage: Investigating programmed sociality on Facebook. *Television & New Media*, 14, pp. 479–493.

Bucher, T. & Helmond, A. (2018) The affordances of social media platforms. In *The SAGE handbook of social media* (Eds, Burgess, J., Poell, T. & Marwick, A.) Sage Publications, London, pp. 233–253.

Bunz, M. (2009) *Die Geschichte des Internet: Vom Speicher zum Verteiler*. Kadmos, Berlin.

Bunz, M. & Meikle, G. (2018) *The Internet of things*. Polity Press, Cambridge.

Burkhardt, M. (2015) *Digitale Datenbanken: Eine Medientheorie im Zeitalter von Big Data*. transcript, Bielefeld.

Burston, J., Dyer-Witheford, N. & Hearn, A. (2010) Digital labour: Workers, authors, citizens. *Special issue, Ephemera: Theory and Politics in Organization*, 10, pp. 214–221.

Bush, V. (1945) As we may think. *The Atlantic Monthly*, 176, pp. 101–108.

Butsch, R. & Livingstone, S.M. (Eds.) (2014) *Meanings of audiences: Comparative discourses*. Routledge, London.

Carlson, M. (2007) Order versus access: News search engines and the challenge to traditional journalistic roles. *Media, Culture and Society*, 29, pp. 1014–1030.

Carlson, M. (2015) The robotic reporter. *Digital Journalism*, 3, pp. 416–431.

Carlson, M. (2016) Metajournalistic discourse and the meanings of journalism: Definitional control, boundary work, and legitimation. *Communication Theory*, 26, pp. 349–368.

Carlson, M. & Usher, N. (2016) News startups as agents of innovation. *Digital Journalism*, 4, pp. 563–581.

Carneiro, H.A. & Mylonakis, E. (2009) Google trends: A web-based tool for real-time surveillance of disease outbreaks. *Clinical Infectious Diseases*, 49, pp. 1557–1564.

Carr, N. (2009) *The big switch: Rewiring the world, from Edison to Google*. W.W. Norton, New York.

Castells, M. (1996) *The rise of the network society. The information age: Economy, society and culture. Vol. 1.* Blackwell, Oxford.

Castells, M. (2001) *The Internet galaxy: Reflections on the internet, business, and society.* Oxford University Press, Oxford.

Castells, M. (2009) *Communication power.* Oxford University Press, Oxford.

Caswell, D. & Dörr, K. (2018) Automated journalism 2.0: Event-driven narratives. *Journalism Practice*, 12, pp. 477–496.

Chadha, M. (2016) Work and identity negotiation in hyperlocal news startups. *Journalism Practice*, 10, pp. 697–714.

Chadwick, A. (2017) *The hybrid media system: Politics and power. Second edition.* Oxford University Press, Oxford.

Chapman, J.L. (2005) *Comparative media history: An introduction - 1789 to the present.* Polity Press, Cambridge.

Chen, B.X. (2011) *Always on.* Da Capo Press, Philadelphia.

Cheney-Lippold, J. (2017) *We are data: Algorithms and the making of our digital selves.* New York University Press, New York.

Child, J.T. & Westermann, D.A. (2013) Let's be Facebook friends: Exploring parental Facebook friend requests from a communication privacy management (CPM) perspective. *Journal of Family Communication*, 13, pp. 46–59.

Choi, H. & Varian, H. (2012) Predicting the present with Google trends. *Economic Record*, 88, pp. 2–9.

Christensen, M. & Jansson, A. (2015) Complicit surveillance, interveillance, and the question of cosmopolitanism: Toward a phenomenological understanding of mediatization. *New Media & Society*, 17, pp. 1473–1491.

Clark, L.S. (2012) *The parent app: Understanding families in the digital age.* Oxford University Press, Oxford.

Clerwall, C. (2014) Enter the robot journalist: Users' perceptions of automated content. *Journalism Practice*, 8, pp. 519–531.

Coleman, G.E. (2013) *Coding freedom: The ethics and aesthetics of hacking.* Princeton University Press, Princeton.

Cormen, T. (2013) *Algorithms unlocked.* MIT Press, Cambridge, MA, London.

Correa, T. et al. (2015) Brokering new technologies: The role of children in their parents' usage of the Internet. *New Media & Society*, 17, pp. 483–500.

Cottle, S. & Ashton, M. (1999) From BBC newsroom to BBC newscentre: On changing technology and journalist practices. *Convergence*, 5, pp. 22–43.

Couldry, N. (2004) Theorising media as practice. *Social Semiotics*, 14, pp. 115–132.

Couldry, N. (2006) Transvaluing media studies: Or, beyond the myth of the mediated centre. In *Media and cultural theory* (Eds, Curran, J. & Morley, D.) Routledge, London u. a., pp. 177–194.

Couldry, N. (2009) Does "the media" have a future? *European Journal of Communication*, 24, pp. 437–450.

Couldry, N. (2012) *Media, society, world: Social theory and digital media practice.* Polity Press, Cambridge, Oxford.

Couldry, N. (2014a) A necessary disenchantment: Myth, agency and injustice in a digital world. *Social Review*, 62, pp. 880–897.

Couldry, N. (2014b) The myth of 'us': Digital networks, political change and the production of collectivity. *Information, Communication & Society*, 18, pp. 608–626.

Couldry, N. & Hepp, A. (2013) Conceptualising mediatization: Contexts, traditions, arguments. *Communication Theory*, 23, pp. 191–202.

Couldry, N. & Hepp, A. (2017) *The mediated construction of reality.* Polity Press, Cambridge.

Couldry, N. & Kallinikos, J. (2017) Ontology. In *The SAGE handbook of social media* (Eds, Burgess, J., Marwick, A. & Poell, T.) Sage, London, pp. 146–159.

Couldry, N., Livingstone, S.M. & Markham, T. (2007) *Media consumption and public engagement: Beyond the presumption of attention.* Palgrave, Houndmills.

Couldry, N. & Markham, T. (2006) Public connection through media consumption: Between oversocialization and de-socialization. *The Annals of the American Academy of Political and Social Science*, 608, pp. 251–269.

Couldry, N. & Mejias, U.A. (2019a) Data colonialism: Rethinking big data's relation to the contemporary subject. *Television & New Media*, 20, pp. 336–349.

Couldry, N. & Mejias, U.A. (2019b) *The costs of connection: How data is colonizing human life and appropriating it for capitalism.* Stanford University Press, Stanford.

Couldry, N. & Turow, J. (2014) Advertising, big data and the clearance of the public realm: Marketers' new approaches to the content subsidy. *International Journal of Communication*, 8, pp. 1710–1726.

Coupland, D. (1992) *Generation X - tales from an accelerated culture.* St. Martin's Press, New York.

Crawford, K., Gray, M.L. & Miltner, K. (2014) Critiquing big data: Politics, ethics, epistemology. Special section introduction. *International Journal of Communication*, 8, 10, pp. 1663–1672.

Crawford, K. & Joler, V. (2018) Anatomy of an AI system. The Amazon Echo as an anatomical map of human labor, data and planetary resources. *AI Now Institute and Share Lab*, September 7th, retrieved from: https://anatomyof.ai (Last accessed: 15th August 2019).

Crawford, K., Lingel, J. & Karppi, T. (2015) Our metrics, ourselves: A hundred years of self-tracking from the weight scale to the wrist wearable device. *European Journal of Cultural Studies*, 18, pp. 479–496.

Crawford, K. & Robinson, P. (2013) Beyond generations and new media. In *A companion to new media dynamics*. Wiley-Blackwell, Malden, MA, Oxford, West Sussex, pp. 472–479.

Creech, B. & Mendelson, A.L. (2015) Imagining the journalist of the future: Technological visions of journalism education and newswork. *The Communication Review*, 18, pp. 142–165.

Cubitt, S. (2017) Ecologies of fabrication. In *Sustainable media: Critical approaches to media and environment* (Eds, Starosielski, N. & Walker, J.) Routledge, London, pp. 163–179.

Curran, J. (2016) The Internet of history: Rethinking the Internet's past. In *Misunderstanding the Internet. Second edition* (Eds, Curran, J., Fenton, N. & Freedman, D.) Routledge, Milton Park, New York, pp. 48–84.

Dahlberg-Grundberg, M., Lundström, R. & Lindgren, S. (2016) Social media and the transnationalization of mass activism: Twitter and the labour movement. *First Monday*, 21, August 1st, retrieved from: https://firstmonday.org/ojs/index.php/fm/article/view/6729/5601 (Last accessed: 15th August 2019).

Dalen, A.V. (2012) The algorithms behind the headlines. *Journalism Practice*, 6, pp. 648–658.

Davenport, T. (2012) Submarine communications cables and law of the sea: Problems in law and practice. *Ocean Development & International Law*, 43, pp. 201–242.

Davies, S.R. (2017) *Hackerspaces: Making the maker movement.* Polity Press, Cambridge.

Davis, C.H. & Michelle, C. (2011) Q methodology in audience research: Bridging the qualitative/quantitative 'divide'? *Participations: Journal of Audience and Reception Studies*, 8, pp. 559–593.

De Maeyer, J. et al. (2015) Waiting for data journalism: A qualitative assessment of the anecdotal take-up of data journalism in French-speaking Belgium. *Digital Journalism*, 3, pp. 432–446.

Deacon, D. & Stanyer, J. (2014) Mediatization: Key concept or conceptual bandwagon? *Media, Culture & Society*, 36, 1032–1044.

Dencik, L. (2018) Surveillance realism and the politics of imagination: Is there no alternative? *Krisis: Journal for Contemporary Philosophy*, 2018, pp. 31–43.

Dencik, L., Hintz, A. & Cable, J. (2016) Towards data justice? The ambiguity of anti-surveillance resistance in political activism. *Big Data & Society*, Online first, pp. 1–12. doi: 2053951716679678.

Deuze, M. (2007) *Media work.* Polity Press, Cambridge.

Deuze, M. (2008) The changing context of news work: Liquid journalism for a monitorial citizenry. *International Journal of Communication*, 2, pp. 848–865.

Deuze, M. (2011) Media life. *Media, Culture & Society*, 33, pp. 137–148.

Deuze, M. & Witschge, T. (2018) Beyond journalism: Theorizing the transformation of journalism. *Journalism*, 19, pp. 165–181.

Didžiokaitė, G., Saukko, P. & Greiffenhagen, C. (2018) The mundane experience of everyday calorie trackers: Beyond the metaphor of quantified self. *New Media & Society*, 20, pp. 1470–1487.

Dimock, M. (2019) Defining generations: Where Millennials end and Generation Z begins. *Pew Research Center*, January 17th, retrieved from: https://www.pewresea

rch.org/fact-tank/2019/01/17/where-and-generation-z-begins/ (Last accessed: 15th August 2019).

Dolata, U. & Schrape, J.-F. (2015) Masses, crowds, communities, movements: Collective action in the Internet Age. *Social Movement Studies*, 15, pp. 1–18.

Donges, P. & Jarren, O. (2014) Mediatization of political organizations: Changing parties and interest groups? In *Mediatization of politics: Understanding the transformation of Western democracies* (Eds, Esser, F. & Strömbäck, J.) Palgrave Macmillan, Houndmills, pp. 181–199.

Dörr, K.N. (2016) Mapping the field of algorithmic journalism. *Digital Journalism*, 4, pp. 700–722.

Dougherty, D. & Conrad, A. (2016) *Free to make: How the maker movement is changing our schools, our jobs, and our minds.* North Atlantic Books, Berkeley, CA.

Dourish, P. (2015) Protocols, packets, and proximity. The materiality of internet routing. In *Signal traffic: Critical studies of media infrastructures* (Eds, Parks, L. & Starosielski, N.) University of Illinois Press, Urbana, Chicago, Springfield, pp. 183–204.

Draper, N.A. (2017) From privacy pragmatist to privacy resigned: Challenging narratives of rational choice in digital privacy debates. *Policy & Internet*, 9, pp. 232–251.

Draper, N.A. & Turow, J. (2019) The corporate cultivation of digital resignation. *New Media & Society*, 21, pp. 1824–1839.

Driessens, O. (2014) *The celebritisation of culture and society: A theoretical inquiry and empirical exploratioon of celebrity culture.* Department of Communication studies (dissertation), Ghent University Press, Ghent.

Driessens, O. et al. (Eds.) (2017) *Dynamics of mediatization.* Palgrave, London.

Edstrom, M. & Ladendorf, M. (2012) Freelance journalists as a flexible workforce in media industries. *Journalism Practice*, 6, pp. 711–721.

Ekström, M. et al. (2016) Three tasks for mediatization research: Contributions to an open agenda. *Media, Culture & Society*, 38, pp. 1090–1108.

Elias, N. (1978) *What is sociology?* Hutchinson, London.

Elias, N. (1991) *The symbol theory.* Sage, London, Newbury Park, New Delhi.

Elias, N. (2000) *The civilizing process.* Wiley-Blackwell, Oxford, Malden.

Elmer, G., Langlois, G. & Redden, J. (Eds.) (2015a) *Compromised data: From social media to big data.* Bloomsbury Academic, London.

Elmer, G., Langlois, G. & Redden, J. (2015b) Introduction: Compromised data - from social media to big data. In *Compromised data: From social media to big data* (Eds, Elmer, G., Langlois, G. & Redden, J.) Bloomsbury Academic, London. pp. 11–13.

Eskjær, M.F. (2018) Mediatization as structural couplings: Adapting to media logic(s). In *Media logic(s) revisited: Modelling the interplay between media institutions, media technology and societal change* (Eds, Thimm, C., Anastasiadis, M. & Einspänner-Pflock, J.) Palgrave Macmillan, London, pp. 85–109.

Eslami, M. et al. (2015) "I always assumed that I wasn't really that close to [her]": Reasoning about invisible algorithms in news feeds. In *Proceedings of the 2015 Annual Conference on Human Factors in Computing Systems* (Eds, Begole, B. & Kim, J.) ACM Press, Seoul, Republic of Korea, pp. 153–162.

Esposito, A., Fortunati, L. & Lugano, G. (2014) Modeling emotion, behavior and context in socially believable robots and ICT interfaces. *Cognitive Computation*, 6, pp. 623–627.

Esposito, E. (2017) Artificial communication? The production of contingency by algorithms. *Zeitschrift für Soziologie*, 46, pp. 249–265.

Esser, F. & Matthes, J. (2013) Mediatization effects on political news, political actors, political decisions, and political audiences. In *Democracy in the age of globalization and mediatization* (Eds, Kriesi, H. et al.) Macmillan, London, pp. 177–201.

Esser, F. & Strömbäck, J. (Eds.) (2014) *Mediatization of politics: Understanding the transformation of Western democracies*. Palgrave Macmillan, Houndmills.

Eubanks, V. (2017) *Automating inequality: How high-tech tools profile, police, and punish the poor*. St. Martin's Press, New York.

Evans, E. (2011) *Transmedia television: Audiences, new media, and daily life*. Routledge, London.

Fenton, N. et al. (2010) *Meeting the news needs of local communities*. Goldsmiths University of London, London.

Ferrara, E. et al. (2016) The rise of social bots. *Communications of the ACM*, 59, pp. 96–104.

Fidler, D. (Ed.) (2015) *The Snowden reader*. Indiana University Press, Bloomington, IN.

Fink, K. & Anderson, C.W. (2015) Data journalism in the United States: Beyond the "usual suspects". *Journalism Studies*, 16, pp. 1–15.

Fink, R.D. & Weyer, J. (2014) Interaction of human actors and non-human agents. A sociological simulation model of hybrid systems. *Science, Technology & Innovation Studies*, 10, pp. 47–64.

Finnemann, N.O. (2014) Digitalization: New trajectories of mediatization? In *Mediatization of communication* (Ed, Lundby, K.) de Gruyter, Berlin, New York, pp. 297–322.

Fiske, J. (1987) *Television culture*. Routledge, London, New York.

Flew, T. et al. (2012) The promise of computational journalism. *Journalism Practice*, 6, pp. 157–171.

Flyverbom, M. & Murray, J. (2018) Datastructuring - organizing and curating digital traces into action. *Big Data & Society*, 5, pp. 1–12.

Fortunati, L. (2018) Robotization and the domestic sphere. *New Media & Society*, pp. 2673–2690.

Foucault, M. (1988) *The history of sexuality: The care of the self*. Vintage, New York.

Foucault, M. (1991) *Discipline and punish: The birth of the prison*. Penguin, London.

Frau-Meigs, D. (2000) A cultural project based on multiple temporary consensus identity and community in Wired. *New Media & Society*, 2, pp. 227–244.

Fredriksson, M. & Pallas, J. (2017) The localities of mediatization: How organizations translate mediatization into everyday practices. In *Dynamics of mediatization* (Eds, Driessens, O. et al.) Palgrave Macmillan, London, pp. 119–136.

Fredriksson, M., Schillemans, T. & Pallas, J. (2015) Determinants of organizational mediatization: An analysis of the adaptation of Swedish government agencies to news media. *Public Admin*, 93, pp. 1049–1067.

Freedman, D. (2009) The political economy of the 'new' news environment. In *New media, old news: Journalism and democracy in the digital age* (Ed, Fenton, N.) Sage, Los Angeles, London, New Delhi, Singapore, pp. 35–50.

Friedland, R. & Alford, R.R. (1991) Bringing society back in: Symbols, practices and institutional contradictions. In *The new institutionalism in organizational analysis* (Eds, Powell, W.W. & DiMaggio, P.J.) University of Chicago Press, Chicago, pp. 232–263.

Fromm, E. (1941) *Escape from freedom*. Avon Books, New York.

Frosh, P. (2015) The gestural image: The selfie, photography theory, and kinesthetic sociability. *International Journal of Communication*, 9, 22, pp. 1607–1628.

Fuchs, C. (2014) Digital prosumption labour on social media in the context of the capitalist regime of time. *Time & Society*, 23, pp. 97–123.

Galloway, A.R. (2004) *Protocol: How control exists after decentralization*. MIT Press, Cambridge, MA.

Gardner, H. & Davis, K. (2013) *The app generation: How today's youth navigate identity, intimacy, and imagination in a digital world*. Yale University Press, New Haven, London.

Garfinkel, H. (1967) *Studies in ethnomethodology*. Prentice-Hall Inc., Englewood Cliffs.

Gauntlett, D. (2018) *Making is connecting: The social power of creativity, from craft and knitting to digital everything. Second expanded edition*. Polity Press, Cambridge.

Gaved, M., & Mulholland, P. (2008) Pioneers, subcultures, and cooperatives: The grassroots augmentation of urban places. In *Augmented urban spaces: Articulating the physical and electronic city. Design and the Built Environment* (Eds, Aurigi, A. & de Cindio, F.) Ashgate Publishing, Farnham, pp. 171–184.

Gaver, W. (1996) Situating action II: Affordances for interaction: The social is material for design. *Ecological Psychology*, 8, pp. 111–129.

Gehl, R.W. & Bakardjieva, M. (2016) Socialbots and their friends. In *Socialbots and their friends: Digital media and the automation of sociality* (Eds, Gehl, R.W. & Bakardjieva, M.) Routledge, London, pp. 1–16.

Gentili, R.J. et al. (2015) A neural architecture for performing actual and mentally simulated movements during self-intended and observed bimanual arm reaching movements. *International Journal of Social Robotics*, 7, pp. 371–392.

Gentzel, P. et al. (Eds.) (2019) *Das vergessene Subjekt: Subjektkonstitutionen in mediatisierten Alltagswelten*. VS Springer, Wiesbaden.

Gerhard, U. & Hepp, A. (2018) Appropriating digital traces of self-quantification: Contextualising 'pragmatic' and 'enthusiast' self-trackers. *International Journal of Communication*, 11, pp. 683–700.

Gershenfeld, N. (2005) *Fab: The coming revolution on your desktop - from personal computers to personal fabrication*. Basic Books, New York.

Gibson, J. (1967) Theory of affordances. In *Perceiving, acting, knowing* (Eds, Shaw, R. & Bransford, J.) Erlbaum, New York, pp. 67 82.

Giddens, A. (1984) *The constitution of society: Outline of the theory of structuration*. Polity Press, Cambridge, Oxford.

Giddens, A. (1990) *The consequences of modernity*. Polity Press, Cambridge.

Gillespie, M. (Ed.) (2005) *Media audiences*. Open University Press, Berkshire.

Gillespie, T. (2010) The politics of platforms. *New Media & Society*, 12, pp. 347–364.

Gillespie, T. (2014) The relevance of algorithms. In *Media technologies: Essays on communication, materiality, and society* (Eds, Gillespie, T., Boczkowski, P.J. & Foot, K.A.) MIT Press, Cambridge, MA, London, pp. 167–194.

Gillespie, T. (2018) *Custodians of the Internet: Platforms, content moderation, and the hidden decisions that shape social media*. Yale University Press, New Haven, London.

Gitelman, L. & Jackson, V. (2013) Introduction. In *"Raw data" is an oxymoron* (Ed, Gitelman, L.) MIT Press, Cambridge, MA, pp. 1–13.

Goffman, E. (1974) *Frame analysis: An essay on the organization of experience*. Harvard University Press, Cambridge, MA.

Goffman, E. (1978) *The presentation of self in everyday life*. Harmondsworth, London.

Goggin, G. (2011) *Global mobile media*. Routledge, London.

Good, I.J. (1965) *The estimation of probabilities*. MIT Press, Cambridge, MA.

Goodman, I. (1983) Television's role in family interaction: A family systems perspective. *Journal of Family Issues*, 4, pp. 116–137.

Göttlich, U. (1996) *Kritik der Medien: Reflexionsstufen kritisch-materialistischer Medientheorien*. Westdeutscher Verlag, Opladen.

Goulden, M. et al. (2018) Living with interpersonal data: Observability and accountability in the age of pervasive ICT. *New Media & Society*, 20, pp. 1580–1599.

Granovetter, M. (1983) The strength of weak ties. A network theory revisited. *Sociological Theory*, 1, pp. 203–233.

Graves, L. (2007) The affordances of blogging: A case study in culture and technological effects. *Journal of Communication Inquiry*, 31, pp. 331–346.

Gray, J., Chambers, L. & Bounegru, L. (Eds.) (2012) *The data journalism handbook: How journalists can use data to improve the news*. O'Reilly Media, Beijing, Cambridge.

Greenbaum, J. & Kyng, M. (1991) *Design at work: Cooperative design of computer systems*. Lawrence Erlbaum Ass., Hillsdale, NJ.

Greenfield, A. (2010) *Everyware: The dawning age of ubiquitous computing*. New Riders, San Francisco.

Greenfield, D. (2016) Deep data. Notes on the n of 1. In *Quantified: Biosensing technologies in everyday life* (Ed, Nafus, D.) MIT Press, Cambridge, MA, London, pp. 123–146.

Greengard, S. (2015) *The internet of things*. MIT Press, Cambridge, MA, London.

Greenstein, S. (2015) *How the internet became commercial: Innovation, privatization and the birth of a new network*. Princeton University Press, Princeton.

Greenwald, G. (2014) *No place to hide: Edward Snowden, the NSA, and the US surveillance state*. Hamish Hamilton, London.

Grenz, T. & Kirschner, H. (2016) Unravelling the app store: Toward an interpretative perspective on tracing. *International Journal of Communication*, 12, pp. 612–628.

Greschke, H., Dreßler, D. & Hierasimowicz, K. (2017) Die Mediatisierung von Eltern-Kind-Beziehungen im Kontext grenzüberschreitender Migration. In *Mediatisierung als Metaprozess* (Eds, Krotz, F., Despotovic, C. & Kruse, M.-M.) VS Verlag, Wiesbaden, pp. 59–80.

Grisot, M., Parmiggiani, E. & Geirbo, H.C. (2018) Infrastructuring internet of things for public governance. *Research-in-Progress Papers*, 66, pp. 1–8.

Guzman, A.L. (2018) Introduction: What is human-machine-communication anyway? In *Human-machine communication: Rethinking communication, technology, and ourselves* (Ed, Guzman, A.L.) Peter Lang, New York, pp. 1–28.

Guzman, A.L. & Lewis, S.C. (2019) Artificial intelligence and communication: A human-machine communication research agenda. *New Media & Society*, pp. 1–17. doi: 1461444819858691.

Habermas, J. (1984) *The theory of communicative action [1981]*. Beacon Press, Boston.

Habermas, J. (1989) *The structural transformation of the public sphere: An inquiry into a category of bourgeois society*. MIT Press, Cambridge, MA.

Habermas, J. (1992) *The theory of communicative action. Vol. 2 [1981]*. Beacon Press, Boston.

Haggerty, K.D. & Ericson, R.V. (2000) The surveillant assemblage. *British Journal of Sociology*, 51, pp. 605–622.

Hahn, A. (2000) *Konstruktionen des Selbst, der Welt und der Geschichte*. Suhrkamp, Frankfurt a. M.

Hall, M.M. & Link, J. (2004) From the "power of the norm" to "flexible normalism": Considerations after Foucault. *Cultural Critique*, 57, pp. 14–32.

Hall, S. (1992) The question of cultural identity. In *Modernity and its futures* (Eds, Hall, S., Held, D. & McGrew, T.) Polity Press, Cambridge, pp. 273–326.

Hall, S. (1997) The centrality of culture: Notes on the cultural revolutions of our time. In *Media and cultural regulation* (Ed, Thompson, K.) Sage, London, pp. 207–238.

Halpern, S. (2018) Cambridge Analytica, Facebook, and the revelations of open secrets. *The New Yorker*, March 21st, retrieved from: https://www.newyorker.com /news/news-desk/cambridge-analytica-facebook-and-the-revelations-of-open-se crets (Last accessed: 15th August 2019).

Hargittai, E. & Marwick, A.E. (2016) "What can I really do?" Explaining the privacy paradox with online apathy. *International Journal of Communication*, 10, pp. 3737–3757.

Hartmann, M. (2013) *Domestizierung*. Nomos, Baden-Baden.

Hasebrink, U. (2003) Nutzungsforschung. In *Öffentliche Kommunikation: Handbuch Kommunikations- und Medienwissenschaft* (Eds, Bentele, G., Brosius, H.-B. & Jarren, O.) Westdeutscher Verlag, Wiesbaden, pp. 101–127.

Hasebrink, U. (2014) Die kommunikative Figuration von Familien: Medien, Kommunikation und Informationstechnologie im Familienalltag. In *Zukunft der Familie - Anforderungen an Familienpolitik und Familienwissenschaft. Tagungsband zum 4. Europäischen Fachkongress Familienforschung* (Eds, Rupp, M., Kapella, O. & Schneider, N.F.) Verlag Barbara Budrich, Opladen, Berlin, Toronto, pp. 225–240.

Hasebrink, U. (2015) Kommunikationsrepertoires und digitale Öffentlichkeiten. In *Digitale Öffentlichkeit(en)* (Eds, Hahn, O., Hohlfeld, R. & Knieper, T.) UVK Verlagsgesellschaft, Konstanz, pp. 35–50.

Hasebrink, U. (2019) *Public connection: Individuals' media repertoires and the re-figuration of publics*. Unpublished manuscript, Hamburg.

Hasebrink, U. & Domeyer, H. (2010) Zum Wandel von Informationsrepertoires in konvergierenden Medienumgebungen. In *Die Mediatisierung der Alltagswelt* (Ed, Hartmann, M. & Hepp, A.) VS, Wiesbaden, pp. 49–64.

Hasebrink, U. & Domeyer, H. (2012) Media repertoires as patterns of behaviour and as meaningful practices: A multimethod approach to media use in converging media environments. *Participations: Journal of Audience & Reception Studies*, 9, pp. 757–783.

Hasebrink, U. & Hepp, A. (2017) How to research cross-media practices? Investigating media repertoires and media ensembles. *Convergence*, 23, pp. 362–377.

Hasebrink, U. & Hölig, S. (2014) Topografie der Öffentlichkeit. *APuZ*, 22–23, pp. 16–22.

Hasebrink, U. & Popp, J. (2006) Media repertoires as a result of selective media use. A conceptual approach to the analysis of patterns of exposure. *Communications*, 31, pp. 369–387.

Hasebrink, U. et al. (2015) Changing patterns of media use across cultures: A challenge for longitudinal research. *International Journal of Communication*, 9, 1, pp. 435–457.

Hatch, M. (2014) *The maker movement manifesto: Rules for innovation in the new world of crafters, hackers, and tinkerers.* McGraw Hill Professional, New York.

Helberger, N., Pierson, J. & Poell, T. (2018) Governing online platforms: From contested to cooperative responsibility. *The Information Society*, 34, pp. 1–14.

Hemphill, D. & Leskowitz, S. (2012) DIY activists: Communities of practice, cultural dialogism, and radical knowledge sharing. *Adult Education Quarterly*, 63, pp. 57–77.

Hepp, A. (2013) *Cultures of mediatization.* Polity Press, Cambridge.

Hepp, A., Alpen, S. & Simon, P. (2018a) Zwischen Utopie und Dystopie: Der öffentliche Diskurs um die Pioniergemeinschaften der Maker- und Quantified-Self-Bewegung in Deutschland und Großbritannien. *Communicative Figurations Working Paper*, 22, pp. 1–25.

Hepp, A., Berg, M. & Roitsch, C. (2014a) *Mediatisierte Welten der Vergemeinschaftung: Kommunikative Vernetzung und das Gemeinschaftsleben junger Menschen.* VS, Wiesbaden.

Hepp, A., Berg, M. & Roitsch, C. (2014b) Mediatized worlds of communitization: Young people as localists, centrists, multi-localists and pluralists. In *Mediatized worlds: Culture and society in a media age* (Eds, Hepp, A. & Krotz, F.) Palgrave, London, pp. 174–203.

Hepp, A., Berg, M. & Roitsch, C. (2017a) A processual concept of media generation: The media-generational positioning of elderly people. *Nordicom Review*, 38, 109–122.

Hepp, A., Bozdag, C. & Suna, L. (2011) *Mediale Migranten: Mediatisierung und die kommunikative Vernetzung der Diaspora.* VS, Wiesbaden.

Hepp, A., Bozdag, C. & Suna, L. (2012) Mediatized migrants: Media cultures and communicative networking in the diaspora. In *Migrations, diaspora, and information technology in global societies* (Eds, Fortunati, L., Pertierra, R. & Vincent, J.) Routledge, London, pp. 172–188.

Hepp, A., Breiter, A. & Friemel, T. (2018b) Digital traces in context. An introduction. *International Journal of Communication*, 12, pp. 439–449.

Hepp, A., Breiter, A. & Hasebrink, U. (Eds.) (2017b) *Communicative figurations: Transforming communications in times of deep mediatization*. Palgrave Macmillan, London.

Hepp, A. & Hasebrink, U. (2017) Researching transforming communications in times of deep mediatization: A figurational approach. In *Communicative figurations: Transforming communications in times of deep mediatization* (Eds, Hepp, A., Breiter, A. & Hasebrink, U.) Palgrave Macmillan, London, pp. 51–80.

Hepp, A. & Hitzler, R. (2016) Collectivities in change: The mediatisation and individualisation of community building from a subjective and figurational perspective. In *Politics, civil society and participation: Media and communications in a transforming environment* (Eds, Kramp, L. et al.) Edition Lumière, Bremen, pp. 133–150.

Hepp, A., Hjarvard, S. & Lundby, K. (2015) Mediatization: Theorizing the interplay between media, culture and society. *Media, Culture & Society*, 37, pp. 314–324.

Hepp, A. & Krotz, F. (Eds.) (2014) *Mediatized worlds: Culture and society in a media age*. Palgrave, London.

Hepp, A. & Loosen, W. (2019) Pioneer journalism: Conceptualizing the role of pioneer journalists and pioneer communities in the organizational re-figuration of journalism. *Journalism*, Online first, pp. 1–19. doi: 1464884919829277.

Hepp, A., Looser, W., Hasebrink, U., Reichertz, J. (2017c) Konstruktivismus in der Kommunikationswissenschaft. Über die Notwendigkeit einer (erneuten) Debatte. *Medien & Kommunikationswissenschaft*, 65, pp. 181–206.

Hepp, A., Lunt, P. & Hartmann, M. (2015) Communicative figurations of the good life: Ambivalences surrounding the mediatization of homelessness and the transnational family. In *Communication and "the good life"* (Ed, Wang, H.) Peter Lang, Berlin, New York, pp. 181–196.

Herman, E.S. & McChesney, R.W. (1997) *The global media: The new missionaries of corporate capitalism*. Cassell, London.

Hern, A. (2019) A 'privacy-focused' Facebook would kill Zuckerberg's business model. *The Guardian*, March 7th, retrieved from: https://www.theguardian.com/ commentisfree/2019/mar/07/privacy-focused-facebook-kill-zuckerbergs-busi ness-model (Last accessed: 15th August 2019).

Hess, T., Köster, A. & Steiner, R. (2014) Journalistic startups in the online world. *Management Report*, 3, retrieved from: https://www.wim.bwl.uni-muenchen.de/ download/epub/mreport_2014_3.pdf (Last accessed: 15th August 2019).

Hintz, A., Dencik, L. & Wahl-Jorgensen, K. (2019) *Digital citizenship in a datafied society*. Polity Press, Cambridge.

Hitzler, R. & Niederbacher, A. (2010) *Leben in Szenen. Formen juveniler Vergemeinschaftung heute. Dritte, vollständig überarbeitete Auflage*. VS, Wiesbaden.

Hjarvard, S. (2009) Soft individualism: Media and the changing social character. In *Mediatization: Concept, changes, consequences* (Ed, Lundby, K.) Peter Lang, New York, pp. 159–177.

Hjarvard, S. (2013) *The mediatization of culture and society*. Routledge, London.

Hjarvard, S. (2017) Mediatization. In *International encyclopedia of media effects* (Eds, Höffner, C.A. & Zoonen, L.V.) Wiley-Blackwell, New York, pp. 1221–1240.

Hjarvard, S. (2018) The logics of the media and the mediatized conditions of social interaction. In *Media logic(s) revisited: Modelling the interplay between media institutions, media technology and societal change* (Eds, Thimm, C., Anastasiadis, M. & Einspänner-Pflock, J.) Palgrave Macmillan, London, pp. 63–84.

Hoffman, B. (2019) Generation AI: Teaching a new kind of tech savvy. *Medium*, MIT Media Lab, retrieved from: https://medium.com/mit-media-lab/generation-ai-tea ching-a-new-kind-of-tech-savvy-623e6821032f (Last accessed: 15th August 2019).

Hoffmann, C.P., Lutz, C. & Ranzini, G. (2016) Privacy cynicism: A new approach to the privacy paradox. *Cyberpsychology: Journal of Psychosocial Research on Cyberspace*, 10, 4. doi: 10.5817/CP2016-4-7.

Höflich, J.R. (2003) *Mensch, Computer und Kommunikation: Theoretische Verortungen und empirische Befunde*. Peter Lang, Frankfurt a. M.

Höflich, J.R. (2016) *Der Mensch und seine Medien. Mediatisierte interpersonale Kommunikation. Eine Einführung*. VS, Wiesbaden.

Honneth, A. (2008) *Reification: A new look at an old idea*. Oxford University Press, Oxford.

Honneth, A. (2012) *The I in the we: Studies in the theory of recognition*. Polity Press, London.

Hopkins, J. (2015) Assembling blog affordances: Theorising affordances and agency in new media. *EASA Media Anthropology Network*, pp. 1–17.

Hovden, J.F. & Moe, H. (2017) A sociocultural approach to study public connection across and beyond media: The example of Norway. *Convergence: The International Journal of Research into New Media Technologies*, 23, pp. 391–408.

Hughes, T.P. (1983) *Networks of power: Electrification in Western society, 1880–1930*. Johns Hopkins University Press, Baltimore, MD.

Hunsinger, J. & Schrock, A. (2016) The democratization of hacking and making. *New Media & Society*, 18, pp. 535–538.

Hutchby, I. (2001) Technologies, texts and affordances. *Sociology*, 35, pp. 441–456.

Innis, H.A. (1951) *The bias of communication*. Toronto University Press, Toronto.

Jameson, F. (1991) *Postmodernism, or the cultural logic of late capitalism*. Verso, London.

Jansson, A. (2015a) Interveillance: A new culture of recognition and mediatization. *Media and Communication*, 3, pp. 81–90.

Jansson, A. (2015b) Polymedia distinctions. The sociocultural stratification of interpersonal media practices in couple relationships. *Nordicom Review*, 36, pp. 33–50.

Jansson, A. (2016) Critical communication geography: Space, recognition, and the dialectic of mediatization. In *Communications/Media/Geographies* (Eds, Adams, P. et al.) Routledge, London, pp. 107–143.

Jansson, A. (2018) *Mediatization and mobile lives: A critical approach*. Routledge, London.

Jasanoff, S. & Kim, S.-H. (Eds.) (2015) *Dreamscapes of modernity: Sociotechnical imaginaries and the fabrication of power*. University of Chicago Press, Chicago.

Jenkins, H. (2006) *Convergence culture: Where old and new media collide*. New York University Press, New York.

Jensen, K.B. (2010) *Media convergence: The three degrees of network, mass and interpersonal communication*. Routledge, London.

Jensen, K.B. (2013) Definitive and sensitizing conceptualizations of mediatization. *Communication Theory*, 23, pp. 203–222.

Jensen, K.B. & Helles, R. (2015) Audiences across media. A comparative agenda for future research on media audiences. *International Journal of Communication*, 9, pp. 291–298.

Johansson, J. (2013) The early days of radio in Sweden, Ernst FW Alexanderson and Grimeton radio station SAQ, UNESCO world heritage. *Antennas and Propagation (EuCAP)*, pp. 3148–3152.

John, N.A. (2017) *The age of sharing*. Polity Press, Cambridge.

Jones, S.G. (Ed.) (1998) *Cybersociety 2.0: Revisiting computer-mediated communication and technology*. Sage, London.

Just, N. & Latzer, M. (2017) Governance by algorithms: Reality construction by algorithmic selection on the internet. *Media, Culture & Society*, 39, pp. 238–258.

Kaerlein, T. (2015) The social robot as fetish? Conceptual affordances and risks of neo-animistic theory. *International Journal of Social Robotics*, 7, pp. 361–370.

Kangas, S. (Ed.) (2011) *Digital pioneers: Tracing the cultural drivers of future media culture*. Nuorisotutkimusverkosto, Helsinki.

Kannengießer, S. (2019) Reflecting on and engaging with the materiality of media technologies: Repairing and fair producing. *New Media & Society*, Online first, pp. 1–7. doi: 1461444819858081.

Kannengießer, S. & Kubitschko, S. (2017) Acting on media: Influencing, shaping and (re)configuring the fabric of everyday life. *Media and Communication*, 5, pp. 1–4.

Karanasios, S. et al. (2013) Making sense of digital traces: An activity theory driven ontological approach. *Journal of the Association for Information Science and Technology*, 64, pp. 2452–2467.

Karasti, H. & Baker, K.S. (2004) Infrastructuring for the long-term: Ecological information management. *37th Annual Hawaii International Conference on System Sciences*. doi: 10.1109/HICSS.2004.1265077.

Katzenbach, C. (2012) Technologies as institutions: Rethinking the role of technology in media governance constellations. In *Trends in communication policy research: New theories, methods and subjects* (Eds, Just, N. & Puppis, M.) Intellect, Bristol, pp. 117–138.

Kaulingfreks, R. & Warren, S. (2010) SWARM: Flash mobs, mobile clubbing and the city. *Culture and Organization*, 16, pp. 211–227.

Kavada, A. (2015) Creating the collective: Social media, the Occupy Movement and its constitution as a collective actor. *Information, Communication & Society*, 18, pp. 872–886.

Kavada, A. (2016) Social movements and political agency in the digital age: A communication approach. *Media and Communication*, 4, pp. 8–12.

Keen, A. (2007) *The cult of the amateur.* Doubleday, New York.

Kelly, K. (2016) *The inevitable: Understanding the 12 technological forces that will shape our future.* Viking, New York.

Kelty, C.M. (2008) *Geeks and recursive publics: How the internet and free software make things public,* retrieved from: http://kelty.org/or/papers/unpublishable/Kelty.Rec ursivePublics-short.pdf (Last accessed: 15th August 2019).

Kesselring, S. & Vogl, G. (2004) Mobility pioneers. Networks, scapes and flows between first and second modernity. In *Mobility and the cosmopolitan perspective. A workshop at the reflexive modernization research centre* (Eds, Bonß, W., Kesselring, S. & Vogl, G.) SFB 536, München, pp. 47–67.

Klein, J., Schimank, U. & Walter, M. (2017) How to interview about media repertoires as tacit components of practices - problems and empirical experiences. In *Communicative figurations: Transforming communications in times of deep mediatization* (Eds, Hepp, A., Breiter, A. & Hasebrink, U.) Palgrave Macmillan, London, pp. 363–386.

Klinger, U. & Svensson, J. (2015) The emergence of network media logic in political communication: A theoretical approach. *New Media & Society,* 17, pp. 1241–1257.

Klinger, U. & Svensson, J. (2018) The end of media logics? On algorithms and agency. *New Media & Society,* 121, pp. 4653–4670.

Knight, M. (2015) Data journalism in the UK: A preliminary analysis of form and content. *Journal of Media Practice,* 16, pp. 55–72.

Knoblauch, H. (2008) Kommunikationsgemeinschaften. Überlegungen zur kommunikativen Konstruktion einer Sozialform. In *Posttraditionale Gemeinschaften. Theoretische und ethnographische Erkundungen* (Eds, Hitzler, R., Honer, A. & Pfadenhauer, M.) VS, Wiesbaden, pp. 73–88.

Knoblauch, H. (2013) Communicative constructivism and mediatization. *Communication Theory,* 23, pp. 297–315.

Knoblauch, H. (2017) *Die kommunikative Konstruktion der Wirklichkeit.* VS, Wiesbaden.

Knoblauch, H. & Löw, M. (2017) On the spatial re-figuration of the social world. *Sociologica,* 11, pp. 1–27.

Knorr Cetina, K. (2014) Scopic media and global coordination: The mediatization of face-to-face encounters. In *Mediatization of communication* (Ed, Lundby, K.) de Gruyter, Berlin, pp. 39–62.

Knorr Cetina, K. & Preda, A. (2007) The temporalization of financial markets: From network to flow. *Theory, Culture & Society,* 24, pp. 116–138.

Knorr Cetina, K. & Reichmann, W. (2015) Living data in financial markets: Concepts and consequences. In *Die Gesellschaft der Daten: Über die digitale Transformation der sozialen Ordnung* (Ed, Süssenguth, F.) Transcript, Bielefeld, pp. 147–172.

Kobbernagel, C. & Schrøder, K.C. (2016) From everyday communicative figurations to rigorous audience news repertoires: A mixed method approach to cross-media news consumption. *MedieKultur: Journal of media and communication research,* 60, pp. 6–31.

Kohler, T. et al. (2011) Co-creation in virtual worlds: The design of the user experience. *MIS Quarterly,* 35, pp. 773–788.

Kostakis, V., Niaros, V. & Giotitsas, C. (2015) Production and governance in hackerspaces: A manifestation of commons-based peer production in the physical realm. *International Journal of Cultural Studies*, 18, pp. 555–573.

Krajina, Z., Moores, S. & Morley, D. (2014) Non-media-centric media studies: A cross-generational conversation. *European Journal of Cultural Studies*, 17, pp. 682–700.

Krebs, M. (2014) Manufacturing expertise for the people: The open source hardware movement in Japan. *Ethnographic Praxis in Industry Conference Proceedings 2014*, pp. 20–35.

Krotz, F. (2007a) *Mediatisierung: Fallstudien zum Wandel von Kommunikation*. VS, Wiesbaden.

Krotz, F. (2007b) The meta-process of mediatization as a conceptual frame. *Global Media and Communication*, 3, pp. 256–260.

Krotz, F. (2014) Mediatization as a mover in modernity. In *Mediatization of communication* (Ed, Lundby, K.) de Gruyter, Berlin, New York, pp. 131–161.

Krotz, F. (2017) Pfade der Mediatisierung: Bedingungsgeflechte für die Transformationen von Medien, Alltag, Kultur und Gesellschaft. In *Mediatisierung als Metaprozess* (Eds, Krotz, F., Despotovic, C. & Kruse, M.-M.) VS Verlag, Wiesbaden, pp. 347–364.

Krotz, F. (2018) Media logic and the mediatization approach: A good partnership, a mésalliance, or a misunderstanding? In *Media logic(s) revisited: Modelling the interplay between media institutions, media technology and societal change* (Eds, Thimm, C., Anastasiadis, M. & Einspänner-Pflock, J.) Palgrave Macmillan, London, pp. 41–61.

Kunelius, R. & Reunanen, E. (2016) Changing power of journalism: The two phases of mediatization. *Communication Theory*, 26, pp. 369–388.

Kurzweil, R. (2005) *The singularity is near: When humans transcend biology*. Viking, New York.

Lahire, B. (2011) *The plural actor*. Polity Press, Cambridge.

Landerer, N. (2013) Rethinking the logics: A conceptual framework for the mediatization of politics. *Communication Theory*, 23, pp. 239–258.

Lange, B. (2015) Fablabs und Hackerspaces. Die Rolle der Maker-Community für eine nachhaltige Wirtschaft. *Ökologisches Wirtschaften*, 30, pp. 8–9.

Larkin, B. (2008) *Signal and noise: Media, infrastructure, and urban culture in Nigeria*. Duke University Press, Durham, London.

Lazer, D.M.J. et al. (2018) The science of fake news. *Science*, 359, pp. 1094–1096.

Leonardi, P.M. (2012) Materiality, sociomateriality, and socio-technical systems: What do these terms mean? How are they related? Do we need them? In *Materiality and organizing: Social interaction in a technological world* (Eds, Leonardi, P.M., Nardi, B.A. & Kallinikos, J.) Oxford University Press, Oxford, pp. 25–48.

Levy, S. (1984) *Hackers: Heroes of the computer revolution*. Doubleday, New York.

Lewis, S.C. (2014) Journalism in an era of big data: Cases, concepts, and critiques. *Digital Journalism*, 3, pp. 321–330.

Lewis, S.C. & Usher, N. (2013) Open source and journalism: Toward new frameworks for imagining news innovation. *Media, Culture & Society*, 35, pp. 602–619.

Lewis, S.C. & Usher, N. (2014) Code, collaboration, and the future of journalism: A case study of the hacks/hackers global network. *Digital Journalism*, 2, pp. 383–393.

Lewis, S.C. & Westlund, O. (2014) Big data and journalism: Epistemology, expertise, economics, and ethics. *Digital Journalism*, 3, pp. 447–466.

Lievrouw, L.A. (2014) Materiality and media in communication and technology studies: An unfinished project. In *Media technologies: Essays on communication, materiality, and society* (Eds, Gillespie, T., Boczkowski, P.J. & Foot, K.A.) MIT Press, Cambridge, MA, London, pp. 21–51.

Lindlof, T.R. (1988) Media audiences as interpretive communities. *Communication Yearbook*, 11, pp. 81–107.

Lindlof, T.R., Shatzer, M.J. & Wilkinson, D. (1988) Accommodation of video and television in the American family. In *World families watch television* (Ed, Lull, J.) Sage, London, Thousand Oaks, New Delhi, pp. 158–192.

Ling, R. & Donner, J. (2009) *Mobile communication*. Polity Press, Cambridge.

Linke, C. (2011) Being a couple in a media world: The mediatization of everyday communication in couple relationships. *Communications*, 36, pp. 91–111.

Livingstone, S. (2005) On the relation between audiences and publics. In *Audiences and publics: When cultural engagement matters for the public sphere* (Ed, Livingstone, S.M.) Intellect, Bristol, pp. 17–41.

Livingstone, S. (2014) The mediatization of childhood and education: Reflections on the class. In *Media practice and everyday agency in Europe* (Eds, Kramp, L. et al.) Edition Lumière, Bremen, pp. 55–68.

Livingstone, S. (2019) Audiences in an age of datafication: Critical questions for media research. *Television & New Media*, 20, pp. 170–183.

Livingstone, S. & Lunt, P. (2014) Mediatization: An emerging paradigm for media and communication research? In *Mediatization of communication* (Ed, Lundby, K.) de Gruyter, Berlin, New York, pp. 703–724.

Livingstone, S.M. (2001) Children and their changing media environment. In *Children and their changing media environment: An European comparative study* (Eds, Livingstone, S.M. & Bovill, M.) Lawrence Erlbaum, London, pp. 307–333.

Livingstone, S.M. (2004) The challenge of changing audiences. Or, what is the audience researcher to do in the age of the Internet? *European Journal of Communication*, 19, pp. 75–86.

Livingstone, S.M. (2009) On the mediation of everything. *Journal of Communication*, 59, pp. 1–18.

Lohmeier, C. (2014) The researcher and the never-ending field: Reconsidering big data and digital ethnography. In *Studies in qualitative methodology* (Eds, Hand, M. & Hillyard, S.) Emerald Group Publishing Limited, pp. 75–89.

Lohmeier, C. & Böhling, R. (2017) Communicating family memory: Remembering in a changing media environment. *Communications*, 42, pp. 277–292.

Lomborg, S. & Frandsen, K. (2015) Self-tracking as communication. *Information, Communication & Society*, 19, pp. 1015–1027.

Loosen, W. (2005) Zur medialen Entgrenzungsfähigkeit journalistischer Arbeitsprozesse: Synergien zwischen Print-, TV-und Online-Redaktionen. *Publizistik*, 50, pp. 304–319.

Loosen, W. (2018a) Data-driven gold-standards: What the field values as award-worthy data journalism and how journalism co-evolves with the datafication of society. In *The data journalism handbook 2: Towards a critical data practice* (Eds, Gray, J. & Bounegru, L.) European Journalism Centre and Google News Initiative, London.

Loosen, W. (2018b) Four forms of datafied journalism. Journalism's response to the datafication of society. *Communicative Figurations Working Paper*, 18, pp. 1–10.

Loosen, W., Reimer, J. & De Silva-Schmidt, F. (2017) Data-driven reporting - an on-going (r)evolution? An analysis of projects nominated for the data journalism awards 2013-2016. *Journalism*, Online first, pp. 1–18. doi: 1464884917735691.

Loosen, W. & Schmidt, J.-H. (2012) (Re-)discovering the audience. The relationship between journalism and audience in networked digital media. *Information, Communication & Society*, 15, pp. 1–21.

Loosen, W. & Schmidt, J.-H. (2017) Between proximity and distance: Including the audience in journalism (research). In *The Routledge companion to digital journalism studies* (Eds, Franklin, B. & Eldridge II, S.A.) Routledge, Abingdon, Oxon, pp. 354–363.

Loosen, W. & Scholl, A. (2017) Journalismus im Zeitalter algorithmischer Wirklichkeitskonstruktion. *Medien & Kommunikationswissenschaft*, 65, pp. 348–366.

Lopatovska, I. et al. (2018) Talk to me: Exploring user interactions with the Amazon Alexa. *Journal of Librarianship and Information Science*, 51, pp. 984–997. doi: 0961000618759414.

Lounsbury, M. & Kaghan, W.N. (2001) Organizations, occupations and the structuration of work. In *The transformation of work* (Ed, Vallas, S.) Emerald, pp. 25–50.

Luckmann, B. (1970) The small life-worlds of modern man. *Social Research*, 37, pp. 580–596.

Luhmann, N. (2012) *Theory of society. 2 volumes.* Stanford University Press, Stanford.

Lull, J. (Ed.) (1988) *World families watch television.* Sage, London, Thousand Oaks, New Delhi.

Lull, J. (1990) *Inside family viewing: Ethnographic research on television's audiences.* Routledge, London, New York.

Lundby, K. (2009) Media logic: Looking for social interaction. In *Mediatization: Concept, changes, consequences* (Ed, Lundby, K.) Peter Lang, New York, pp. 101–119.

Lundby, K. (Ed.) (2014a) *Mediatization of communication.* de Gruyter, Berlin, New York.

Lundby, K. (2014b) Mediatization of communication. In *Mediatization of communication* (Ed, Lundby, K.) de Gruyter, Berlin, New York, pp. 3–35.

Lundby, K. (2016) Where are audiences in mediatization research? *Paper Presented at the 6th ECREA Conference*, Prague, 9–12 November 2016.

Lunt, P. & Livingstone, S. (2012) *Media regulation: Governance and the interests of citizens and consumers.* Sage, London.

Lunt, P. & Livingstone, S. (2013) Media studies' fascination with the concept of the public sphere: Critical reflections and emerging debates. *Media, Culture & Society*, 35, pp. 87–96.

Lunt, P. & Livingstone, S. (2016) Is 'mediatization' the new paradigm for our field? A commentary on Deacon and Stanyer (2014, 2015) and Hepp, Harvard and Lundby (2015). *Media, Culture & Society*, 38, pp. 462–470.

Lupton, D. (2012) M-health and health promotion: The digital cyborg and surveillance society. *Social Theory & Health*, 10, pp. 229–244.

Lupton, D. (2014) Self-tracking cultures: Towards a sociology of personal informatics. *OzCHI '14 Proceedings of the 26th Australian Computer-Human Interaction Conference on Designing Futures: The Future of Design.* pp. 77–86. doi: 2686612.2686623.

Lupton, D. (2015) *Digital sociology.* Routledge, London.

Lupton, D. (2016) *The quantified self.* Polity Press, Cambridge.

Lury, C. & Day, S. (2019) Algorithmic personalization as a mode of individuation. *Theory, Culture & Society*, 36, pp. 17–37.

Lyon, D. (2014) Surveillance, Snowden, and big data: Capacities, consequences, critique. *Big Data & Society*, 1, pp. 1–13.

Lyon, D. (2017) Surveillance culture: Engagement, exposure, and ethics in digital modernity. *International Journal of Communication*, 11, pp. 824–842.

MacCormick, J. (2012) *Nine algorithms that have changed the world: The ingenious ideas that drive today's computers.* Princeton University Press, Princeton, Oxford.

MacKenzie, D. (2019) How algorithms interact: Goffman's 'interaction order' in automated trading. *Theory, Culture & Society*, 36, pp. 39–59.

Madianou, M. (2014) Polymedia communication and mediatized migration: An ethnographic approach. In *Mediatization of communication* (Ed, Lundby, K.) de Gruyter, Berlin, New York, pp. 323–348.

Madianou, M. & Miller, D. (2012) *Migration and new media: Transnational families and polymedia.* Routledge, London.

Madianou, M. & Miller, D. (2013) Polymedia: Towards a new theory of digital media in interpersonal communication. *International Journal of Cultural Studies*, 16, pp. 169–187.

Majchrzak, A. et al. (2013) The contradictory influence of social media affordances on online communal knowledge sharing. *Journal of Computer-Mediated Communication*, 19, pp. 38–55.

Mannheim, K. (1952) The problem of generations. In *Essays on the sociology of knowledge* (Ed, Kecskemeti, P.) Oxford University Press, Oxford, pp. 276–320.

Manovich, L. (2013) *Software takes command.* Bloomsbury, New York, London, New Delhi, Sydney.

Mansell, R. (2004) Political economy, power and new media. *New Media & Society*, 6, pp. 96–105.

Marcinkowski, F. (2014) Mediatisation of politics: Reflections on the state of the concept. *Javnost - The Public*, 21, pp. 5–22.

Marr, B. (2015) *Big data: Using smart big data, analytics and metrics to make better decisions and improve performance.* Wiley, Chichester.

Marshall, A. (2017) Elevating an industry: The stocksy united story. *Co-operatives First*, June 23rd, retrieved from: https://cooperativesfirst.com/blog/2017/06/23

/2017622elevating-an-industry-the-stocksy-united-story/ (Last accessed: 15th August 2019).

Martín-Barbero, J. (1993) *Communication, culture, and hegemony: From the media to mediations*. Sage, London, Thousand Oaks, New Delhi.

Marwick, A. (2012) The public domain: Surveillance in everyday life. *Surveillance & Society*, 9, pp. 378–393.

Mascheroni, G. (2018) Datafied childhoods: Contextualising datafication in everyday life. *Current Sociology*. doi: 0011392118807534.

Mattoni, A. & Treré, E. (2014) Media practices, mediation processes, and mediatization in the study of social movements. *Communication Theory*, 24, pp. 252–271.

Mau, S. (2017) *Das quantifizierte Wir*. Suhrkamp, Berlin.

Maxigas, P. (2012) Hacklabs and hackerspaces - tracing two genealogies. *Journal of Peer Production*, 2, peerproduction.net/issues/issue-2.

Maxwell, R. & Miller, T. (2012) *Greening the media*. Oxford University Press, Oxford.

Mayer-Schönberger, V. & Cukier, K. (2013) *Big data: A revolution that will transform how we live, work and think*. John Murray, New York.

Mazzoleni, G. (2008) Media logic. In *The international encyclopedia of communication, vol VII* (Ed, Donsbach, W.) Blackwell Publishing, Oxford, pp. 2930–2932.

Mazzucato, M. (2013) *The entrepreneurial state*. Anthem Press, London, New York.

McChesney, R.W. (2013) *Digital disconnect: How capitalism is turning the internet against democracy*. New Press, New York.

McGrenere, J. & Ho, W. (2000) Theory of affordances. *Proceedings of Graphics Interface Conference Montreal, May 2000*, pp. 179–186.

Meister, M. (2014) When is a robot really social? An outline of the robot sociologicus. *Science, Technology & Innovation Studies*, 10, pp. 107–134.

Mensing, D.H. & Ryfe, D.M. (2013) Blueprint for change: From the teaching hospital to the entrepreneurial model of journalism education. *#ISOJ The Official Research Journal of the International Symposium on Online Journalism*, 2, pp. 144–161.

Merzeau, L. (2009) Présence numérique: Les médiations de l'identité. *Les Enjeux de l'information et de la communication*, 1, pp. 79–91.

Meyrowitz, J. (2009) Medium theory: An alternative to the dominant paradigm of media effects. In *The SAGE handbook of media processes and effects* (Eds, Nabi, R.L. & Oliver, M.B.) Sage, Thousand Oak, CA, pp. 517–530.

Milan, S. (2017) Data activism as the new frontier of media activism. In *Media activism in the digital age* (Eds, Pickard, V. & Yang, G.) Routledge, New York, pp. 151–163.

Milan, S. & ten Oever, N. (2017) Coding and encoding rights in internet infrastructure. *Internet Policy Review*, 6, pp. 1–17.

Milan, S. & Velden, L.V.D. (2016) The alternative epistemologies of data activism. *Digital Culture & Society, special issue 'The Politics of Big Data'*, retrieved from: https://ssrn.com/abstract=2850470 (Last accessed: 15th August 2019).

Miller, J. (2014) Intensifying mediatization: Everyware media. In *Mediatized worlds: Culture and society in a media age* (Eds, Hepp, A. & Krotz, F.) Palgrave Macmillan, Houndmills, Basingstoke, pp. 107–122.

Miller, J. (2017) Mediatization of the automobile. In *Dynamics of mediatization* (Eds, Driessens, O. et al.) Palgrave, London, pp. 203–223.

Miller, J. (2019) Mediatization and the internet of things. *Cultural Science Journal*, 11, pp. 1–12.

Moores, S. (2016) Non-media-centric media studies and non-representational theories of practice. *New Media, Everyday Life and Social Change*, 17, pp. 682–700.

Morley, D. (1986) *Family television: Cultural power and domestic leisure*. Comedia, London.

Morley, D. (2000) *Home territories: Media, mobility and identity*. Routledge, London, New York.

Morley, D. (2007) *Media, modernity and technology: The geography of the new*. Routledge, London, New York.

Morley, D. (2009) For a materialist, non-media-centric media studies. *Television & New Media*, 10, pp. 114–116.

Morley, D. & Silverstone, R. (1990) Domestic communication: Technologies and meanings. *Media, Culture & Society*, 12, pp. 31–55.

Mosco, V. (2014) *To the cloud: Big data in a turbulent world*. Paradigm Publishers, St. Paul.

Mosco, V. (2017) *Becoming digital: Toward a post-internet society*. Emerald Publishing, Bingley.

Mueller, M. (2010) *Networks and states: The global politics of internet governance*. MIT Press, Cambridge, MA.

Murdock, G. (2017) Mediatisation and the transformation of capitalism: The elephant in the room. *Javnost - The Public*, 24, pp. 119–135.

Murthy, D. (2011) Twitter: Microphone for the masses? *Media, Culture & Society*, 33, pp. 779–789.

Nafus, D. (Ed.) (2016) *Quantified: Biosensing technologies in everyday life*. MIT Press, Cambridge, MA, London.

Nagy, P. & Neff, G. (2015) Imagined affordance: Reconstructing a keyword for communication theory. *Social Media + Society*. doi: 10.1177/2056305115603385.

Nambisan, S. & Nambisan, P. (2013) *Engaging citizens in co-creation in public services lessons learned and best practices*. IBM Center for The Business of Government, Washington, DC.

Napoli, P.M. (2014) Automated media: An institutional theory perspective on algorithmic media production and consumption. *Communication Theory*, 24, pp. 340–360.

Naughton, J. (1999) *A brief history of the future: The origins of the internet*. Weidenfeld and Nicolson, London.

Neff, G. & Nafus, D. (2016) *Self-tracking*. MIT Press, Cambridge, MA.

Neff, G. & Stark, D. (2003) Permanently beta. Responsive organization in the internet era. In *Society online* (Eds, Howard, P.N. & Jones, S.) Sage, New Delhi, London, pp. 173–188.

Neff, G. et al. (2017) Critique and contribute: A practice-based framework for improving critical data studies and data science. *Big Data*, 5, pp. 85–97.

Negroponte, N. (1995) *Being digital*. Alfred A. Knopf, New York.

Negus, K. (2002) The work of cultural intermediaries and the enduring distance between production and consumption. *Cultural Studies*, 16, pp. 501–515.

Neuman, W.R. (2010) Theories of media evolution. In *Media technology and society: The challenge of digital convergence* (Ed, Neuman, W.R.) University of Michigan Press, Ann Arbor, pp. 1–21.

Neuman, W.R. & Guggenheim, L. (2011) The evolution of media effects theory: A six-stage model of cumulative research. *Communication Theory*, 21, pp. 169–196.

Neumann-Braun, K. & Autenrieth, U.P. (Eds.) (2011) *Freundschaft und Gemeinschaft im Social Web. Bildbezogenes Handeln und Peergroup-Kommunikation auf Facebook & Co.* Nomos, Baden-Baden.

Newman, N. et al. (2018) *Reuters institute digital news report 2018.* Reuters Institute for the Study of Journalism, Oxford.

Nieborg, D.B. & Helmond, A. (2018) The political economy of Facebook's platformization in the mobile ecosystem: Facebook messenger as a platform instance. *Media, Culture & Society*, 41, pp. 196–218.

Nimmo, B. (2018) Robot wars: How bots joined battle in the gulf. *Journal of International Affairs*, 71, pp. 87–96.

Nixon, S. & du Gay, P. (2002) Who needs cultural intermediaries? *Cultural Studies*, 16, pp. 495–500.

Noble, S.U. (2018) *Algorithms of oppression: How search engines reinforce racism.* NYU Press, New York.

Nölleke, D. & Scheu, A.M. (2018) Perceived media logic: A point of reference for mediatization. In *Media logic(s) revisited: Modelling the interplay between media institutions, media technology and societal change* (Eds, Thimm, C., Anastasiadis, M. & Einspänner-Pflock, J.) Palgrave Macmillan, London, pp. 195–216.

Nwankwo, A.O. & Ogbu, S.U. (2018) Mediatization of life: Exploring the influence of the mobile and other media in Nigeria. *Observatorio*, 12, pp. 72–84.

O'Connor, J. (2013) Intermediaries and imaginaries in the cultural and creative industries. *Regional Studies*, 49, pp. 374–387.

O'Hara, K., Tuffield, M.M. & Shadbolt, N. (2008) Lifelogging: Privacy and empowerment with memories for life. *IDIS*, 1, pp. 155–172.

Ong, S. & Suplizio, A. (2016) Unpacking the breakout success of the Amazon Echo. *Experian.com*, September 7th, retrieved from: https://www.experian.com/innov ation/thought-leadership/amazon-echo-consumer-survey.jsp (Last accessed: 15th August 2019).

Opermann, S. (2014) *Generational use of news media in Estonia: Media access, spatial orientations and discursive characteristics of the news media.* Södertörns högskola, Huddinge.

Oremus, W. (2014) The first news report on the LA earthquake was written by a robot. *Slate.com*, March 17th, retrieved from: https://slate.com/technology/2 014/03/quakebot-los-angeles-times-robot-journalist-writes-article-on-la-earthqua ke.html (Last accessed: 15th August 2019).

Oudshoorn, N. & Pinch, T.J. (2003) *How users matter: The co-construction of users and technologies.* MIT Press, Cambridge, MA.

Øyvind, I. & Pallas, J. (2014) Mediatization of corporations. In *Mediatization of communication* (Ed, Lundby, K.) de Gruyter, Berlin, New York, pp. 423–442.

Palfrey, J. & Gasser, U. (2008) *Born digital: Understanding the first generation of digital natives.* Basic Books, New York.

Parasie, S. & Dagiral, E. (2013) Data-driven journalism and the public good: 'Computer-assisted-reporters' and 'programmer-journalists' in Chicago. *New Media & Society*, 15, pp. 853–871.

Parks, L. & Starosielski, N. (2015a) Introduction. In *Signal traffic: Critical studies of media infrastructures* (Eds, Parks, L. & Starosielski, N.) University of Illinois Press, Illionois, pp. 1–27.

Parks, L. & Starosielski, N. (Eds.) (2015b) *Signal traffic: Critical studies of media infrastructures.* University of Illinois Press, Urbana, Chicago, Springfield.

Pasquale, F. (2015) *The black box society: The secret algorithms that control money and information.* Harvard University Press, Cambridge, MA.

Passoth, J.-H., Sutter, T. & Wehner, J. (2014) The quantified listener: Reshaping providers and audiences with calculated measurement. In *Mediatized worlds* (Eds, Hepp, A. & Krotz, F.) Palgrave, London, pp. 271–287.

Pauen, M. & Welzer, H. (2015) *Autonomie: Eine Verteidigung.* Fischer Verlag, Frankfurt a.M.

Pfadenhauer, M. (2014) On the sociality of social robots. A sociology-of-knowledge perspective. *Science, Technology & Innovation Studies*, 10, pp. 135–153.

Pfadenhauer, M. & Dukat, C. (2015) Robot caregiver or robot-supported caregiving? The performative deployment of the social robot PARO in dementia care. *International Journal of Social Robotics*, 7, pp. 393–406.

Piller, F.T., Ihl, C. & Vossen, A. (2010) A typology of customer co-creation in the innovation process. *Social Science Research Network*, retrieved from: https://ssrn.com/abstract=1732127 (Last accessed: 15th August 2019).

Pinch, T.J. & Bijker, W.E. (1984) The social construction of facts and artefacts: Or how the sociology of science and the sociology of technology might benefit each other. *Social Studies of Science*, 14, pp. 399–441.

Plantin, J.-C. & Punathambekar, A. (2019) Digital media infrastructures: Pipes, platforms, and politics. *Media, Culture & Society*, 14, pp. 163–174.

Postigo, H. (2016) The socio-technical architecture of digital labor: Converting play into YouTube money. *New Media & Society*, 18, pp. 332–349.

Powell, W.W. & DiMaggio, P.J. (Eds.) (1991) *The new institutionalism in organizational analysis.* University of Chicago Press, Chicago.

Prensky, M. (2001) Digital natives, digital immigrants. *On the horizon*, 9, pp. 1–6.

Prokop, D. (2001) *Der Kampf um die Medien. Das Geschichtsbuch der neuen kritischen Medienforschung.* VSA-Verlag, Hamburg.

Purington, A. et al. (2017) Alexa is my new BFF: Social roles, user satisfaction, and personification of the Amazon Echo. *Proceedings of the 2017 CHI Conference Extended Abstracts on Human Factors in Computing Systems*, pp. 2853–2859.

Puschmann, C. & Burgess, J. (2014) Metaphors of big data. *International Journal of Communication*, 8, pp. 1690–1709.

Qiu, J.L. (2016) *Goodbye iSlave.* University of Illinois Press, Urbana, IL.

Quandt, T. (2005) *Journalisten im Netz*. VS, Wiesbaden.

Radway, J. (1984) Interpretive communities and variable literacies: The functions of romance reading. *Daedalus*, 113, pp. 49–73.

Rainie, H. & Wellman, B. (2012) *Networked: The new social operating system*. MIT Press, Cambridge, MA.

Rao, H., Monin, P. & Durand, R. (2003) Institutional change in Toque Ville: Nouvelle cuisine as an identity movement in French gastronomy. *American Journal of Sociology*, 108, pp. 795–843.

Ratto, M. & Boler, M. (Eds.) (2014) *DIY citizenship: Critical making and social media*. MIT Press, Cambridge, MA, London.

Reckwitz, A. (2002) Toward a theory of social practices. A development in culturalist theorizing. *European Journal of Social Theory*, 5, pp. 245–265.

Reichertz, J. (2008) *Die Macht der Worte und der Medien. Zweite Auflage*. VS, Wiesbaden.

Reichertz, J. (2009) *Kommunikationsmacht: Was ist Kommunikation und was vermag sie? Und weshalb vermag sie das?* VS, Wiesbaden.

Reichertz, J. (2011) Communicative power is power over identity. *Communications*, 36, pp. 147–168.

Reichmann, W. (2013) Epistemic participation: How to produce knowledge about the economic future. *Social Studies of Science*, 43, pp. 852–877.

Reigeluth, T.B. (2014) Why data is not enough: Digital traces as control of self and self-control. *Surveillance & Society*, 12, pp. 243–254.

Rheingold, H. (1994) *The virtual community: Finding connection in a computerised world*. Martin Secker & Warburg Ltd, London.

Rheingold, H. (2003) *Smart mobs: The next social revolution*. Perseus Publishing, Cambridge, MA.

Rieder, B. (2012) ORDER BY column_name: The relational database as pervasive cultural form. *"Lived logics of database machinery" workshop at the wellcome collection*, June 28th, retrieved from: https://de.slideshare.net/bernhardrieder/presentation-database-13498016 (Last accessed: 15th August 2019).

Riesman, D. (1950) *The lonely crowd: A study of the changing American character*. Yale University Press, New Haven, London.

Rogers, E.M. (2003) *Diffusion of innovations. Fifth edition*. Free Press, New York, London.

Roitsch, C. (2017) *Kommunikative Grenzziehung. Herausforderungen und Praktiken junger Menschen in einer vielgestaltigen Medienumgebung*. ZeMKI (doctoral dissertation), Universität Bremen, Bremen.

Rosa, H. (2013) *Social acceleration: A new theory of modernity*. Columbia University Press, New York.

Rosenblat, A. (2018) *Uberland: How algorithms are rewriting the rules of work*. University of California Press, Oakland.

Röser, J. et al. (2017) Häusliches Medienhandeln zwischen Dynamik und Beharrung: Die Domestizierung des Internets und die Mediatisierung des Zuhauses 2008-2016. In *Mediatisierung als Metaprozess* (Eds, Krotz, F., Despotovic, C. & Kruse, M.-M.) VS Verlag, Wiesbaden.

Rossetto, L. (1993) Why Wired? *Wired*, 1, retrieved from: https://www.wired.com/sto ry/original-wired-manifesto/ (Last accessed: 15th August 2019).

Rössler, B. (2017) *Autonomie: Ein Versuch über das gelungene Leben*. Suhrkamp, Berlin.

Ruckenstein, M. (2014) Visualized and interacted life: Personal analytics and engagements with data doubles. *Societies*, 4, pp. 68–84.

Rühl, M. (1969) *Die Zeitungsredaktion als organisiertes soziales System*. Bertelsmann Universitätsverlag, Düsseldorf.

Ruppert, E. (2011) Population objects: Interpassive subjects. *Sociology*, 45, pp. 218–233.

Ryan, M. (2005) Micro-macro-integration. In *Encyclopedia of social theory, Vol. 1 [A-M]* (Ed, Ritzer, G.) Sage, Thousand Oaks, pp. 501–503.

Sanders, E.B.-N. & Stappers, P.J. (2008) Co-creation and the new landscapes of design. *CoDesign*, 4, pp. 5–18.

Scannell, P. (1989) Public service broadcasting and modern public life. *Media, Culture and Society*, 11, pp. 135–166.

Schäfer, M.T. & van Es, K. (Eds.) (2017) *The datafied society: Studying culture through data*. Amsterdam University Press, Amsterdam.

Schatzki, T.R., Knorr Cetina, K. & von Savigny, E. (Eds.) (2001) *The practice turn in contemporary theory*. Routledge, New York.

Schimank, U. (2010) *Handeln und Strukturen: Einführung in die akteurstheoretische Soziologie, 4. Auflage*. Juventa, Weinheim, Basel.

Schimank, U. (2013) *Gesellschaft*. transcript, Bielefeld.

Schmidt, D.C. (2018) Google data collection. *Digital Content Next*, retrieved from: https://digitalcontentnext.org/blog/2018/08/21/google-data-collection-resea rch/ (Last accessed: 15th August 2019).

Schmidt, J. (2019) Öffentliche Kindheit in Elternblogs? Ergebnisse einer Befragung von deutschsprachigen Elternbloggerinnen und -bloggern. *merz*, 1, pp. 63–69.

Schnapp, J.T. & Tiews, M. (Eds.) (2006) *Crowds and collectivities in networked electoral politics*. Stanford University Press, Stanford.

Scholz, T. (2013) Introduction: Why does digital labour matter now? In *Digital labor: The internet as playground and factory* (Ed, Scholz, T.) Routledge, New York, pp. 1–9.

Scholz, T. (2017) *Uberworked and underpaid: How workers are disrupting the digital economy*. Polity Press, Cambridge.

Scholz, T. & Schneider, N. (Eds.) (2017) *Ours to hack and to own: The rise of platform cooperativism, a new vision for the future of work and a fairer internet*. OR Books, New York, London.

Schrock, A.R. (2015) Communicative affordances of mobile media: Portability, availability, locatability, and multimediality. *International Journal of Communication*, 9, pp. 1229–1246.

Schrøder, K. (2016) Q-method and news audience research. In *The SAGE handbook of digital journalism* (Eds, Witschge, T. et al.) Sage, New Delhi, London, New York, pp. 528–545.

Schrøder, K. (2017) Towards the 'audiencization' of mediatization research? Audience dynamics as co-constitutive of mediatization processes. In *Dynamics of mediatization* (Eds, Driessens, O. et al.) Palgrave, London, pp. 85–115.

Schrøder, K.C. & Gulbrandsen, I.T. (2018) Audience. In *The international encyclopedia of strategic communication* (Eds, Heath, R.L. & Johansen, W.) Wiley-Blackwell, Boston, pp. 54–63.

Schröder, K.C. (1994) Audience semiotics, interpretive communities and the 'ethnographic turn' in media research. *Media, Culture & Society*, 16, pp. 337–347.

Schrott, A. (2009) Dimensions: Catch-all label or technical term. In *Mediatization: Concept, changes, consequences* (Ed, Lundby, K.) Peter Lang, New York, pp. 41–61.

Schulz, W. (2004) Reconstructing mediatization as an analytical concept. *European Journal of Communication*, 19, pp. 87–101.

Schütz, A. (1967a) *Collected papers I. The problem of social reality. Second edition.* Martinus Nijhoff, Leiden.

Schütz, A. (1967b) *The phenomenology of the social world.* Northwestern University Press, New York.

Schütz, A. & Luckmann, T. (1973) *The structures of the life-world. 2 volumes.* Northwestern University Press, Evanston.

Sciuto, A. et al. (2018) Hey Alexa, what's up? A mixed-methods studies of in-home conversational agent usage. *Proceedings of the 2018 on Designing Interactive Systems Conference 2018*, pp. 857–868.

Scolari, C.A. (2013) Media evolution: Emergence, dominance, survival and extinction in the media ecology. *International Journal of Communication*, 7, pp. 1418–1441.

Scott, S.V. & Orlikowski, W.J. (2014) Entanglements in practice: Performing anonymity through social media. *MIS Quarterly*, 38, pp. 873–893.

Scott, W.R. (2001) *Organizations: Rational, natural, and open systems.* Prentice-Hall, Upper Saddle River.

Scott, W.R. et al. (2000) *Institutional change and healthcare organizations: From professional dominance to managed care.* University of Chicago Press, Chicago.

Selke, S. (2016) Quantified Self statt Hahnenkampf. *Bundesgesundheitsblatt, Gesundheitsforschung, Gesundheitsschutz*, 59, pp. 963–969.

Sen, A. (1992) *Inequality reexamined.* Oxford University Press, Oxford.

Sen, A. (1999) *Development as freedom.* Oxford University Press, Oxford.

Shibutani, T. (1955) Reference groups as perspectives. *American Journal of Sociology*, 60, pp. 562–569.

Siibak, A., Vittadini, N. & Nimrod, G. (2014) Generations as media audiences: An introduction. *Participations*, 11, 2, pp. 100–107.

Silverstone, R. & Haddon, L. (1998) Design and domestication of information and communication technologies: Technical change and everyday life. In *Communication by design: The politics of information and communication technologies* (Eds, Mansell, R. & Silverstone, R.) Oxford University Press, Milton Keynes, pp. 44–74.

Silverstone, R. & Hirsch, E. (Eds.) (1992) *Consuming technologies: Media and information in domestic spaces.* Routledge, London, New York.

Simmel, G. (1972) *On individuality and social forms*, edited by and with an introduction by Donald Levine. University of Chicago Press, Chicago.

Stage, C. (2013) The online crowd: A contradiction in terms? On the potentials of Gustave Le Bon's crowd psychology in an analysis of affective blogging. *Distinktion: Scandinavian Journal of Social Theory*, 14, pp. 211–226.

Star, S.L. & Ruhleder, K. (1996) Steps toward an ecology of infrastructure: Design and access for large information spaces. *Information Systems Research*, 7, pp. 111–134.

Stark, L. & Levy, K. (2018) The surveillant consumer. *Media, Culture & Society*, 40, pp. 1202–1220.

Starosielski, N. (2015) Fixed flow. Undersea cables as media infrastructure. In *Signal traffic: Critical studies of media infrastructures* (Eds, Parks, L. & Starosielski, N.) University of Illinois Press, Urbana, Chicago, Springfield, pp. 53–70.

Starosielski, N. (2017) Pipeline ecologies: Rural entanglements of fiber-optic cables. In *Sustainable media: Critical approaches to media and environment* (Eds, Starosielski, N. & Walker, J.) Routledge, London, pp. 38–55.

Storsul, T. & Stuedahl, D. (Eds.) (2007) *Ambivalence towards convergence: Digitalization and media change.* Nordicom, Göteborg.

Strate, L. (2017) *Media ecology: An approach to understanding the human condition.* Peter Lang, New York.

Strauss, A. (1978) A social world perspective. *Studies in Symbolic Interaction*, 1, pp. 119–128.

Stray, J. (2011) What's with this programmer-journalist identity crisis? retrieved from: http://jonathanstray.com/whats-with-this-programmer-journalist-identity-crisis (Last accessed: 15th August 2019).

Striphas, T. (2015) Algorithmic culture. *European Journal of Cultural Studies*, 18, pp. 395–412.

Strömbäck, J. & Esser, F. (2014a) Introduction. *Journalism Practice*, 8, pp. 245–257.

Strömbäck, J. & Esser, F. (2014b) Mediatization of politics: Towards a theoretical framework. In *Mediatization of politics: Understanding the transformation of Western democracies* (Eds, Esser, F. & Strömbäck, J.) Palgrave Macmillan, Houndmills, pp. 3–28.

Strübing, J. et al. (Eds.) (2016) *Leben nach Zahlen: Self-Tracking als Optimierungsprojekt?* transcript, Bielefeld.

Stukal, D. et al. (2017) Detecting bots on Russian political Twitter. *Big Data*, 5, pp. 310–324.

Stukal, D. et al. (2019) The use of Twitter bots in Russian political communication. *PONARS Eurasia Policy Memo*, 564, pp. 1–10.

Suchman, L., Trigg, R. & Blomberg, J. (2002) Working artefacts: Ethnomethods of the prototype. *British Journal of Sociology*, 53, pp. 163–179.

Sumantran, V., Fine, C. & Gonsalzez, D. (2017) *Faster, smarter, greener: The future of the car and urban mobility.* MIT Press, Cambridge, MA, London.

Tapscott, D. (1998) *Growing up digital: The rise of the net generation.* McGraw-Hill, New York.

Taylor, L. (2017) What is data justice? The case for connecting digital rights and freedoms globally. *Big Data & Society*, doi: 205395171773633.

Thimm, C. (2018) Media technology and media logic(s): The media grammar approach. In *Media logic(s) revisited: Modelling the interplay between media institutions, media technology and societal change* (Eds, Thimm, C., Anastasiadis, M. & Einspänner-Pflock, J.) Palgrave Macmillan, London, pp. 111–132.

Thimm, C., Anastasiadis, M. & Einspänner-Pflock, J. (2018a) Media logic or media logics? An introduction to the field. In *Media logic(s) revisited: Modelling the interplay between media institutions, media technology and societal change* (Eds, Thimm, C., Anastasiadis, M. & Einspänner-Pflock, J.) Palgrave Macmillan, London, pp. 1–8.

Thimm, C., Anastasiadis, M. & Einspänner-Pflock, J. (Eds.) (2018b) *Media logic(s) revisited: Modelling the interplay between media institutions, media technology and societal change.* Palgrave Macmillan, London.

Thompson, J.B. (1995) *The media and modernity: A social theory of the media.* Cambridge University Press, Cambridge.

Thornham, H. (2019) Algorithmic vulnerabilities and the datalogical: Early motherhood and tracking-as-care regimes. *Convergence: The International Journal of Research into New Media Technologies*, 25, pp. 171–185.

Thornton, P., Ocasio, W. & Lounsbury, M. (2012) *The institutional logics perspective: A new approach to culture, structure, and process.* Oxford University Press, Oxford.

Thurman, N., Dörr, K. & Kunert, J. (2017) When reporters get hands-on with robo-writing. *Digital Journalism*, 5, pp. 1240–1259.

Tifentale, A. & Manovich, L. (2016) Competitive photography and the presentation of the self. In *Exploring the selfie: Historical, analytical, and theoretical approaches to digital self-photography* (Eds, Ruchatz, J., Wirth, S. & Eckel, J.) Palgrave Macmillan, New York, pp. 167–187.

Toffler, A. (1970) *Future shock.* Random House, New York.

Torres, E.C. & Mateus, S. (Eds.) (2015) *From multitude to crowds: Collective action and the media.* Peter Lang, Berlin.

Townley, B. (1997) The institutional logic of performance appraisal. *Organization Studies*, 18, pp. 261–285.

Tsvetkova, M. et al. (2017) Even good bots fight: The case of Wikipedia. *PLoS One*, 12, e0171774.

Turkle, S. (2002) Sociable technologies: Enhancing human performance when the computer is not a tool but a companion. In *Converging technologies for improving human performance* (Eds, Roco, M.C. & Bainbridge, W.S.) National Science Foundation, Arlington, Virginia, pp. 150–158.

Turkle, S. (2015) *Reclaiming conversation: The power of talk in a digital age.* Penguin, New York.

Turner, F. (2006a) *From counterculture to cyberculture: Stewart Brand, the Whole Earth network, and the rise of digital utopianism.* University of Chicago Press, Chicago.

Turner, F. (2016) Prototype. In *Digital keywords: A vocabulary of information, society and culture* (Ed, Peters, B.) Princeton University Press, Princeton, Oxford, pp. 256–268.

Turner, F. (2018) Millenarian tinkering: The puritan roots of the maker movement. *Technol Cult*, 59, pp. 160–182.

Turner, J. (2006b) Micro-macro theory. In *The Cambridge dictionary of sociology* (Ed, Turner, B.S.) Cambridge University Press, Cambridge, pp. 383–384.

Turner, P. (2005) Affordance as context. *Interacting with Computers*, 17, pp. 787–800.

Turow, J. (2011) *The daily you: How the new advertising industry is defining your identity and your worth*. Yale University Press, New Haven, London.

Turow, J. (2017) *The aisles have eyes: How retailers track your shopping, strip your privacy and define your power*. Yale University Press, New Haven, London.

Ulam, S. (1958) Tribute to John von Neumann 1903–1957. *Bulletin of the American Mathematical Society*, 64, pp. 1–49.

Ullman, E. (1997) *Close to the machine: Technophilia and its discontents*. City Lights Books, San Francisco.

Usher, N. (2016) *Interactive journalism: Hackers, data, and code*. University of Illinois Press, Urbana, Chicago, Springfield.

Usher, N. (2017) Venture-backed news startups and the field of journalism. Challenges, changes, and consistencies. *Digital Journalism*, 5, pp. 1116–1133.

van Dijck, J. & Poell, T. (2013) Understanding social media logic. *Media and Communication*, 1, pp. 2–14.

van Dijck, J., Poell, T. & de Waal, M. (2018) *The platform society*. Oxford University Press, Oxford.

Varol, O. et al. (2017) Online human-bot interactions: Detection, estimation, and characterization. *arXiv*. doi: arXiv:1703.03107.

Vázquez Schaich, M.J. & Klein, J.S. (2013) Entrepreneurial journalism education: Where are we now? *Observatorio (OBS*)*, 7, pp. 185–211.

Vinge, V. (1993) *Technological singularity*. Department of Mathematical Sciences, San Diego State University, San Diego.

Vittadini, N. et al. (2013) Generations and media: The social construction of generational identity and differences. In *Transforming audiences* (Eds, Carpentier, N., Schröder, K. & Hallet, L.) Routledge, London, pp. 65–81.

Volkmer, I. (2006) Globalization, generational entelechies, and the global public space. In *News in public memory: An international study of media memories across generations* (Ed, Volkmer, I.) Peter Lang, New York, pp. 251–268.

Vos, T.P. & Singer, J.B. (2016) Media discourse about entrepreneurial journalism. *Journalism Practice*, 10, pp. 143–159.

Wachelder, J. (2019) Regeneration: Generations remediated. *Time & Society*, 28, pp. 883–903.

Wagemans, A., Witschge, T. & Deuze, M. (2016) Ideology as resource in entrepreneurial journalism. *Journalism Practice*, 10, pp. 160–177.

Wagemans, A., Witschge, T. & Harbers, F. (2019) Impact as driving force of journalistic and social change. *Journalism*, (20) pp. 552–567. doi: 146488491877053.

Wahl-Jorgensen, K. (2009) News production, ethnography and power. On the challenges of newsroom-centricity. In *Journalism and anthropology* (Ed, Bird, S.E.) Indiana University Press, Bloomington, pp. 21–35.

Walde, C.-H. (2006) Swedish submarine communication during 100 years, the role of Ernst FW Alexanderson, and how the Royal Swedish Navy helped Varberg radio at Grimeton (SAQ) to world heritage status. *Tidskrift i Sjöväsendet*, 4, pp. 379–392.

Wang, H. (Ed.) (2015) *Communication and "the good life"*. Peter Lang, New York.

Wang, S. (2018) This hyperlocal news site in San Francisco is reinventing itself with an automated local news wire. *Nieman Journalism Lab*, February 5th, retrieved from: https://www.niemanlab.org/2018/02/ this-hyperlocal-news-sit e-in-san-francisco-is-reinventing-itself-with-an-automated-local-news-wire/ (Last accessed: 15th August 2019).

Waxman, O.B. (2016) It's been 10 years since you were named TIME's person of the year. *TIME.com*, December 7th, retrieved from: https://time.com/4586842/perso n-of-the-year-2006-2016/ (Last accessed: 15th August 2019).

Weber, M. (1988) *Gesammelte Aufsätze zur Wissenschaftslehre. Siebte Auflage.* Mohr Verlag (UTB), Tübingen.

Wehner, J. (2010) 'Numerische Inklusion' – Wie die Medien ihr Publikum beobachten. In *Medienwandel als Wandel von Interaktionsformen* (Eds, Sutter, T. & Mehler, A.) VS, Wiesbaden, pp. 183–210.

Weick, K.E. (1979) *The social psychology of organizing. Second edition.* McGraw, New York.

Weick, K.E., Sutcliffe, K.M. & Obstfeld, D. (2005) Organizing and the process of sensemaking. *Organization Science*, 16, pp. 409–421.

Weissman, C.G. (2018) How Amazon helped Cambridge Analytica harvest Americans' Facebook data. *Fastcompany.com*, March 27th, retrieved from: https://www.fas tcompany.com/40548348/how-amazon-helped-cambridge-analytica-harvest-am ericans-facebook-data (Last accessed: 15th August 2019).

Wellman, B. et al. (2003) The social affordances of the Internet for networked individualism. *Journal of Computer-Mediated Communication*, 8. doi: j.1083-6101.2003.tb00216.x.

Wenger, E. (1999) *Communities of practice: Learning, meaning, and identity.* Cambridge University Press, Cambridge.

Wilke, J. (2003) The history and culture of the newsroom in Germany. *Journalism Studies*, 4, pp. 465–477.

Williams, R. (1983) Problems of the coming period. *New Left Review*, 140, pp. 7–18.

Williams, R. (1990) *Television: Technology and cultural form.* Routledge, London, New York.

Winter, R. & Eckert, R. (1990) *Mediengeschichte und kulturelle Differenzierung. Zur Entstehung und Funktion von Wahlnachbarschaften.* Leske + Budrich, Opladen.

Witschge, T. (2014) Passive accomplice or active disruptor. The role of audiences in the mediatization of politics. *Journalism Practice*, 8, pp. 342–356.

Wittel, A. (2012) Digital Marx. Toward a political economy of distributed media. *tripleC*, 10, pp. 313–333.

Wohlrab-Sahr, M. (2002) Säkularisierungsprozesse und kulturelle Generationen. In *Lebenszeiten. Erkundungen zur Soziologie der Generation* (Eds, Burkart, G. & Wolf, J.) VS Verlag für Sozialwissenschaften, Wiesbaden, pp. 209–228.

Wolf, G. (2009) Know thyself: Tracking every facet of life, from sleep to mood to pain. *Wired Magazine*, June 22nd, retrieved from: https://www.wired.com/2009/06/lbnp-knowthyself/ (Last accessed: 15th August 2019).

Young, M.L. & Hermida, A. (2015) From Mr. and Mrs. Outlier to central tendencies: Computational journalism and crime reporting at the Los Angeles Times. *Digital Journalism*, 3, pp. 381–397.

Zelfman, I. (2017) Bot traffic report 2016. *Imperva Incapsula Blog*, January 24th, retrieved from: https://libguides.ioe.ac.uk/harvard/newspaperonline (Last accessed: 15th August 2019).

Zervas, G., Proserpio, D. & Byers, J. (2014) The rise of the sharing economy: Estimating the impact of Airbnb on the hotel industry. *Boston U. School of Management Research Paper No. 2013-16*, retrieved from: https://papers.ssrn.com/sol3/papers.cfm?abstract_id=2366898 (Last accessed: 15th August 2019).

Zillien, N. (2008) Die (Wieder-)Entdeckung der Medien. Das Affordanzkonzept in der Mediensoziologie. *Sociologia Internationalis*, 46, pp. 161–181.

Zuboff, S. (2019a) Surveillance capitalism and the challenge of collective action. *New Labor Forum*, 28, pp. 10–12.

Zuboff, S. (2019b) *The age of surveillance capitalism: The fight for the future at the new frontier of power*. Profile Books, London.

Zuckerberg, M. (2019) The Internet needs new rules. Let's start in these four areas. *The Washington Post*, March 30th, retrieved from: https://beta.washingtonpost.com/opinions/mark-zuckerberg-the-internet-needs-new-rules-lets-start-in-these-four-areas/2019/03/29/9e6f0504-521a-11e9-a3f7-78b7525a8d5f_story.html?noredirect=on (Last accessed: 15th August 2019).

INDEX

Figures are indicated by page numbers in *italics* and tables are indicated by page numbers in **bold**.

For Product Safety Concerns and Information please contact our EU
representative GPSR@taylorandfrancis.com
Taylor & Francis Verlag GmbH, Kaufingerstraße 24, 80331 München, Germany

www.ingramcontent.com/pod-product-compliance
Lightning Source LLC
Chambersburg PA
CBHW050637280326
41932CB00015B/2682